Rubles

Dollars
TO

Rubles to Dollars

MAKING MONEY ON RUSSIA'S EXPLODING FINANCIAL FRONTIER

Dr. Alexander Elder

NEW YORK INSTITUTE OF FINANCE

NEW YORK • TORONTO • SYDNEY • TOKYO • SINGAPORE

Library of Congress Cataloging-in-Publication Data

Elder, Alexander.
　　Rubles to dollars : making money on Russia's exploding financial frontier　/
by Alexander Elder.
　　　　p.　cm.
　　Includes bibliographical references and index.
　　ISBN 0-7352-0062-9 (hardcover)
　　　1. Russia (Federation)—Economic conditions—1991–　2. Investments—Russia
(Federation)　I. Title.
　　HC340.12.E6　1998
　　332.67'3'0947—dc21

98-34349
CIP

Acquisitions Editor: *Ellen Schneid Coleman*
Production Editor: *Sharon L. Gonzalez*
Formatting/Interior Design: *Robyn Beckerman*
Jacket Design: *Henrik Langsdorf*

Printed in the United States of America

10 9 8 7 6 5 4 3 2 1

ISBN 0-7352-0062-9

This publication is designed to provide accurate and authoritative information in regard to the subject
matter covered. It is sold with the understanding that the publisher is not engaged in rendering legal,
accounting, or other professional service. If legal advice or other expert assistance is required, the services of a competent professional person should be sought.
　　　. . . *From the Declaration of Principles jointly adopted by a Committee of the American Bar
Association and a Committee of Publishers and Associations.*

ATTENTION: CORPORATIONS AND SCHOOLS

Prentice Hall books are available at quantity discounts with bulk purchase for educational, business, or sales promotional use. For information, please write to:
Prentice Hall Special Sales, 240 Frisch Court, Paramus, New Jersey 07652. Please
supply: title of book, ISBN, quantity, how the book will be used, date needed.

 NEW YORK INSTITUTE OF FINANCE
An Imprint of Prentice Hall Press
Paramus, NJ 07652
A Simon & Schuster Company

On the World Wide Web at http://www.phdirect.com

Prentice Hall International (UK) Limited, *London*
Prentice Hall of Australia Pty. Limited, *Sydney*
Prentice Hall Canada, Inc., *Toronto*
Prentice Hall Hispanoamericana, S.A., *Mexico*
Prentice Hall of India Private Limited, *New Delhi*
Prentice Hall of Japan, Inc., *Tokyo*
Simon & Schuster Asia Pte. Ltd., *Singapore*
Editora Prentice Hall do Brasil, Ltda., *Rio de Janeiro*

To four men, who in the midst of the triumphant Soviet empire opened my eyes to its evil and gave me a start in learning to think for myself—my grandfather, Professor Isai Landsman, who taught me to listen to Western radio; George Orwell, the author of *Animal Farm*; Boris Pasternak, the author of *Doctor Zhivago*; and Garik Superfin, a college friend, linguist, and historian. The first three are dead, but Garik survived Soviet labor camps and keeps the fires of Russian culture burning in distant Bremen.

AUTHOR'S FOREWORD

By an accident of fate, I had two special advantages in writing this book. I am bicultural, rather than bilingual—equally at ease in the US and Russia. I did my research for this book in Russian, but wrote it in English. The people I interviewed related to me like one of their own, and gave me the information that most foreigners never get. At the same time, I could see changes in Russia more clearly than locals by coming in from the US and commuting between Moscow and New York. I saw Russia from the inside, but viewed it as an American. Add a third advantage—I am a psychiatrist, and after more than 20 years of practicing my craft I have an ingrained habit of looking for the hard core of reality beneath the cover of external details.

One of my friends in Moscow recently asked a sales clerk in a bakery to pack her pastries all facing the same way. The clerk, smiling, quoted a passage from Yesenin, a Russian poet—*Litsom k litsu litsa ne uvidat*—"When face to face you cannot see the face." My friend laughed, telling me of her encounter with yet another out-of-work linguist, but it reminded me that by being outside the box of daily life where most face the same way, I could see the face of Russia more clearly than most locals.

The key idea of this book—that Russia is in an early stage of a freedom-fueled boom and its stocks are a screaming buy—sounds less outrageous with each passing month. The value of the Russian stock market has doubled in each of the last two years, but the markets of Hong Kong and Brazil, which in many ways are its forerunners, have risen more than 40-fold from their humble beginnings. There is still plenty of money left on the table.[1]

Russia is a huge country, with vast natural resources and an educated and cultured population. Its people were kept down for centuries by brutal and incompetent rulers. The collapse of the communist system in 1991 left Russians free for the first time in a millennium. Freedom has unleashed the creative energy of a nation, propelling it into a headlong rush to catch up with the industrial West—and even try to overtake it—in a single generation.

Russia still has many problems, as any Russian will promptly tell you. We take openness and willingness to face problems for granted in the West, but it is a huge change for Russia. The Potemkin village—a fake showpiece erected to impress a visiting dignitary—has been torn down. After centuries of hiding in fear of their overlords, the Russians are talking; complaining about problems is the first step toward solving them.

The severe depression of the 1990s has beaten false pride out of most Russians, forcing them to roll up their sleeves and work harder than ever. Their banks and financial companies—the first industries to rise from the rubble of the communist collapse—are already within range of their Western counterparts, with others starting to emerge from the communist morass. The government has begun to purge itself of visibly corrupt officials. Organized crime is down from its post-Soviet peak.

When I first thought of writing this book, at the bottom of the Russian depression, the idea of a freedom-fueled boom seemed bizarre to most people. Now it is becoming widely accepted. Russia is developing amazingly fast—what seemed impossible a year ago

---

[1]The Russian stock market was the best performing market in the world in 1997—and the worst performing in 1998. Russian markets are thin and their liquidity is low, making them especially subject to swings as the international investors pile in or out of them. The decline of 1998 does not change the fundamentally bullish case for Russia.

looks normal today. When Transaero, a large Russian airline, made a takeover bid for TWA in 1997, it reflected the emergence of confident, Western-style capitalism in Russia.

Russia's economy has stopped declining, bottomed out, and started to grow while this book was being written. The Russians, facing their second millennium, are determined not to fail—"We wanted the best and got the usual." Nobody can tell how high the economy will rise, but Russia has a democracy, an emerging system of modern law, a huge market, and vast natural, financial, and human wealth. An investment boom is unavoidable, like spring and summer after a long winter.

Read on if you are interested in learning how the largest country in the world has reversed its course from totalitarianism and stagnation toward democracy, freedom, and prosperity. Not only Russians, but Westerners, too, can profit from these changes. Very rarely in life can you profit, have fun, and do good at the same time. That time in Russia is now!

Dr. Alexander Elder
Moscow, April 1998

CONTENTS

Pearls in the Dirt 169

In with Caution, Out with Money 221

The Wild West
Has Moved East

1

ESCAPE AND RETURN

Two nights after Christmas, 1973, I ran up the gangplank of a ship in the Tallinn harbor. I was the ship's doctor, and we were about to leave for Africa in a few hours. Wet snow melted on the dirty pier, sharp gusts of wind blew in from the Baltic. I turned at the top of the gangplank to take the last look at my old city—its incongruous mixture of dark medieval towers and brightly lit billboards with Lenin's profile.

I had already smuggled my documents aboard ship, given away most of my possessions, visited friends I never expected to see again. I was going to jump ship—and dash for America. An escape was a capital crime in the Soviet Union. The state owned us, the slaves of communism. My shipmates would try to catch or kill me when I ran. If I managed to escape and survive I could never go back.

The mighty Soviet empire was advancing across the globe in those years, acquiring mass as it went, gaining new allies and satellites in Latin America, Asia, and Africa. The empire appeared unstoppable, as late-stage bull markets usually do. I bucked its trend and became involved in the democratic movement. After seeing my friends carted off to prisons or thrown out of jobs or universities, I realized—that there was no life for me in the USSR. Soon after graduating from medical school, I got a job as a ship's doctor, in order to escape.

I turned at the top of the gangplank and spat at the pier. A winter gale blew my spit into the strip of dirty water between the ship and the shore. As I stepped inside, wet wind slammed the door behind me.

The strip of dirty water between the ship and the pier grew wider. We circled Europe, and headed for Africa. As the air grew warmer, I went to the upper deck to skip rope for several hours each day. Men tend to grow flabby aboard modern ships; there is good food and little physical work. I knew I would have to run for my life and was determined to be in better physical shape than any other man on that ship.

I jumped ship in Abidjan, Ivory Coast. My shipmates chased me, but could not catch me. I outran them, then hailed a taxi and took it to the US Embassy. They hid me in a "safe house," until the State Department granted me political asylum. A week later, after a night flight across the Atlantic, I saw, for the first time, the lights of New York from the window of a Pan Am plane.

The Soviets did not look kindly upon escapees. Running away was a capital offense, which earned me a spot on the KGB's "Wanted List." Whenever I flew to the Caribbean in the 1970s I used to feel uneasy. Planes were being hijacked to Cuba in those years and I feared that if it happened to us, I'd be taken off the plane, shipped to Moscow, and once there, either shot or sent to the camps.

Communism was in a strong uptrend in the old country, and I built a new life for myself in America, never expecting to return. I trained as a psychiatrist, practiced, taught at Columbia University, then learned to trade, started a company, and even wrote a financial bestseller—*Trading for a Living*. My private bull market was quietly going on while the Soviet empire had topped out and entered a vicious bear market.

In 1989 the Berlin Wall came down, then the Baltics became independent, and then the Communist Party was briefly outlawed in Russia. I followed the news in *The New York Times* and talked to a few friends who still had contacts in the old country, but it felt like looking at an old grainy photograph. I had already said my final goodbyes. Then, at a conference in New York in the autumn of 1994, I ran into a group of Russian bankers. They kept buying cases of my American book for their currency traders back in Moscow.

They were surprised when I spoke to them in fluent unaccented Russian and asked me to fly to Moscow to teach their traders. Things tend to move either excruciatingly slowly or extremely quickly when you deal with Russians; there is little middle ground. A few weeks later I was looking down from an airplane window on the land I never expected to see again.

It was still warm when I left New York, but here the ground was covered with snow. As the plane rolled to a stop at Sheremetyevo airport, I recognized the bundled up slow-moving *muzhiki* on the runway. The workers who chucked the wheels and drove refueling trucks hadn't changed a bit. The country had a new flag and its border guards gave me no problems.

My seminars in Moscow drew crowds. The financial and currency markets were just opening up, and there hadn't been anyone yet who could teach trading in Russian. Hundreds of men and women packed the auditoriums, and to this day many financial people in Russia tell me that their involvement with trading and technical analysis began at my seminars.

I never lost my ability to speak Russian. After living in America for over 20 years and even dreaming in English, I continued to speak Russian like a native. I went to visit old friends who were still around, teachers, ex-lovers; it was a sentimental journey. People I had not seen in over 20 years took me back as one of their own, but with a fantastic twist—a local boy who had escaped and made good in the West.

The Moscow bankers kept inviting me to teach their traders several times each year, creating great opportunities to observe the flood of changes in Russia. At first, in the early '90s, it was like visiting a zoo—interesting but wild. The old communist system had collapsed, but the new one had not yet emerged, and most people were just trying to survive amid the ruins. My so-called luxury suite had roaches, and handles came off drawers when I tried to open them. Lawlessness was rampant. My hotel was encircled by barbed wire, with two submachine gunners at the gate.

Russian jokes are the best in the world, and one of them captured the mood of those days: A woman wakes up, moves her hand about the nightstand, flicks the switch, and the light comes on. She gets up and goes to the bathroom, and there is running water. She rushes back into the bedroom and shakes her husband—"Wake up, quick, the communists are back!"

People on the streets of Moscow in the early '90s appeared downcast and beaten, as if the country had lost a war. They were grim; nobody smiled or was helpful. You could walk with both hands full of packages and someone would slam a door in your face. People weren't hostile, simply exhausted, with no energy to think of anything but day-to-day survival. Even the Russian language became polluted with mangled, twisted Americanisms when perfectly good Russian words existed.

I now call the period of 1991–1996 the Depression of the 1990s. Moscow was filthy, with potholed streets and crumbling buildings. Long lines of destitute people, many of them old, stood for hours near subway stops. A few begged, but most were trying to sell a loaf of bread, or a herring, or a pair of socks—anything to make a few rubles, to survive another day. Inflation wiped out most people's savings, and salaries were not being paid on time.

The new economic elite was emerging—exporting commodities, importing consumer goods, privatizing anything that wasn't nailed down. The press, freed from Soviet oppression, was lively. I remember freezing in my tracks seeing a picture of Solzhenitsyn—the Nobel prize winner imprisoned in 1945 and exiled by the Soviets in 1974—on the front page of *Pravda*, the former Communist Party newspaper. New imported cars roared on the streets and you could buy fresh fruits and vegetables in winter—nonexistent luxuries in the planned Soviet economy.

Russians kept looking ahead, and saw a better future. When communists attempted their coups, first in 1991 and again in 1993, people rose to resist—and won. The nation whose average per-capita income had shrunk by half refused to go back to the communist model.

Sometimes the most important messages are spoken in a very soft voice. I heard mine in the spring of 1996, while riding down an escalator. The Moscow subway is very deep, and on that long ride a woman's voice on the public address system kept saying softly, "Ladies and gentlemen (she was using a particularly endearing Russian form of address), be kind and attentive to one another." Kind and attentive? That was not what I grew up with. We had to be vigilant and militant. What if I was kind and attentive to someone and he turned out to be a class enemy?

Moscow was full of good cheer that summer. Russia's first ever presidential campaign was in full swing. The smart money bet on Yeltsin and against the communists, who went down to defeat several months later. They received only 40% of the vote, against 52% for the democrats. The communists lost as Russians voted for the future, against a return to the past.

In the runup to that election, the Russian Exchange introduced a futures contract based on the election's outcome. The wisdom and the power of free markets had been affirmed in the heart of the old Soviet empire. The final spread on the floor of the exchange came closer to the actual results than any opinion poll. The president of the exchange told me that he entered a betting pool at his club with $10,000 based on those results, and won the pot.

Moscow looked shiny and green, with construction everywhere, its streets and plazas cleaner than in New York. The stock market was booming; it doubled in the summer of '96, with many stocks rallying 3- and 4-fold.

I realized that traveling to Russia was no longer a sentimental journey, or a visit to a zoo. A modern country awoke from centuries of slumber and was confidently moving into the future. Freedom was up, crime was down, and business opportunities seemed amazing. A month later I bought my first ticket to Moscow. Instead of flying there on a bankers' ticket for a few days, teaching a seminar, and flying back, I took an apartment in Moscow and went to live there, exploring the city and learning about its business opportunities. Since then, I have been dividing my time between Moscow and New York.

Moscow is growing rich. Its concentration of money, power, arts, and sciences has no parallel in the US. Imagine the power of Washington, the money of New York, the entertainment industry of Los Angeles, the exchanges of Chicago, and much more rolled into a single city. Moscow has more Mercedes Benz cars than any other city outside of Germany and many restaurants where you can drop $200 per person for dinner. Its magazines advertise vacations in Thailand, real estate in the Mediterranean, and currency brokerage in Switzerland. The city pulsates with the excitement of money being made.

You can feel changes on the streets of Moscow and underground on its metro. People are well dressed, they make eye contact with one another, they hold doors for each other—friendly "Western" behavior, in striking contrast to the old Soviet gruffness.

The economic system is rapidly normalizing—moving toward a rational capitalist economy, away from the bizarre distortions of the communist era. Changing rubles into dollars used to be a crime in 1989, a risky deal with a 20% spread between the buy and the sell in 1995. Now it is a casual transaction with the spread of less than half of one percent (much better than you can get in New York City).

Russians are working harder than they have in generations. They earn, save, spend, and improve their lot. The Soviet Union used to have a horrendous rate of alcoholism—stuporous drunks used to lie on sidewalks even before noon. Now vodka is cheap; you can buy a pint for about $1, but falling-down drunks are almost gone. Workers have better things to do with their lives.

Russia had been ill with communism for 74 years. Today, the country is like a patient who just got out of bed after a long and severe illness. He is still weak, he cannot walk very fast, and he still holds onto the walls—but he is out of bed and he is not going back! Russia is irreversibly on the road to recovery.

Life in Russia is still hard—and downright brutal for many people. Some old folks rummage through garbage bins—that never used to happen in the Soviet Union. The old communist government cheated those who worked for it all their lives. Many workers outside of Moscow still go without pay for months. But this is a stage that many developing countries pass through. If you cannot see through the grime and crime, you have no business in Russia.

Are you a forward-looking investor? Do you try to look into the future and profit from it—or do you follow yesterday's news? Do you remember the fantastic bull markets of Asia Pacific in the 1980s and '90s, after the "emerging tigers" threw off their shackles of feudalism and became modern capitalist dynamos? Have you made money in Singapore, Hong Kong, and Taiwan? Did you profit in the stock markets of Latin America in the mid-1990s when one country after another went from a sleepy oligarchic statism to free enterprise?

Today, Russia has turned the corner. It is poised for takeoff, the way Asian tigers were in the 1960s.

Early fortunes have already been made, the easy money stolen in privatizations. There are still huge profits in the ongoing rush to economic normalization and prosperity. I wrote this book to give you basic information on the economic, political, and social changes in today's Russia. We will take a look at Russia's financial markets and review the dos and don'ts for investors and traders. If you believe in the future of freedom, you can help it advance in one huge country—and make money in the process.

I invite you on a journey to Russia. We will learn about this huge, rich country and look for investment and trading opportunities in its emerging markets. Russia today is a country of great opportunities—if you know how to exploit them and not become a financial statistic.

I will share my knowledge with you. Please question everything you read. Only by challenging and testing my ideas can you make them your own.

Let us begin our journey to Russia in search of profit opportunities.

2

THE ALMOST BLOODLESS REVOLUTION

There was little political violence in Russia when the country, like some huge ocean liner, reversed its course to steam away from the totalitarian dead end, toward the democratic opening. A few individuals were shot in the ensuing disorder, a handful of government bigwigs shot themselves, but there were very few tanks in the streets, no crowds storming government palaces. The Czechs, to the west of Russia, whose turn to democracy was even softer, called theirs a Velvet Revolution. The reason for this remarkable softness was that the change came from the top. The totalitarian government simply ran out of energy—it lost its will. As repression crumbled, free enterprise started to emerge, and democratic reformers entered the government.

Even a brief look at Russia's history reveals centuries of brutal oppression. Today, the nation that succeeded in liberating itself is in the midst of a democratic revolution.

More than six centuries ago the nomad hordes of Ghengis Khan erupted from the steppes (prairies) of Mongolia, riding west for thousands of miles. They burned, looted, raped, and killed until they came to a halt in what is now Austria. Their devastating and murderous sweep across Russia was followed by two hundred years of brutal occupation. The Mongols burned towns and villages, killed men and boys, and raped such masses of local women that to this day many Russian faces have prominent Mongol features.

In the 1500s, when Western Europe was blossoming with the Renaissance, the Russians were being hunted like animals by the invading nomads. One of the main forces holding Russia together at that time was the church. In 988 A.D., the country converted from paganism to the Byzantine branch of Christianity—perhaps the largest mass conversion in the history of the church. Russia's recent conversion to capitalism looks like a replay of this earlier change.

The Mongol occupation collapsed after two centuries, although their raids continued for another century. The Russian nobles and bishops remembered all too well the horrible price they had paid for their disjointed and ineffective defense. They wanted a strong central power, and for the next 300 years Russia was saddled with one of the most repressive dynasties in Europe.

The tsar of a hundred million people rode the streets of his capital in a carriage looking for nobles who might be smoking in public. (Sniffing tobacco was considered a healthy Russian habit, while smoking was a noxious foreign influence.) While Western Europe was booming with the Industrial Age, most Russians still lived as serfs (indentured peasants) in remote villages, whipped at will by their masters. The tiny ruling elite found it easy to extract enough wealth from the huge country, so they had no interest in developing its economy. There was no middle class to speak of—just masses of serfs and a small landed aristocracy. The tsars repressed, exiled, or chased out of the country many of its best creative minds, especially writers—Pushkin, Lermontov, Dostoyevsky, Turgenev. Amazingly, in that repressive atmosphere, Russia developed and sustained one of the most vibrant cultures anywhere in the world.

The Russian tsars expanded their empire over three centuries as far west as Poland, deep enough into Eastern Siberia to grab land from China and fight with Japan, north into Finland, and far enough south to clash with Turkey. In the 19th Century the tsars became rabid defenders of the geopolitical status quo, earning the nickname, "the gendarmes of Europe."

In 1918, the last members of the hapless Romanov dynasty ended their lives at the bottom of a Siberian mine shaft with bullet holes in their skulls. The murder of any individual is a tragedy, but recent attempts by Russian monarchists to elevate the last tsar to the status of a saint ignore the fact that his ineptitude helped bring the Bolshevik cruelty not just upon the royal family, but upon the entire nation. The monarchists are daydreaming of a restoration, even though in the 1990s Dmitry Lihachev, the nation's most respected historian, unearthed conclusive proof that the branch of the Russian royal family trying to weasel its way back into Moscow had lost its right of succession even by its own rules.

The communists who overthrew the tsar made him look like an amateur in the business of repression. Where a tsar hung five military officers for demonstrating against him, Trotsky and Lenin put thousands of officers, guilty only of having served in the tsar's army, into barges, towed them offshore, and sank them. Where the tsars hanged revolutionary gunrunners off telegraph poles, the communists hanged thousands of men and women in villages and towns that dared to resist their rule.

Six centuries of brutal repression did not break the Russian spirit. After two centuries of Mongol rule, three centuries of a repressive monarchy, and nearly a century of bloodthirsty communists, long-suffering Russia was liberated in 1991. It was an almost bloodless revolution. The old system crumbled after the government could no longer hold the empire together. There had been no general uprising, simply the falling apart of the old, and a spontaneous emergence of a democracy. Russia had freed itself not just from communism—it liberated itself from six centuries of repression. Since then, would-be strongmen tried to roll back the clock twice—and the nation rose to resist them and kept its freedom.

THE EVIL EMPIRE[2]

Casual visitors cannot comprehend the depth and speed of changes in Russia in recent years. Even locals, caught in their daily grind, often lose sight of the fantastic changes in their country.

---

[2] When Ronald Reagan slapped this movie term on the Soviets, many liberals snickered at him as simplistic—but the words stuck. In today's Russia, people use this term whenever they talk of their recent past.

Visitors see Coca-Cola signs, people in jeans, *The Wall Street Journal* on newsstands, and a chain of religious stores owned by the Moscow Patriarchy. It seems like a pretty normal landscape, with some local color.

These and other seemingly casual signs reflect profound political, social, and economic changes. The Soviet empire fiercely fought change; it jailed, exiled, and killed its opponents. The Soviet Union was a repressive behemoth whose ham-fisted control of its people grew like a cancer, metastasizing at a crazy speed, following a sick logic of its own. It began at birth—the state laid down the rules for a family's first contact with its newborn. It continued after death—if a family dared to arrange a religious funeral, the state punished the survivors.

A baby born in the USSR was kept for ten days in a "birthing house," a maternity ward where women sometimes had to wash their own bloody bedsheets. New mothers could touch their newborns only during feeding times, and no visitors were allowed. The Health Ministry laid down those rules, and no one could argue with the ministry! Fathers and relatives across the country lined up under the windows of the birthing houses, hoping for a glimpse of their new baby, kept at bay by an idiotic decree.

A child old enough to go to school would come for the first time into the field of vision of the KGB, the dreaded secret police. Private schools were outlawed,[3] and public schools promoted the cult of Pavlik Morozov. When city communists came to his village to confiscate grain in the 1920s, Pavlik showed them where his parents hid theirs. They were arrested and exiled to Siberia, and Pavlik's uncle slit the boy's throat. The Soviet propaganda machine sanctified the informer boy.

I was six years old when my parents and grandparents began to warn me, "Do not tell anyone what you hear at home." They listened to the Voice of America behind closed doors and drawn curtains, spoke highly of the West, and laughed at the government, but both my parents were communist party members. At their jobs, they

---

[3]Today, there is an amazing proliferation of private schools in Russia—Christian and Jewish, English and Latin, and so on. I have met several owners—few are making any money, but all are having a lot of fun.

sat at party meetings and raised their hands in approval of party resolutions. Several generations of Soviet children grew up like that,
learning to hide and lay low. No wonder so many Soviets grew up
stiff and suspicious.

At the same time, many people in the USSR learned to enjoy
intense closeness with the few people they could trust. Loyalties and
friendships were and still are much deeper in Russia than in the
West—strengthened by the knowledge of shared dangers.

Those of us who went to universities after high school were
split into groups of 15 to 25 students—with a KGB informer in each
group. The Russian word for an informer was *stukach* (literally, the
one who knocks). You never knew who it was; you always tried to
guess, but could never be sure. You'd be sharing jokes with friends
when someone would rap his knuckles on a table—beware of those
who knock. Was your *stukach* a quiet girl listening in the corner or
a loudmouth guy trying to provoke others to speak their minds?
There was a *stukach* in every factory unit and every office; some
reported out of fear, others hoped for future favors from the KGB.

Where are those *stukachi* today? The state has no more use for
them, but keeps protecting their identities. Their files remain locked
in secret archives. When you deal with a person over 35 in Russia
today, you can never be sure whether he or she used to be a KGB
stukach—there are millions of those lost souls.

Out on the streets of the Soviet Union, groups of *druzhinniki*,
(police auxiliaries), harassed people whose clothes were politically
incorrect. They could catch a *stilyaga* (sharp dresser) and cut open
his tight pant legs, or mess up a tall hairdo on a girl, or break her
spike heels. I grew up in Estonia, the formerly independent Baltic
state, whose national blue-black-and-white flag had been outlawed.
The police could toss a person into the slammer for 15 days, if they
caught him in the street wearing a blue-black-and-white sweater.

It was a crime to be in business or even to be self-employed.
An elderly neighbor who helped my parents buy a good winter coat
and two spare tires had been arrested, convicted of being a *makler*
(broker) and sent to a labor camp for two years. The government
had the monopoly on the means of production. Underground businessmen could make astronomic profits, but had to hide. Every

entrepreneur was a criminal by definition because he used equipment that belonged to the state. All businessmen risked their freedom, but the reward for the most successful was death. If you made a million and the government caught you, it called that "an extra large theft of state property," and could shoot you after a show trial.

Stalin, the supreme leader from the early 1920s until his death in 1953, proclaimed that a Soviet man was a cog in the machinery of the state; and the state stuck its nose deep into people's private affairs. If a man wanted a divorce, his wife could ask his bosses to haul him to a workers' meeting and grill him about his "antisocial tendencies."[4] It could have been funny if it weren't so sad. A divorced couple often had nowhere to go. The perennial housing shortage meant they continued to live together and even date other people, sharing the only room they had, divided in two by a blanket hanging from a rope.

Each citizen above the age of 16 had to carry an "internal passport" stamped with his or her address. It was a crime to live away from one's assigned place for more than three days without registering with the police. The law was rarely enforced against vacationers or tourists, but often used to harass dissidents and keep peasants down on collective farms.

The "Iron Curtain" that surrounded the USSR not only limited foreigners' access to the country, it imprisoned Soviet citizens. The entire country was ringed with barbed wire, tripwires, and a 6-meter (18 ft.) wide strip of specially smoothed dirt to detect the tracks of would-be escapees. No wonder political prisoners called labor camps "the small zone" and the country "the big zone." Half a million guards patrolled the border with dogs, searchlights, and helicopters. Running away was a capital offense, but desperate men, such as myself, kept taking chances.

Permission to travel abroad was one of the greatest perks of the Soviet elite. The rulers went shopping in the West, but prevented

---

[4] A typical Russian joke from those days: A man marries a hooker, but can no longer tolerate her behavior and files for divorce. She hauls him to a party meeting.
—Why do you want to divorce your wife?
—She does not satisfy me.
—Rubbish! She satisfies all of us, whaddya mean she doesn't satisfy you?

ordinary people from seeing how their counterparts lived. They kept foreign newspapers and magazines out of the USSR. In August 1968, after the Soviets invaded Czechoslovakia, I ran to the newsstands to see what the West had to say, but *The Morning Star*, the British Communist Party newspaper, had already been removed.

The government not only owned all the mass media, it ringed most cities with stubby "suppression towers." They broadcasted noise at the wavelengths of Radio Liberty, the BBC, and the Voice of America, drowning them out. Hando, my neighbor, returning from prison, said that the USSR was like a steamboat that could not move forward because it wasted its steam tooting its horn.

As I write these lines in Moscow, my radio is tuned to a local station, broadcasting the BBC in Russian. The station whose signal used to be suppressed has its own transmitter in the city! The Voice of America, Die Deutsche Welle (The German Wave), even South Korean radio all have local offices in Moscow. Radio Liberty, formerly funded by the CIA, has moved from Munich to Prague, and its commentators often appear on Russian TV. It is a fantastic change for a returning refugee!

The Soviet Union prevented its people from traveling abroad–unless they went in tanks and armored personnel carriers. The history of the USSR is a chronicle of crude threats, intimidation, gunrunning, and naked aggression against its neighbors. The Soviets invaded Mongolia in 1930, Finland and Poland in 1939, Hungary in 1956, Czechoslovakia in 1968, Afghanistan in 1981—this is just a short list of some of the most brazen attacks.

When Europe was stumbling toward World War II in 1939, Stalin signed a friendship pact with Hitler, attacked Poland and invaded and annexed Estonia, Latvia, and Lithuania. After the two buddies fell out, Russia was plunged into a bloody war, which it won at a cost of 19 million lives.

Millions had been killed during the 74-year war the Soviet government waged against its own people. Entire layers of society had been summarily sentenced to death and imprisonment—tsarist military officers, priests, aristocrats, Cossacks, successful peasants, political dissidents. They were shot, or hanged, or died a slow death in labor camps.

THE COMMUNIST COLLAPSE

The Communist Party and the KGB held the Soviet Empire by its gills, while a huge army protected it from any external threat. The system had been built to last and even to try to conquer the world. The ship of the state sank after its captain cracked open the door to reform—and the flood of change rushed in.

Mikhail Gorbachev, who came into power in 1985, was the last communist tsar. He may have been more inclined to liberalize the system because his and his wife's families had been victimized during the Stalin era. In trying to revive the stagnant Soviet economy, Gorbachev introduced two new concepts—*glasnost* and *perestroika*. *Glasnost* (literally, "voice-ness") meant speaking up and criticizing mistakes. This may sound normal to a Westerner, but it was a revolutionary concept in the USSR, where many generations had been brutally subdued into silence. *Perestroika* (literally, rebuilding) permitted a small degree of private enterprise.

Once the people could speak with impunity, the shouts suppressed for over 70 years broke from their throats. Once they got a chance to run their own businesses, they started abandoning their state jobs. The old system could not take the stress of change and began to crumble. Gorbachev, who remained a card-carrying communist, had nothing against the Soviet system. He was its product and its beneficiary and only tried to improve it. He was flabbergasted when, in response to his reforms, the Soviet system began falling apart.

Magazines and newspapers started publishing political exposés. The mass murders of political opponents, the massacre of Polish officers at Katyn, the century-long history of communist lies, repression, and exploitation were opened up to the public. At first, many journalists feared arrest, but when nobody came after them, the media grew bold and its revelations helped wash away the last remaining shreds of the system's legitimacy. The communists were like Dracula—both drank blood in the dark and could not survive the light of day.

Private businesses began to open up in the late 1980s. Their right to exist was still uncertain—the laws against them were still on the books. A vice-president of the Russian Exchange said to me lightheartedly in April 1997, while we were waiting for the annual meeting to begin, "For the first four years we all worked under the article of the Criminal Code—ten years imprisonment with confiscation of property."

As the dam of prohibitions erected over 74 years began to crumble, new opportunities came in like a flood. Interest rates rocketed above 100%, but businesses could earn 100% in three months. The impregnable Iron Curtain became more like Swiss cheese. Imports and exports soared, nobody paid any taxes, the government treasury was emptied. Without subsidies, inefficient state industries started grinding to a halt.

Democrats and nationalists in Eastern Europe began to stir. The communist regimes of Czechoslovakia and Poland imploded and fell. Germany became reunited just months after the last two men had been shot trying to scale the Berlin Wall. The earlier Soviet rulers would have ruthlessly repressed their satellites, but Gorbachev's government lost its sense of purpose. The military literally ran out of gas. The men in the Kremlin stared in a groggy stupor at the changes they had unleashed, but could no longer control.

As the empire started to disintegrate, the increasingly restive Soviet parliament had scheduled a crucial vote. No longer a rubber stamp for the Central Committee of the Communist Party, it was going to vote whether to maintain the Soviet Union or let its restive members go. The Communist Party of the Soviet Union had a century-long history of armed intervention on the eve of important votes. On the eve of the 1991 vote, a group of old communist bosses staged a coup, trying to turn back the tide.

In August 1991, while Gorbachev was vacationing at a Black Sea *dacha* (summer house), they seized control of the central government. The *putchists,* as the plotters came to be called, hoped to swing Gorbachev to their side, but, just in case they could not, they put him and his family under house arrest. The *putchists* had been just as incompetent running a coup as they had been running the country in their earlier days. The first thing they did after announcing their takeover on TV was to have a party and drink themselves into a stupor. They never secured the Moscow TV tower, its City Hall, or most other potential resistance centers. Boris Yeltsin, the firebrand president of the Russian Republic, the largest component of the Soviet Union, fired by Gorbachev from the central government just a year earlier, rapidly emerged as the leader of the democratic resistance.

Yeltsin had been away from Moscow on the day of the coup. With great personal courage, he flew back into Moscow to organize resistance. He managed to land and get into his office because the incompetent plotters had forgotten to seal the airports.

Yeltsin rallied the democrats from his office in the Russian White House, ringed by a thin line of loyal police and armed guards sent by private security agencies. An American hotel owner loaned Yeltsin his cell phone, allowing him to keep in touch with the media even after his phone lines had been cut. Volunteers streamed to the White House and built barricades against the assault—but it never came. The plotters, bruised by fierce public resistance turned to the military; but the Russian army has no tradition of coups. When the army refused to join the fight, the rebellion collapsed.

Three persons were killed in the coup. The *putchists* were released after a few years in jail and an unsuccessful prosecution. There was an emotional backlash against the communists, and their party was briefly outlawed. Gorbachev was widely perceived as having lost control and prestige. Yeltsin met with the presidents of Ukraine and Belarus, the two largest Slavic republics. The three had agreed to separate, effectively ending the existence of the Soviet Union. Gorbachev, the president of the USSR, no longer had a country—and Yeltsin, who had publicly resigned from the Communist Party, remained president of the largest, richest, and most powerful component of the old Soviet empire.

The tsars had built their empire for over three centuries and the communists had expanded it for nearly a century, but the entire structure collapsed in just a few years. One ex-Soviet republic after another bolted and declared its independence. The population of the Soviet Union used to be over 250 million, but after the republics split up only 150 million people remained in Russia.

When Humpty Dumpty fell off the wall, he left jagged shards all over the place. Local fights for power flared into nasty national-ist wars along Russia's periphery, especially its southern borders. Armed bands chased each other in Moldova (the Trans-Dniestr region), in Georgia (the civil war in Abhazia), in Armenia and Azerbaidjan (the fight for Nagorno-Karabakh), and elsewhere. Moscow kept sending its paratroops to extricate Russian refugees, but lost surprisingly few men, thanks to the troops' speed and the limited scope of their operations.

Two years later Russia was in for another communist coup attempt. In 1993 Boris Yeltsin came to loggerheads with the *Duma* (the Russian parliament). Its communist deputies were blocking his reforms and trying to roll them back. Yeltsin publicly questioned the legitimacy of those deputies, since half of them had been appointed under the old regime rather than elected.

Russia's new constitution was still too raw and did not have a clear mechanism for resolving such conflicts between the branches of government (it now does). Yeltsin was prepared to wait for the next election, but the communist members of *Duma* had other plans. They stockpiled weapons in the Parliament building and called on their supporters to come join them. Moscow communists rushed to the Duma and attacked the TV center in Ostankino on the outskirts of Moscow. The city saw another night of skirmishes: firefights between rebels and the city police, crowds of democracy supporters rallying to build barricades and protect the Ostankino TV tower.

The old communists' planning had been slipshod and inefficient as usual. They counted on the support of the army whose officer corps was heavily communist—but the army remained in its barracks.[5] Yeltsin ordered a tank unit from the elite Kantemirov Guards division into the city. The tanks circled the *Duma* building in the center of Moscow, gave its defenders an ultimatum, and opened fire. The rebels surrendered, their leaders were arrested, but released after two years without a trial. In 1996 Alexander Rutskoi, one of the coup leaders, won a democratic gubernatorial election in the Kursk region, southwest of Moscow, in the heart of Russia.

Speaking of beating back the coup, there are several thousand persons in Moscow who recognize one another from the barricades

---

[5] While driving to a friend's *dacha* outside Moscow in 1996, I saw a handmade plywood memorial to a traffic cop who had been killed in 1993 after he stopped several truckloads of soldiers driving to the city to join the rebels. They murdered him but lost heart, turned and drove back to their barracks.

of 1991 and 1993. They risked their lives and the future of their families to protect the fledgling democracy and fight communism—and
won. Victory was far from certain in those days, and a strong sense
of camaraderie persists. I have noticed in recent years that more and
more people speak of having been there (the barricades are becoming more crowded with the passage of time). It reminds me of
Americans claiming descent from the Mayflower, which has been
called "the largest ship in history."

In 1996, Russia held its first democratic presidential election—
a watershed event in the nation's history. The establishment threw
its support to Yeltsin, who won with 52% of the popular vote,
against 40% for Zyuganov, the communist candidate. Communists
hinted darkly at a social disorder if they lost the election, but in the
end were remarkably gracious in their defeat.

WILL THEY RETURN?

Many casual observers in the US, Australia, Europe, and Asia have
said to me they feared that Russia's anticommunist revolution of 1991
will become undone. They think a new strongman may emerge, grab
power, roll back the clock and return us all to the days of living
under the threat of Russian intercontinental ballistic missiles.

These are empty fears.

Russian reforms are irreversible—the country will not tolerate
a new strongman. As the waves of democratic elections roll across
the land, people keep voting time and again for democracy and
capitalism. The communist opposition is splintered, broke, devoid
of ideas, and has lost its access to the mass media. The majority,
not only the elite, are benefiting from the reforms. The Russian
army never staged a coup, and its military machine is a broken,
rusting hulk.

The Russian army is in a sad state today, hungry and demoralized. It lost the war in Chechnya, its officers are selling blood to help
feed their families, and suicide is the largest cause of death among
the military. The Russian army has never been very good at offensive operations, although it had always been an extremely tough

defender of the homeland. Bismarck, Germany's so-called Iron Chancellor, once said, "It is not enough to kill the Russian soldier—you still have to knock him down."

NATO has not been gracious in its new aggressive push towards Russia's borders. The former satellites, liberated from Soviet tanks are about to see American armor rolling on their soil. NATO's eastward expansion preserves the military's jobs but feeds Russia's fears. NATO plays into the hands of the worst right-wing nationalists—against the liberal, pro-Western circles of Russia.

On May 9, 1997, Victory Day, an emotional public holiday in the country that had lost 19 million people in World War II, the army did not have enough money for its customary parade of military hardware in Red Square. They could afford only a 50-minute march by several units, representing different services. The fatal weakness of the military machine is good for the young democracy.

Free, vigorously contested elections are taking place all over the vast expanse of Russia. Not just Presidential elections, but many local ones, for governors and mayors. Communists rarely win; most winners are young reformers, with no strong party affiliation, running on the platform of economic growth and democratic reform. An occasional good showing by a potential strongman, such as Zhirinovsky[6] is no more than a flash in the pan. The Russians have had their fill of strongmen and will not tolerate another one.

The transition from the old Soviet system to the free markets merits its own book; most topics in this volume merit their own books. Three groups made out best: businesspeople, the young, and the members of the Soviet power structure.[7] Businesspeople flourished because they could concentrate on making money without

---

[6] Zhirinovsky is an extreme right-wing Russian nationalist. He promised to expand Russia into Germany and south to the Indian Ocean. He promised profits for businesspeople and good salaries to workers; support for families with children and respect for homosexuals. He promised to lock up or shoot criminals (which is probably why for one brief moment he became the second highest polling politician in the country) before his antics and grandiose empty promises made him the laughingstock of the country.

[7] I know a man who used to be a career KGB officer, spying on NATO out of Riga. When the Soviet Union collapsed, his entire intelligence unit took off their uniforms, "privatized" their building, and went into business importing computers, using their connections at the border. He used part of his new fortune to buy a green card, and is now a prosperous businessman in San Francisco.

hiding from the KGB. Young people have found it easier than their parents to adjust, learn English (which opens a window to the West), and acquire new working skills. Members of the Soviet elite already had their hands on many levers of power, which meant they could make more money in the new economy.

Revolutions and riots are the work of young men who feel disenfranchised. In Russia the young are the main beneficiaries of the reform. They can earn more money than their parents, buy Western goods, and travel abroad. They do not go to political meetings or demonstrations; they are too busy learning English and saving to buy apartments and cars. Many of the older folks who worked all their lives for the Soviet Union are hurt and disgruntled. The reforms have left them with no jobs, no money, and miserable pensions. But poor *babushkas* do not make revolutions.

The political/government/KGB elite that used to run the old Soviet Union has made out very well in the *perestroika*. They lost their monopoly on power, but gained a great deal of wealth by grabbing some of the choicest assets during Russia's privatization. A Communist Party boss could privatize the party building—which was often the best, most central building in the city—and become a major commercial landlord. The question of what happened to the Communist Party money is one of the greatest mysteries of life in modern Russia (you sometimes get a whiff of that money while visiting people in high places).

Some members of the old communist elite are still in the government, while others have moved into banking, big business, and big time import and export. They dominate areas that require government licenses, and use their old connections. They no longer have to hide their wealth. Now, they can own private planes, live ostentatiously, and send their wives to shop in the toniest boutiques of Europe.

A woman who came to work for me in New York described the transition at her old Soviet job at a programming center in Riga. The government paychecks stopped, and the executives turned the center into a private business, doing anything they could to earn money—from computer programming to exporting souvenirs and importing watches. The party members at the firm had a meeting at which they decided to continue paying their dues to the party cell chairman, who'd keep their cash in his office safe. Should the old system come back, they'd have proof of their loyalty, but should the USSR collapse for good, they would use that money for a huge party—which is exactly what they did several months later.

An investor, who stays out of Russia today because he fears the return of communism, is still paying dues into that old party safe—while the rest of us are having a party!

Russia is rapidly developing into a modern liberal capitalist state. It has been on this road for only a few years, and already has free enterprise, free media, and free elections. Sure, the country has many problems. Many enterprises are inefficient and plagued with outmoded regulations. Some of the new mega-rich are buying up media outlets, trying to control and slant their coverage. Some elections have been marred by claims of restricted access to the media and improper financial support. But these are normal problems of a young democracy.

As recently as 1990, the KGB still held the country in its grip; the Soviet troops, armed to the teeth, faced NATO in divided Germany; the single-party system was enshrined in the constitution, and free enterprise was a crime. In just a few years Russian society has made a huge leap forward. It accomplished this historic transition in a remarkably peaceful manner, with very little bloodshed.

"Buy when blood is running in the streets," said Baron Rothschild. You will not see blood on the streets of Russia—just a lot of potholes—but the memory of recent troubles keeps investment values low, creating great opportunities.

Russians have a saying, "There is good fishing in murky waters." Eventually, Russia's financial markets will become less murky and as sedate as the markets in the US or Germany, but, by that time, the great opportunities will no longer be there. Investors who buy low today will make their money by selling high to the crowds that will rush in later.

3

THE DEPRESSION
OF THE 1990S

The rulers of the Soviet Union held the country in an iron grip, trying to achieve two major goals: to build up the military and take care of the elite. It hardly mattered to them that people's incomes were abysmally low and stagnant or that consumer goods were always in short supply. When the rulers' grandiose plans clashed with reality, they simply raised production quotas and made workers push harder. People lived in shabby apartments with paper-thin walls, several families sharing a single bathroom. People could buy fruits and vegetables only for a few short months in summer, and women spent endless hours each day on food lines. None of that mattered to the elite, who lived in guarded compounds, with their own stores and fleets of cars, and relaxed at special resorts.

The Soviet state, led by the Communist Party, owned everything in the USSR, from the deepest gold mine to the shabbiest shoeshine stand. After the party was outlawed in the aftermath of its 1991 coup attempt, the assets of the entire country were suddenly left without an owner. Everything was up for grabs. The savvy operators joined the gold rush, while the enfeebled economy began to sink.

Russia's Gross National Product (GNP) shrank nearly in half from 1989 to 1996. The purchasing power of the ruble went down the drain, as inflation wiped out more than 99% of its value. Most Russians lost their life savings, while a handful of speculators made quick fortunes. Many industries crumbled, factories and research institutes shut down, and throngs of the unemployed lined the streets trying to sell a few loaves of bread or a pair of socks in order to eat for another day.

Amazingly, there were no riots among the destitute—another proof of the legendary patience of the Russian people.[8] Imagine what would have happened in the US if the nation's income had been cut in half! The Russians got rid of the communist system and expected their lives to improve—only no one knew how long the Depression would last.

. The collapse of the communist system liberated Russia, but the drastic change pushed its economy over the brink. The nation became impoverished, its savings were wiped out, entire industries run into the ground. The pain of the Depression of the 1990s was so intense that even Russia's birthrate collapsed, while its mortality rate shot up. It had an effect similar to that of the carpet bombings of Germany and Japan in World War II. Those bombings pulverized industries and killed civilians, but, by wiping the slate clean, they allowed the countries that lost the war to emerge as economic super-powers after it ended. The Depression of the 1990s forced Russians to abandon their old ways, change their laws and mindsets, and get into a position to become world-class economic competitors.

In November 1996, I visited a friend who served as a chief care-taker and deacon at a local monastery. The autumn sun played on the Moscow River while a gang of workers lazily swung mallets at a low brick wall in the courtyard. The city sent them to work off their unemployment benefits, and my friend had them remove "the wall of honor." I laughed. The wall of honor was a typical Soviet struc-ture, erected at factories and offices to display slogans and portraits of their best workers. What was it doing at a monastery? Igor

---

[8] In a Stalin-era joke, a factory director tells a foreign visitor about how cooperative his work-ers are: "I could hang them if I wanted, and they wouldn't complain." The visitor looks doubtful, so the director calls a factory meeting and announces: "Comrades, we have an overproduction problem and need to reduce our labor force. Since we can't lay people off in our socialist homeland, we will hang redundant workers, starting with those in Building A, tomorrow. Any questions? Suddenly, a lone hand shoots up, "I have a question!" "What's that?" frowns the director. "Will the factory provide the rope or do we bring our own?"

explained that the communists confiscated most of his monastery's buildings and gave them to the State Pricing Committee. Hordes of faceless bureaucrats used to sit in the monks' chambers, dictating prices of tractors in Siberia or shoelaces in Leningrad. The photos of the best price setters went on the wall of honor. A few months before my visit, the last holdouts from the Price Committee had been booted out. They set a fire as their going away present. Now the monastery was reclaiming its grounds—just as the free market reclaimed its right to set its own prices.

THE CENTER COULD NOT HOLD

Even after beating back the 1991 communist coup attempt, the central government was weak and disorganized. It was made up of an odd mixture of reform-minded democrats still learning the ropes and old *apparatchiki* (Soviet officials) trying to hold on to their jobs.

Daniel Cloud, a New York money manager, remarked: "Power deflation has a built-in positive feedback. Since there are only so many KGB agents and so many prisons, the more people defy or ignore the authority of the state, the safer it is for the marginal person to do so, while the perceived legitimacy of the state and its laws is increasingly damaged by the sight of powerful people using them for a doormat." He added, "Reform . . . makes the leader who initiates it vulnerable precisely because he has abandoned the traditional sources of legitimacy and power on which his regime has heretofore been based." Mikhail Gorbachev, who attempted to liberalize the Soviet Union, was swept out of office and became one of the most hated men in Russia.

The Communist Party ruthlessly suppressed all the rival power centers in the country—its ethnic and religious movements, its businesspeople and independent farmers, its dissident writers and artists. As the system began to crumble, members of those groups became increasingly vocal, and, after seeing they could act with impunity, increasingly bold.

Angry crowds pulled down statues of Lenin and other communist saints. The first president of the Russian Exchange left the crowd and called the Moscow city hall as men began tying ropes around the neck of the statue of Dzerzhinsky, the founder of the KGB (the Soviet secret police). He asked for a truck-mounted crane to yank away the statue, whose violent fall could injure demonstrators. When bureaucrats balked, he offered them money—and so, a belated hanging of the founder of the KGB was paid for by a commodities trader! Thick smoke came out of the KGB office windows facing the statue, as panicked officers burned secret papers, expecting the crowd to storm their buildings.

Nationalists on the periphery of the Soviet empire had risen, as one republic after another proclaimed its independence. In some areas, such as Estonia and Ukraine, the parting from the empire was bloodless. In others, such as Tajikistan, shooting continues even today, in 1998.

The breakup of the Soviet Union and the Warsaw Block in Eastern Europe disrupted commercial links built up over decades. Factories, suppliers, and consumers suddenly found themselves on opposite sides of state borders.[9] Instead of rubles, most of them had to deal with new local currencies. Some had an overstock of products they could not sell, others had shortages of goods, parts, and components—and nobody had any money. Even the Westernized Baltics came down from the heady early days of independence with a somber realization that their industrial products were not yet good enough to compete in the West, while their traditional Russian markets had been cut off by the new international borders.

As the state grew weak, its legal system ground to a halt. Nobody paid bills, extortion was rampant, and courts could not enforce contracts. Nobody had any credit. Hundreds of thousands of dollars worth of business was done by paying cash on the spot, usually in dollars. To do business in another city, you'd get on a plane with a briefcase full of $100 bills and bring along two armed bodyguards.

---

[9] An Armenian friend described lustily how he drank fine aged cognacs for only $3 a bottle on a recent trip to his country. Armenia's rail links to Russia—its traditional retail market— had been cut off by its war with Azerbaidjan. Export by air is too expensive, and so the impoverished republic is flooded with good cheap cognac.

It paid to do business only with those you knew and trusted. On a recent visit with a senior Russian executive, I asked about his younger daughter's husband. He sighed, "He was a businessman, Alex. You know what it's like to be a businessman in our country. One day you're driving a Mercedes, the next you have two bullets in your head." Many business disagreements got kicked up to the ubiquitous *kryshas*—bandits who extorted a percentage from businesses and mediated their disputes (more about this in Chapter 4).

THE PEACE DIVIDEND

The Soviet government always allocated the lion's share of its resources to the military, at the expense of a pathetically weak consumer sector. It kept pushing for military superiority over the US, even though its smaller economy made the arms race unaffordable. Communists did develop a powerful military-industrial complex, but ultimately it busted the civilian economy. Gorbachev tried to slow down the arms race, but it was too late. After the Soviet Union fell apart, the military prowess of Russia and other former Soviet republics went into a tailspin.

Americans expected a "peace dividend" at the end of the Cold War. Instead, we had serious economic problems, especially in the states where military industries were concentrated. Unemployment, plant closings, and depressed real-estate values hit the more military-dependent areas of California, New York, Texas, and other states. The closing of the assembly line of F-14 jet fighters on Long Island alone affected more than 10,000 workers in New York state in the mid-1990s. Fortunately, the overall economy was strong enough to pick up the slack. Small towns in North Dakota, whose economy depended on missile forces, went into a deep hibernation after the rocket silos were emptied. This happened in the country that won the Cold War! Russia, which lost it and had a weaker economy to boot, suffered tenfold. Demilitarization was good for world peace, but it helped push the Russian economy into a catastrophic plunge.

Entire cities built around huge tank, rocket, and battleship factories went on the dole after the military stopped buying. To this day, Russia's antiquated real-estate laws make it very difficult to move. People are unlikely to leave their homes to look for jobs elsewhere. The shock of mass unemployment was softer in big cities with diverse industries and better business opportunities, but elsewhere people survived largely on what food they could grow on tiny private plots that circle all Russian cities.

An event in Murmansk, a port city north of St. Petersburg, received some publicity in Russia in 1994, but was largely overlooked in the West. The Russian Navy could not pay for the removal of nuclear reactors from its decommissioned submarines. They berthed several disarmed subs at the Murmansk naval base and used them as floating nuclear waste containers. Those hulks needed electric power from the shore to cool their reactors. The privatized local utility began sending bills to the base.

The navy could not pay, and after a few months the utility pulled the plug on its delinquent customer. As nuclear waste started heating up, an admiral sent a detachment of marines to the power plant to force the electricians at gunpoint to reconnect the power to the base. The local newspapers hailed him as a hero for saving the city from a nuclear disaster. The admiral was bitter, "We are the Navy, we are not here to make money, we can only spend it."

Science and research were hard hit. In Soviet years three quarters of their funding came from the military. Communist rulers kept the best scientists in secret research institutes, away from the universities, reducing the quality of education. Politicians arrogantly "resolved" scientific disputes on the basis of ideology, and restricted international contacts.

After the elite research institutes ran out of money and stopped paying salaries, many appeared as if a neutron bomb had gone off, leaving their peeling walls and old furniture intact, but wiping out most workers. The young ones left—for the West, for private businesses, even to sell vodka in the streets. The older folks still hang on, waiting for their pensions. The woman who cleans my apartment in Moscow has a Ph.D. and used to work for the Soviet space program. I felt uneasy at first having a middle-aged scientist scrub my floors and do laundry, but we became friends and she makes me delicious *blini* (Russian pancakes). Cleaning my apartment is one of several odd jobs this scholar does during her office hours, while waiting for retirement. Her institute is over a year behind on her salary.

The institutes whose very existence used to be a state secret are now begging for any kind of income. A friend of mine rents an office for his investment company from a formerly secret research institute that used to develop long-range radio communications for the Soviet Air Force. They used to plan bombing runs against the US, but now an American can saunter right in, wave a New York-issued credit card instead of an ID, and breeze past an underpaid *babushka* nodding at a checkpoint.

THE HUMAN COST

Russians paid a huge price for the communists' policies of the previous 74 years during the Depression of the 1990s. An average person saw his or her income fall 54% in dollar terms between 1991 and 1996. Huge income disparities emerged, throwing Soviet-era relative egalitarianism out the window. Mercedes Benzes flooded the streets of Moscow at the same time as beggars—the more of one, the more of the other.

Many Russians continue to suffer even today, after the economy has largely bottomed out. The pain of the Depression of the 1990s was so sharp, it left most people immensely skeptical of politicians' promises. A potential strongman in Russia would have a very hard time trying to sell easy fixes. Russians just want to be left alone and earn money.

Back in the spring of 1995, an American friend came to pick me up at the Sheremetyevo airport in Moscow. He told his driver to let us out near the Kremlin for a stroll on Red Square. A flock of *babushki*—old women—rushed toward us, hands outstretched, begging. That could never happen in the old Soviet Union! My friend handed the first one to reach him a 1,000 ruble note, less than 20 American cents. She bent at the waist and kissed his hand. "I've done my *mitzva* (good deed) for the day," he said as we headed for a nearby Chinese restaurant. A pleasant lunch for two with a few beers cost a bit over $100. Outside, old *babushki* were trying to survive on $15 monthly pensions.

In 1996 during Russia's presidential election campaign, Yeltsin promised to take care of pensioners if he won the election. He won and he did—raising old-age pensions from $15 to $19 per month.

The nonpayment of salaries became endemic in Russia. A medieval custom of paying workers "in kind" has returned. Factories that cannot meet their payrolls pay their workers with products which the factory itself cannot sell, such as bookshelves or beer glasses. Driving to a friend's *dacha* north of Moscow in the summer of 1996 I noticed clumps of men and women selling gaudy beach towels along the road. The designs and prices seemed identical, and most roadside sellers appeared grim. My friend explained that a nearby towel factory had paid its workers in kind, and they were selling towels to buy food.

In December 1996 Russian sociologists reported that only 30% of salaries in the country were paid in full and on time that year, mostly in Moscow, St. Petersburg, and other better-off areas (down from 45% in 1995). During that year 39% of salaries never got paid (up from 17% in 1995). The number that follows may shock Westerners—when sociologists asked workers whether they would be willing to demonstrate against those conditions, only 26% answered yes (up from 23% in 1995).

One scenario became so repetitive, it no longer made the front pages of Russian newspapers: salaries would not be paid for several months in the provinces, then miners or teachers would go on strike and bring their region to a halt. The government in the Kremlin would respond by flying in a planeload of cash, pay everyone a month's salary and promise more, and the strikers would go back to work. Sometimes managers really had no money, but as recently as 1996 they could be diverting payrolls into the hugely profitable GKO market (GKO is a Russian acronym for *Gosudarstvenniye Kratkosrochniye Obligatsii* or State Short-Term Obligations—see Chapter 7). Several of my friends among GKO brokers told me they had clients who "borrowed" their workers' payrolls to make themselves 100% profits in GKOs.

Russian workers are not only skilled and educated, they have low expectations. When you pay them a decent salary and pay it on time—a few hundred dollars a month at the time of this writing—

people will gladly work six days a week, for as many hours as you need them.

The Depression of the 1990s physically hurt the nation. The two basic indicators of public health are average longevity and infant mortality. In most countries the average longevity keeps rising and infant mortality keeps falling, but in Russia in the 1990s those trends became reversed.

The average life expectancy in the Soviet Union used to be in a slow uptrend, rising from 68 years in 1959 to 70 years in 1989. It fell to 64 years by 1994 (from 65 years down to 58 for men and from 75 years down to 71 for women). That fall appears to have bottomed out, as in 1995 the average life expectancy rose to 65 years. Mortality in Russia rose from 10.4/1,000 in 1986 to 15.4/1,000 in 1994. It stabilized and began to shrink again, falling to 15.0 in 1995. The Depression of the 1990s was killing people—especially middle-aged men who, left without work, were dropping like flies.

In December 1996 the First Moscow Medical Institute closed its hospitals for lack of supplies and funding. The most prestigious medical center in Russia, built along the grandly named Alley of Life, remained open throughout the revolutions and wars. Now it was sending its patients home.

Russia's population stopped growing and began to shrink during the Depression, falling 0.61% in 1994 and 0.57% in 1995. The birth rate in Russia fell by almost half, from 17.2 per 1,000 population in 1990 to 9.3 in 1995. People were too shell-shocked to procreate. In the early 1990s you saw hardly any babies or young children on the streets of Russia. Giving birth to a second child was called having a large family. Today, one of the more pleasant sights on Moscow streets is the rapidly growing number of baby carriages. I even saw a family once with three smiling young children.

RUBLES IN THE RUBBLE

After democrats beat back the communist coup in 1991, Yeltsin used the power vacuum to issue a series of decrees to legitimize sweeping changes in the society. A decree to remove controls on wages and prices was among them. Central planning—the key tenet of a communist economy—was tossed out the window.

In one fell swoop, Russia's economy was opened to free-market principles. That bold move stunned the economy, like bringing a fish used to living 20,000 feet below the surface right up to sea level. The idiocies of central planning, accumulated during three quarters of a century, were suddenly exposed to market forces.

People did not know how to operate under the new system. The Soviet Union drilled into its people the notion that the economic pie in the free markets was small and shrinking, so that one should grab what he can, and the devil take the hindmost. Communists made sure that Russia had no commercial culture. The first reaction of many to the economic freedom was to try and gouge everyone else.

Following Yeltsin's 1991 decree, wages rose about 50%, but prices jumped 250% in the first month, with most of the increase coming on the first day of decontrol. Those huge price hikes shocked and frightened most Russians. They had one immediate benefit. Suddenly all kinds of scarce consumer goods appeared on the market: fresh fish and dishwashing liquid, fruit and toilet paper, even jeans and cars. Those luxuries had been almost unavailable during the Soviet years. The government kept prices artificially low, leading to horrendous shortages. The abundance of food and consumer goods after price decontrol freed people from standing in lines and gave them something to work for.

Prior to 1991, women used to spend an average of 15 hours per week standing on lines for food. Men and children stood also, but less. Those never-ending lines form the backdrop of my childhood in the Soviet Union. I remember being bundled up on a cold morning before sunrise by my grandmother who put me into a milk line that snaked around three city blocks near her house in Kharkov. But as a rule, I almost never stood in lines, just shuddered and walked by. My mother was a doctor, a specialist in venereal diseases. In those innocent pre-AIDS days a few shots of penicillin cured almost any venereal disease—and she cured many salesgirls in the city, who moonlighted as hookers, from gonorrhea. She'd walk into a store, stride past a long line, and a salesgirl would come out from behind the counter, take her aside and ask: "What would you like today, Doctor?"

A typical Soviet salesclerk or a waiter growled at customers, "There are many of you and one of me." That formula became so ingrained that to this day it amazes me when someone says in Russian: "Thank you for your purchase, enjoy, please come again." In the old Soviet Union salespeople yelled at most customers. Now money is king, and if you have it you are in good shape, but most people had less and less in each passing year of the Depression of the 1990s.

In 1991 the Russian government, broke and unable to pay salaries or feed its troops, revved up the only money-making industry it controlled—its state-of-the-art currency printing press. It began to print truckloads of paper money, rapidly destroying the value of the ruble and stoking the fires of the worst inflation in Russia in 70 years. A government can take a useful commodity, such as paper, and reduce its value by slapping some ink on it. Annual inflation rose as high as 2,510%, while the ruble crashed from a near parity with the dollar to five thousand to a dollar!

My monthly salary as a physician in the USSR in the 1970s used to be 140 rubles! Because I worked on a ship, that money was deposited directly into a bank, and when I jumped I left about 400 rubles there. I could have lived on that money for three months, but today is worth only about 7 cents, not enough for a cup of coffee. In December 1996 my New York firm sent a thousand clients 100 rubles each, as Christmas souvenirs. One hundred thousand rubles cost us about $16, less than the cost of postage. It is easy for me to chuckle about it in New York, but imagine the plight of those who lived through such losses in Russia!

After 1991 many Russian companies, freed from the iron hand of central planners, went on an orgy of price increases. After decades of communist "education," they did not know the difference between freedom and free-for-all. They could tear up old contracts since the legal system stopped functioning and could not enforce them.

Price increases had hit especially hard in the areas where consumers had little or no choice, such as energy and transport. Between 1991 and 1995, prices of refined oil products went up 6,492 times in ruble terms, while prices of light-industry products rose 869 times. Even related industries showed wide disparities: for example, the cost of sea transport rose 5,793 times, while that of rail transport went up 18,476 times. Heavy industry had all but collapsed, unable to raise prices, squeezed by suppliers, cut off from government subsidies.

Sellers of scarce consumer goods raised their prices ahead of the pack, outstripping inflation. Many converted profits into dollars and banked them abroad. People in the sectors that could not raise prices, such as heavy industry, science, and the arts, got squeezed in the inflation spiral. "Inflation became the most powerful tool for the redistribution and polarization of income. Areas late in the price race—primarily agriculture and light industry—did not earn enough to reinvest in their own maintenance," writes Yuri Yakovets, a member of the Russian Academy of Economic Sciences, from whose book many of the above figures were taken.

The most profitable position in Russia in those days was to control commodities which had a ready market in the West. Stealing in Russia and selling in the West made multimillionaires out of a motley crew of savvy businesspeople, former Soviet industrial chiefs (the so-called "Red Directors"), party bosses, and gunmen. If you could refine nickel or aluminum in Russia, or pump oil, or cut timber and deliver your loot to the West, you could collect payment in dollars, marks, or pounds, while paying Russian workers a pittance in near-worthless rubles. Nobody paid taxes on those exports—only bribes and protection money to organized crime.

Some stole by the trainload or the tankerful, with their own teams (*komanda*) handling all stages of stealing, guarding, driving, and selling. Others stole just enough to fill a passenger car or a rickety truck. They would get behind the wheel and drive West, taking their lives in their hands, dodging bandits who waited for them alongside empty stretches of roads.

In 1996, I got off a plane in Warsaw, where a friend drove me to his house outside the city. Poland is sandwiched between Russia and Germany, and all along the way I saw Russian-language signs, inviting drivers to stop and sell "rare metals." When Polish peasants start dealing rhodium or molibdenum, you know that the theft from their Eastern neighbor reached epic proportions.

Breaking the law is not limited to people in poor nations. After 1991, Russians started traveling to Germany, where they bought used cars, drove home across Poland, braving bandits, and sold cars in Russia at huge markups. It did not take prosperous Germans too long to figure out that they could sell a used car to a Russian with no paperwork, give him 24 hours to cross the border, then go to the police, declare their car stolen and collect the insurance.

After Russia lifted restrictions on travel in 1991, many people whose regular jobs stopped paying salaries started looking for temporary work abroad. Cracking the Western job market was hard, but suddenly, after looking down on Poles for generations, Russians found themselves as laborers on Polish farms and construction sites. Facing the depth of their poverty made them take on any work, promoting a major psychological change: losing the false Soviet pride.

In the shortage-ridden Soviet economy, exports were considered bad and were taxed while imports were considered good and came in duty-free. The Soviet Union used to have an impregnable border, but after the USSR collapsed, border guards and customs officers lost their fear of punishment and started taking bribes. Trainloads of stolen commodities left the country with little hindrance. The government began to tax imports, but loopholes were large enough to drive a loaded trailer through them.

The government allowed several organizations to bring in imports without duties. They included its political allies and charitable groups it wanted to subsidize but could not afford to pay. As Maxim Sokolov, a prominent Russian journalist, said, it gave them a few meters of the state border, ostensibly in support of some charitable aim. The beneficiaries included the committee to support sports, the Russian Orthodox Church, the organization of the blind, and so on. In 1996, the church became the largest importer of alcohol and tobacco in the country. None of those organizations had much commercial experience, so they brought in partners, who often included gangsters. In May 1997 Moscow papers and TV were full of news that the chief of the Russian ice hockey organization, a former KGB officer, was gunned down by men who staked out his suburban house. All commentators agreed he was rubbed out because of his role in duty-free liquor imports by his organization.

A huge volume of international trade was done by Russian travelers. A whole new industry sprang up in Russia—*chelnoki*, or shuttle traders. People would fly to Turkey, China, or Abu Dhabi, buy cheap consumer goods and bring them back for sale in Russia, first by the suitcase, later by the crateful. They made a living and provided needed goods, but the large volume of merchandise brought into the country dealt a heavy blow to inefficient domestic industries. The share of imports in the consumer market grew from an already high 23% in 1992 to an astronomical 54% in 1995.

Russia has acquired a huge shadow or gray economy. Even today many legitimate businesses deal in cash to avoid taxes. There is every incentive to cheat, as the laws are onerous and legal protection weak—businesses get little but trouble from filing honest tax returns. The shadow economy amounts to between 20% and 40% of the GNP, depending on whose estimates you believe. The higher number comes from the Federal Security Service, the successor agency of the KGB. It is heartwarming to see it spewing forth negative statistics, just like any Western security agency trying to get better funding. In the Soviet days, when the KGB never had to worry about money, they told us everything was fine and crime was a relic of the past.

Tax collections on an important commodity—vodka—reveal the extent to which Russian businessmen lost their fear of the government. The Soviet Union used to have a horrendous rate of alcoholism. Aimlessness and hopelessness drove people to drink, even though vodka was expensive and one had to stand on line for hours to buy it. The liquor monopoly provided the Soviet state with nearly half its revenues, and moonshining was prosecuted as a major crime. After 1991 new private distilleries went up, untaxed imports streamed in from the West and illegal shipments came in by the trainload from Belarus and the Ukraine. Russia was flooded with cheap vodka, which now sells for as little as $1 per pint. In 1996 the Russian government woke up to the fact that it derived only 3% of its revenue from vodka.

Anatoly Chubais, Yeltsin's former right-hand man, correctly deduced that the nation's budget could be balanced by taxes on alcohol. Now, when you buy a bottle of vodka or wine in Moscow, it is almost always sealed with a paper strip—an excise stamp, indicating that a liquor tax has been paid. Some of those stamps appear homemade and poorly attached, but the trend toward increased government collections is there.

A substantial share of the profits of "shadow businesses" flows out of the country, hiding in European banks or real estate. It is estimated that Russians funnel between 10 and 18 billion dollars out of the country each year. Everyone hopes this money will return after the economic situation in Russia improves. While the outflow continues, organized crime and corrupt officials try to tap into that pipeline.

STEAL, PRIVATIZE, OR PERISH

Russians say about themselves, "We are slow saddlers but fast riders." They take a long time to get going, but once they move, there is no holding them back. Russia spent more years under communist rule than any country in the world, but when it turned capitalist, it privatized its economy faster and more thoroughly than any of its neighbors.

With communists in power, everything—from a street-corner beer stand to a huge shipyard making nuclear-powered icebreakers—had the same owner, the almighty Soviet state. No wonder beer was warm, mugs dirty, the icebreakers even dirtier, only in a radioactive way, so that eventually they had to be scuttled. Russian reformers who gained power in 1991 viewed state enterprises as valuable but grossly mismanaged properties that needed private owners to turn them around.

The reformers began by privatizing small consumer-oriented businesses, selling most of them for cash to managers and employees. Some of those small-scale privatizations worked out spectacularly well, with new owners developing successful restaurants, plumbing businesses, medical clinics, or beauty salons. Many more fizzled out due to a lack of experience and the persisting horrible Soviet mindset. My favorite saleswoman at a food store in Moscow used to be an assistant manager at another store, which she had bought with seven co-workers during the privatization campaign. They pooled their life savings to privatize the store, but the manager promptly bled it dry, bankrupted it and disappeared. The lure of a quick buck proved stronger than owning a piece of a successful business.

Many small retail and service businesses took root, giving Moscow a colorful, bustling look. We take that look for granted in the West, but it is a huge change from the old Soviet drabness. The rapid growth of small businesses, both privatized and started from scratch, is one of the bright spots in the Russian economy in recent years. According to official records, Russian small businesses created 9 million jobs in recent years, but the true figure is probably several times higher. Small businesspeople like to keep the government out of their books. They created millions of islands of stability during the Depression of the 1990s, while large enterprises collapsed all around them.

Privatizing medium-size and large enterprises was a greater challenge for the government, since almost nobody in the country had enough money to buy them. The reformers did not want to run a fire sale for the benefit of a few underground millionaires and foreigners. They designed a program to satisfy the three main groups that claimed interest in any enterprise—workers, managers, and the population at large.

In the autumn of 1992, the Russian government issued a voucher to every citizen, representing his or her share of the nation's wealth. According to the World Bank, "Given the need for privatization efforts to be widespread and quick, as well as the target population's general lack of financial resources, the free distribution of vouchers is argued to be a speedy, feasible, and equitable method for undertaking privatization." Those vouchers could be exchanged for company shares or sold, and several exchanges began to trade vouchers. By the time the voucher stage of privatization had been completed in July 1994, over 19,000 companies were privatized, creating over 40 million new shareholders in less than two years.

The government offered two options for privatization. In Option 1, employees received 35% of the shares—25% preferred (nonvoting but dividend paying) and 10% common stock at reduced prices. Another 5% went to managers, also at reduced prices, with the rest sold to any citizen for vouchers or cash. In Option 2, workers and managers could buy 51% of shares at somewhat higher prices than in Option 1, with the rest sold to the general population. In both options, the government took a packet of shares for itself, pledging to sell it within a few years.

As the economy slid into the Depression of the 1990s, shares in most privatized companies, after an initial flurry of excitement, lost value. The exceptions were few and far between. In May 1997, on a boat ride down the Moscow River, a friend who used to be a broker pointed out to me the building of Mosenergo (see Chapter 11). She said that any worker who invested the entire family's privatization vouchers in shares of Mosenergo made enough money to buy an apartment in Moscow.

Such success stories are few and far between, as most shares issued during mass privatization remain illiquid. Few ordinary people made any money on privatization—those who profited were the more sophisticated financial types and quite a few scam artists. Many vouchers were bought up, especially in the provinces, for a few dollars or even bottles of vodka. If you had a truckload of vodka to barter for vouchers, you could become an important investor.

The more profitable and valuable enterprises were among the first to be privatized. The government lost income from running them, and gained very little in taxes. It essentially gave away profitable properties to new owners who successfully avoided taxes. The losing enterprises found fewer takers and were harder to privatize.

The voucher program boosted Russian financial markets—banks, exchanges, and financial companies. About a quarter of the vouchers ended up in investment funds, which promised to invest in the best companies. "At the end of privatization in July 1994, 536 voucher investment funds existed. Over 1,000 new private banks were also developed. When privatization began, private banks held only 5% of the population's bank deposits, while the state bank held 95%. Although the government insured deposits only in the state bank, private banks held almost 50% of all bank deposits by the end of mass privatization," writes Andrew Spicer, an American finance professor who studied Russian privatization for several years.

He adds: "Since Russian financial markets were created very quickly, they had to be developed from scratch. Other than Russian commercial banks, which had been created during the early 1990s, virtually no private financial organization existed in Russia before 1992, but thousands were established by the end of 1993." The early stage of anything is rarely a pretty sight. Almost all financial operators were inexperienced, many of them unlicensed, and quite a few thieves and scam artists. After 74 years of communism, Russians were like babes in the woods in financial matters.

According to Spicer, up to 2,000 unlicensed financial companies participated in financial markets during the privatization period, and most of those who invested in them lost money. Massive advertising campaigns offered guaranteed returns of thousands of percent in rubles (and hundreds of percent in dollars). For example, the Tibet Company, in a series of nationwide commercials in March 1993, offered an interest rate of 30% a month, yielding over 2,000% a year. It is estimated that over 600,000 investors throughout Russia invested up to 3 billion rubles ($3 million at the then-current rate of exchange) in Tibet. The president of the Tibet Company disappeared in the middle of 1995, and investors did not recover any of their investment.

Getting $3 million from 600,000 people meant taking $50 from an average dupe, reeled in through a nationwide TV campaign. Today, a minute of prime time on Russian TV costs between $20,000 and $35,000, and such a scam could not be pulled off. It could work only in the old days, during a brief period of chaos after the collapse of the Soviet system when a few hundred dollars under the table could buy you plenty of airtime.

The financial company whose crash made the front pages even in the US was MMM. It ". . . advertised its share prices several days in advance, ensuring that the price increased twice every week. It engaged in a massive advertising effort and dominated television commercials. In the six months of its existence, MMM's price increased 6,000% on Moscow's stock markets. It is estimated that between 5 and 10 million Russians invested in MMM certificates. In July 1994, the price of MMM fell on Russian stock exchanges from a high of $62 to a low of 50 cents within two days. The MMM directors were not charged with any breach of securities law because the company argued successfully that it had not broken any parts of

Russian legal code. MMM had not registered as an investment company, and the legal rules which applied to such concerns thus did not apply to it. In short, MMM was not illegal, but nonlegal: it existed outside the current legal code, and could not, or at least would not, be prosecuted under existing laws. In fact, MMM continued to sell its certificates even after its spectacular crash. Although Mavrodi, the president of MMM, faced potential charges on tax fraud, he found a unique way to avoid prosecution: he won a seat in the Russian Duma, where parliamentary deputies were exempt from criminal charges" writes Spicer (whose good grasp of the Russian scene reflects his long stay in the country).

By the time the voucher privatization process had been completed in 1994, Russians became cynical and distrustful of the financial markets. There is a Russian saying, "Get your lips burned by hot water, you'll start blowing even at cold milk." To this day, many people prefer to keep their savings in cash, "under the mattress."

The latest twist—and the latest scandal—in the Russian privatization campaign was the "loans-for-shares" deal in 1996. The government raised money from the top Russian banks by pledging its shares of the best Russian privatized firms as security. The Kremlin could either repay the loans or give up the shares. Since it was clear from the start that the government would not be able to repay, banks fell all over themselves trying to get into the program which amounted to buying stakes in the best firms at knock-down prices. The process was full of dirt, and only the fact that many media outlets were owned by banks prevented the episode from becoming a nationwide scandal. Still, the fallout was so heavy that the program was discontinued—especially after the government found it could raise money more cheaply in the international markets.

Privatization had been an heroic and, on balance, a hugely successful project. It took just a few years to dismantle the malignant totalitarian structure that the communists had cobbled together during their 74 years in power. Privatization is not over yet, as the government owns enterprises producing about 20% of GNP and holds large stakes in many companies. It has publicly committed to divest itself from those holdings, making Russia more capitalist and free-market than many countries in the West.

4

A WEALTHY COUNTRY

Russia is a wealthy country whose former rulers grossly mismanaged its economy for centuries. Various elites kept skimming Russia's immense wealth, squeezing what they wanted out of the repressed majority. The rulers always swam in cash—the tsar's aristocrats kept dropping fortunes at the gambling tables of Monaco and the communist *nomenklatura* (top party members) kept squandering even greater fortunes subsidizing the world revolution. Most Russian people, meanwhile, were consigned to poverty, deprived of what we take for granted in the West.

Russia has enormous natural wealth—huge deposits of gold, oil, and minerals. It has rich agricultural land and forests that stretch literally for thousands of miles. The people of Russia are well educated and hardworking—Russia has more Ph.Ds than the US—but the standard of living remains abysmally low. While annual per capita income in the United States in 1996 was over $20,000, in Russia it was below $2,000 per person.

I recently saw a "60 Minutes" show about a middle-class American family whose pet terrier developed a nervous problem: it barked uncontrollably at bright lights. Rather than put their pooch to sleep, the owners put it on Prozac, at a cost of $15 per week. In 1996, the minimum wage in Russia had been raised from $15 to $19 per *month*. Some Russian workers survive for a month on what a middle-class American family casually spends on its dog in a week.

Why are most Russians vastly poorer than Americans? Their land is rich and the people intelligent. Will the Russians ever rise to the American standard of living—or will they remain mired in economic muck?

THE NATURAL WEALTH

Russia is the largest country in the world, almost twice as big as the US. Russia straddles the continents of Europe and Asia, stretching nearly 6,000 miles from East to West. When you travel from New York to California you cross 3 time zones, but go from Moscow to Chukotka, and you will you cross 10 time zones! Russia's northerly location makes its climate somewhat similar to Canada.

Agricultural land represents 13% of Russia's territory. Under the tsars, Russia and the Ukraine used to be the breadbaskets of Europe, but Stalin's collectivization of 1928 pauperized farmers and turned them into serfs of the Soviet state. Deprived of any incentive to work other than fear, Soviet collective farmers became so unproductive that two generations later, in the 1970s, the USSR started importing grain from the West! While American farmers harvest 5,500 tons of grain per hectare and the more northerly Canadians get 2,620 tons, Russians eke out only 1,480 tons per hectare. During the Depression of the 1990s the country's already low grain harvests fell from 110 million metric tons in 1990 to just 78 in 1995.

Stalin's collectivization of 1928 took away peasants' land, equipment, and farm animals, except for a few chickens and dogs. In a fantastic leap backwards, back to the days when serfs toiled for absentee aristocratic landlords, peasants were made to work on collective farms for the benefit of the Soviet state. Chiefs of collective farms were chosen for political loyalty rather than their knowledge of agriculture. Many were sent to the villages from city communist cells.

Communist rulers kept raping the countryside to shore up their power base in the cities. The government carted off harvests to the cities, often leaving peasants on the verge of starvation. A peasant caught picking up leftover stalks after a harvest on a collective farm could be sent to a labor camp for up to ten years. Peasants who tried to run away were caught and returned. The quality of life of a Soviet collective farmer was just a step above a labor camp inmate. There was no point working; several generations learned to put out just enough to keep their bosses off their backs. Hard drinking by men and women became endemic in villages.

To make sure collective farmers did not run away to the cities, farm bosses took away their internal passports and kept them under lock and key. Since no one was allowed to leave home in the USSR without an internal passport, peasants who left their collective farms would be picked up during the first document check, arrested and deported—either back to the farm or to Siberia. When pauperized peasants tried to escape, their lack of passports made them easy targets for police who patrolled train stations.

"The passport regime" is still the law of the land in Russia. When you come to Moscow, you have three days to register your passport at a local police station. Most hotels will do it for foreigners for a small fee, whether you want it or not. If you stay in a private apartment without registering, nobody will bother you if you appear prosperous. The police use this law today chiefly to keep destitute provincials out of Moscow.

When the government leaves Russian peasants alone, they come across as hardworking and clever. For example, in the 1980s the Soviet regime had allowed peasants to cultivate tiny plots of land for private production. Those minuscule plots comprised only 2.5% of all cultivated land in the country but generated 36% of the nation's agricultural output! When Russian farmers work for themselves—with no machinery and just a bit of fertilizer stolen from collective farms—their productivity grows hundreds of times above average for the country. Just think of Russia's future agricultural production after all of its countryside is privatized!

Russian farmers have very little money and cannot afford machinery or fertilizer, making them less efficient. When I tell my Russian friends how I stayed on farms in New Zealand, where two men manage 400 milk cows with time left over to play tennis or drive to the beach, they sigh and tell me that in Russia 400 cows require a 20-person brigade.

Peasants have long memories, and the memory of mass killings and deportations of successful farmers in 1928 is still alive. It will take a while to convince Russian peasants that if they go out on their own and succeed, they will not wind up being deported to Siberia.

The privatization of Russia's agriculture has been halting and slow. In principle, each farmer has the right to demand his share of land and equipment from the collective farm and go out on his own. A peasant who claims his right may invite ostracism from his neighbors and make a bitter enemy out of the collective farm chief, who still has a tsarlike power in many villages.

After three quarters of a century of collectivization, it is hard to tell who owns what. The land registry for Russia is only now being created. Without a clear title to their land, peasants cannot use land as security for loans. Russian banks have not yet created a system for lending farmers money, with land as security. Once the system is in place, farmers will be able to invest in improvements, fueling a boom not only on the farm but in cities, thanks to their demand for equipment, fertilizer, and consumer goods.

Central planners of the Soviet Union built a network of intercontinental ballistic missiles aimed at the US, but never got a handle on food processing and transportation. Bottlenecks and waste of the Soviet era boggle the mind. Fully one third of fruits and vegetables rotted before reaching processing plants. Local chiefs blamed the weather, a shortage of trucks, poor roads, and lack of refrigeration, but all those excuses skirted the essential fact: commodities spoiled because they had no owner. Fruits and vegetables did not belong to peasants, truckers, or factories. They belonged to the almighty state, which meant they belonged to nobody. Now that the Soviet Union has fallen apart, the efficiency of food processing is certain to improve because commodities have acquired owners. This means food supply in Russia will increase even before farm productivity increases.

On a flight across the Atlantic in 1996, I met an executive of an American food-processing firm working in Moscow. He was excited about the wealth of opportunities in Russia. They had enough projects there, he said, to keep making money for the next 15 years. For example, the Moscow region, the wealthiest in the country, with a population of over 15 million, had only two meat packing plants. You did not have to be a genius to make money building and running another plant there.

Western know-how and a couple hundred thousand dollars can take you very far in today's Russia. That same food executive told me of a collective farm near Moscow whose acreage of greenhouses was the largest in the world. Those greenhouses were gerrybuilt during the Soviet era when fuel was cheap. Today they stand abandoned because nobody can afford to heat them. An Israeli food company leased a small area, fixed up the greenhouses with proper insulation, imported fuel-efficient heaters, and now runs a successful business growing tomatoes year-round on the outskirts of Moscow.

Russians can grow and prepare good food. Whenever I shop in Moscow, I try to buy Russian rather than imported products. I notice that more and more people buy domestic products; they no longer automatically assume that imports are better. Russia's domestic food industry is starting to boom. For example, the Moscow trade show Prodexpo-97 reported that while last year 36 wholesale companies in Moscow carried imported meat and only 14 carried domestic, that ratio reversed in 1997 when 42 wholesalers carried domestic meat and only 38 carried imports. Russians still have a lot of catching up to do in modern packaging but they are learning fast.

Timber is a great natural resource. Trees grow from the soil, fed by the sun and the rain, all by themselves, like interest on capital. Enormous forests cover 45% of Russia's territory, stretching for thousands of miles, their vast expanse broken only by an occasional village or a logging camp.

The Soviet Union had a rapist's approach to timber and other natural resources. Soviets sent inmates to cut down forests along the shores of the tributaries of great Siberian rivers. Tractors pulled tree trunks down to the shores and when they got mired, teams of inmates used ropes to pull tractors out of the mud. Even in the US, logging is the second most dangerous industry, after commercial fishing. The mortality in Soviet logging camps, where underfed, poorly clothed inmates battled huge Siberian forests, was murderously high.

Prisoners dumped huge tree trunks into rivers, which in theory were supposed to carry them downstream where they would be caught and loaded onto freighters. It was a typical Soviet *khalyava*— a scheme for getting something for nothing, or as Russians say, "making candy out of shit" (*Sdelat' iz govna konfetku*). Much of the timber sank and rotted, poisoning rivers, while tractors denuded and tore up shores before moving on to rape another river basin.

Most of Russia's vast natural resources, including timber, are concentrated in the Far North and other remote regions. Those areas represent about two thirds of Russia's territory but hold only 8% of its population. This is similar to Canada, where a majority of the population lives in relative warmth within 50 miles of the US border, leaving vast northern areas underpopulated.

To profit from its wealth, Russia must overcome obstacles of climate and distance. Profiting from Russian timber will require heavy investments in equipment, roads, distribution systems, and support operations. Still, thousands of miles of permafrost are less of an obstacle than the communist system. You cannot build a modern economy on prison labor. The Soviet economy failed, but the capitalist approach has not yet been given a fair chance. Hidebound communists continue to dominate local politics in many faraway timber areas.

Russian geologists have mapped out huge deposits of oil and natural gas, as well as coal, minerals, gold, and diamonds. Russia sits on proven reserves of 50 billion barrels of crude oil—more than twice the reserves of the United States. The country is a net exporter of oil, which it continued to pump even during the Depression of the 1990s. The oil industry suffered less than others from the lack of maintenance because it had a ready product to sell in the West.

The government privatized the oil industry, creating giant oil companies whose shares are among the best performers on the Russian stock market (see Chapter 10). Many Russian oil firms are setting up joint ventures with Western oil firms. Oil exploration declined during the Depression of the 1990s. For the first time in modern history, existing oil reserves were being depleted faster than new reserves were being discovered. Now, with Western companies coming into Russia, exploration is rising sharply.

Russia has proven reserves of 1,467 trillion cubic feet of natural gas, 9 times higher than the US. It supplies nearly half of the natural gas that heats Western Europe. When Gazprom, Russia's largest gas company, floated its ADRs (American Depositary Receipts) in London in 1996, that issue was oversubscribed and ADRs went to a premium of 300% above the price of domestic shares. While the institutional funds bought heavily in London, savvy individuals and hedge funds, working through Russian firms, bought Gazprom shares in the domestic market. They saw a chance to get in on the ground floor of one of the richest energy companies in the world.

Now that the Russian military has collapsed and NATO is pushing into Eastern Europe, Russians joke bitterly that with Gazprom they do not need an army. If NATO tanks come to their borders, all they need to do is turn down the heat in Western Europe a few degrees, and let their public do the rest.

What does the future hold for Russia's agriculture and timber, oil and gas, mining and other resource-based industries? The *Central Intelligence Agency's 1995 Yearbook* points to Russia's weak legal structure, its poor network of social services, pollution in the industrial belt, even permafrost in Siberia and earthquakes in Kamchatka and states: "Russia, a vast country with a wealth of natural resources, a well-educated population, and a diverse industrial base, continues to experience formidable difficulties in moving from its old centrally planned economy to a modern market economy." It nods at Yeltsin, whose ". . . government has made substantial strides in converting to a market economy . . . by freeing nearly all prices, slashing defense spending, eliminating the old centralized distribution system, completing an ambitious voucher privatization program, establishing private financial institutions, and decentralizing foreign trade." Still, the CIA concludes, "Many years will pass before Russia can take full advantage of its natural resources and its human assets."

This comes from the genius agency that kept warning us for years of the imminent Soviet danger and was totally surprised by the communist collapse. In view of the CIA's past spectacular failures to predict Russia's future, let us take its gloomy forecast as a bullish contrarian indicator.

HUMAN WEALTH

The greatest asset of Russia is its people. There are 150 million of them, making Russia the fifth most populous nation in the world, after China, India, the US, and Indonesia. Russia is an industrialized country; three quarters of its people live in cities. People who are ethnically Russian comprise 81.5% of the population, and the rest are minorities. There are hundreds of them, but practically all are literate in Russian as well as their own languages. The 1989 census showed 85 ethnic groups of 10,000 and more, and 37 of 100,000 and more. Minorities participate in the country's economic and cultural life without any affirmative action programs, and minority politicians serve at the highest levels of the Russian government, without the US-style gerrymandering of election districts. There is remarkably little ethnic friction in Russia. The disaster in Chechnya is the proverbial exception that confirms the rule. Russians tend to be tolerant and spiritual, and get along well with others. Even after being twisted for seven decades by communist rule, Russians remain, at the core, ethical and decent.

When the World Bank classified Russia as a developing country in 1996, I saw jubilation in Moscow's financial circles. People were happy to be counted as the Third World because during the Depression of the 1990s they thought they were worse off than that. Russia is still economically backward, but it has one enormous advantage over all developing countries: the cultural level of its people.

All over the world, people in developing countries need to be taught how to read, use toothbrushes, and understand traffic signs. Russia, on the other hand, has a 100% literacy rate and a third of its adult population has been educated beyond high school. Russia has a world-class culture, developed over many centuries, with deep roots in the heritage of Europe.

Russian scholars pioneered many areas of science—
Mendeleyev, the chemist who developed the periodic table of the
elements, and Tsiolkovsky, the pioneer of rocketry, spring to mind.
The latter is an example of what I call Russia's "imperial culture,"—
a culture of a country so big and rich that it attracts scientists and
scholars from its periphery. The United States is an imperial culture;
one third of our Nobel Prize winners are foreign born. Tsiolkovsky,
whose work preceded Goddard's in the US by several decades, was
a Pole by birth.

Some of the greatest inventions of this century have been made
by Russians. Anyone who watches TV today owes that blessing (or
a curse, depending on your viewpoint) to a Russian inventor
Vladimir Zvorykin. The American military has been winning wars
around the globe flying in helicopters originally developed by
another Russian émigré, Igor Sikorsky, who fled Russia for his life
after the communist takeover.

Many scientists and other intellectuals had to run after the communists took power in 1917. Those who remained in the country
faced a stark choice: work for the regime or be persecuted by it. The
state channeled most of its scientific resources into the arms race.
The space race was under military control, and Soviet scientists won
many of its rounds. They launched the first Earth satellite, sent the
first rocket beyond a geocentric orbit, and successfully sent the first
animal, the first man, and the first woman into space. Working from
a relatively poor industrial base, cut off from their colleagues in the
West, Soviet scientists performed miracles of ingenuity (assisted
more than a bit by Soviet intelligence services) and often beat the
US in their feats of science and engineering.

Many Russian scientists became involved in culture and politics,
outside of their scientific disciplines. Andrey Sakharov, the physicist
who was the father of the Soviet hydrogen bomb, eventually grew
into one of the most outspoken opponents of the communist
regime. The Soviets exiled him to a provincial city of Gorky where
the KGB had a free hand isolating him, intimidating his visitors and
even vandalizing his car. Still, he won the Nobel Peace prize and
ended his days, after the communist collapse, as a deputy in the first
democratic Russian parliament.

For centuries Russia produced a steady stream of great writers and other creative artists. Educated people around the world have been reading books by Tolstoy and Dostoyevsky and listening to the music of Tchaikovsky and Rachmaninov. Igor Stravinsky, another illustrious Russian composer who escaped the communists, helped define American classical music for the 20th century. Modern Russian writers, including Boris Pasternak and Aleksandr Solzhenitsyn, both Nobel Prize winners, exposed the moral bankruptcy of the communist regime, contributing to its final collapse.

Intelligentsiya is a Russian word commonly used in the West to denote intellectuals—too narrow a meaning. In Russia, the word refers to people who are not only educated but cultured and ethical (Sakharov is a prime example). Russian *intelligentsiya* feel superior to Western technocrats who may be highly skilled in their craft but are seen as devoid of cultural and spiritual interests. Members of *intelligentsiya* have a strong sense of themselves as the salt of the earth and often look down on those who have more power or money.

Russians tend to respect and admire their writers and creative artists. High culture is much more broadly based than in the US. Russian kids score higher on standardized tests than American kids. It is the norm rather than an exception for them to play a piano or a violin and study foreign languages. Creative life in Russia has remained very active even during the Depression of the 1990s. Russia's vast intellectual energy promises to fuel its drive to greatness.

The communist system wasted the intellectual capital of the nation. The country was like a mother devouring its own children, driving many of the best and the brightest to labor camps in Siberia or to an exile abroad. After coming to the US in 1974 I lived for several months on a suburban New York farm owned by the Tolstoy Foundation. It was set up by the great writer's youngest daughter. I had the privilege of meeting Miss Tolstoy, who was over 80 at that time. She vividly remembered the horrors of a communist prison where she had been incarcerated for several months as a young woman for her crime of having been born into an aristocratic family. She escaped and came to the US where she used what little money she had to set up a foundation named after her father. She dedicated the rest of her life to helping tens of thousands of refugees from communism. I must have been one of the last people she helped.

Many Russian émigrés came to the West with no money and no ability to speak the local language, but succeeded and contributed to their new countries (this book is being written in English by a political refugee from the Soviet Union). Russia's losses became the West's gains, but the brain drain is tapering off. Russia's *intelligentsiya,* no longer harassed by its government, is finding opportunities in its own country. People travel abroad to study and work for a few years, then return to positions of responsibility in Russia, the way they do in any normal country. The intellectual life in Russia today is more exciting and rich than it has been in generations.

The Soviet Union had an economy of shortages. Everything was in short supply. There was not enough food, clothes, apartments, or, once you moved beyond high school, educational opportunities. Education was free, but admission to universities was rationed on the basis of party loyalty, "pull," and ethnicity. People who worked in factories and farms were admitted ahead of bright kids out of high schools. Most universities limited Jews to no more than 2% of any incoming class. Germans, who lived in Russia for centuries (the tsars invited their ancestors to show Russian peasants how to farm), were not allowed into universities at all after 1945, as a "punishment" for Hitler's war. University education under the communists was very rigid. There were no electives, and everybody had to take identical courses designated for their specialties.

Private education has flowered after the collapse of the Soviet Union. At first, private elementary and high schools began to spring up, and now the country has private colleges, which attract paying students by offering Western-style education, relevant to the modern realities of Russia. The older universities, freed from government controls and shaken by severe cuts in subsidies, are rapidly changing their curricula. They now charge tuition to all but the very best students, and feel obliged to offer courses that students want.

The ferment of intellectual life in Russian universities offers a striking contrast to many Asian "emerging tigers" whose economic booms often occurred in an environment of rigid government controls and a general culture of conformity. Many gleaming colleges there look and feel like glorified trade schools. In Russian universities, students sit on rickety chairs under peeling ceilings and share scarce equipment, but there is a feeling of openness, questioning, and intellectual excitement—a good omen for the country's development.

Russian businesses are teeming with Ph.Ds who migrated into private industry after military research centers closed. The scientists who used to build rockets that gave nightmares to generations of Americans are now building businesses that will soon compete in world markets.

The Russian Exchange uses an electronic trading system developed by a team of local programmers that beats any similar system in the West. When I visit a currency trading center at a prosperous Moscow bank, it turns out that two of its three principals have Ph.Ds and all have military backgrounds. A commercial director of a highly profitable publishing house shows me his state-of-the-art program for tracking inventory and sales, better than anything I have seen in the US. His office is decorated with photos of MiG jet fighters. He too has a Ph.D. in engineering and used to work in the defense industry. As recently as two years ago scientists were still bitter at their loss of status at prestigious research institutes and full of false Soviet pride, but the Depression humbled them. They rolled up their sleeves—and Russia's emerging businesses are being supercharged by their brains.

The Soviet Union used to have scores of NII—*Nauchno-Issledovatelskiy Institut*—scientific research institutes, and NPO—*Nauchno-Proizvodstvennoe Ob'edineniye*, or scientific industrial organizations. The latter were research centers attached to various industries, such as chemistry and tool making. Each NPO combined a research center and a factory in either petrochemical, tool making, or other industries, which were supposed to rapidly implement the latest scientific achievements. The idea of coupling research and production was subverted by the typical Soviet secrecy and militarization. Now the marketplace is likely to put the NPO structures to work.

Military factories, destitute and directionless after the Depression of the 1990s, still have some of the country's best engineers, craftsmen, and workers. They built and maintained one of the most powerful military machines in the history of the world. As the Soviet Union imploded and Russia slid into its Depression of the 1990s, the military industry tightened its belt and waited. Now it is disillusioned. The executives of most military plants set their false pride aside and are looking for civilian orders—any orders. Their highly skilled workers will be formidable players in the economic rebirth of Russia.

In 1997 an announcement came out that Transaero, Russia's second largest airline, made a bid to take over TWA. Transaero was formed after the collapse of the Soviet Union by some of the top executives and pilots from Aeroflot, the Soviet state airline. Transaero is regarded as the best domestic airline in Russia, and now they are trying to expand abroad. Russian capitalism is advancing around the globe much more successfully than the Soviet military ever did.

Russians are good craftsmen. One of their national heroes is the Tula Lefty, a southpaw artisan from the city of Tula who, among other feats, made horseshoes for a flea. The Russians are wizards of improvisation. Where Americans say, "Necessity is the mother of invention" Russians grin, "The naked must be clever" (*Gol' na vydumki hitra*). This is how they kept the rickety Soviet machine going for so long with so few resources. An old friend of mine drove a tank from Stalingrad to Vienna in World War II and joked that he maintained it with only three tools—a heavy screwdriver, a sledge-hammer, and a f . . . you.

Some Russians point to their country's remarkable scientific and engineering achievements, from Sputnik onwards, and count on a high-tech boom to leapfrog the US. Maxim Sokolov, one of the country's best journalists, has a different idea: "I do not believe we will have a high-tech boom any time soon. Sure, on the orders of the KGB we created a scanner in the 1960s—but it was a single set built by hand. We always had our Tula Lefties (genius craftsmen), but had a problem with commercial exploitation. We know how to create a single copy of a masterpiece—but not how to have a production line. I do not believe in high-tech pulling us up because in Russia we have not yet mastered the manufacture of screws. I buy screws in Germany for carpenters who are building my country house because when they use Russian screws, the groove in the head always gets stripped. Our Tula Lefties can build a computer-ized phallic microswitch—trouble is, that switch is not connected to anything. In the absence of a proper attitude towards work through-out the entire technological process, that phallic microswitch will simply hang useless. I ask the Germans—why do you screw your screws with a screwdriver—and they say, what else is there to do—and I say, where I come from you gotta hammer them in. Until we start making high-quality screws, we are not going to have a high-tech boom."

Russians are avid gamesmen (that tank driver friend cleaned out a trainload of demobilized soldiers playing blackjack on the ride home from Vienna to Leningrad). The Soviets gained a great deal of profit from that competitive streak. They managed to increase the nation's productivity by setting up the so-called "socialist competi-tions" between brigades, departments, and units in most workplaces. They rarely gave any money to the winners, just a red pennant[10] and bragging rights.

Those competitions entertained and challenged workers, and led to many productivity breakthroughs—until the government choked the goose that laid the golden eggs. The Soviets created a disincentive to compete by raising everyone's production quotas based on the winners' performance and cutting salaries of those who could not keep up. Anyone who won a competition by a large margin created a problem for his/her friends. Winning by a small margin was OK, but a big margin meant your friends might go hun-gry next month. Friendship and loyalty are the quintessential Russian traits. Instead of competing to cut each other's throats, workers took it easy and got drunk together.

Everybody in Russia remarks on how much more productive and hard-working the people have become in recent years. For the first time in their lives, they can compete with each other, produce more, and be rewarded by the marketplace.

---

[10] On my first trip to Moscow after the communist collapse I bought such a pennant in a sou-venir shop for $5. Made of red silk, it showed a soaring rocket, a factory, a wheat field, and Lenin's golden profile with the words "Communist labor collective." My associates laughed when I hung it in our New York office until I pointed to the pennant and said, "Since we are now a communist labor collective, from now on nobody ever gets a raise or a bonus, and you'll have to work for free one Saturday a month."

MUCH BETTER THAN IT LOOKS

The Russian government statisticians tell us the GDP (Gross Domestic Product) declined 48.7% from 1990 to 1994. Had the crash really been that bad? Mark Twain, an American who was not a statistician but a keen observer of the social scene, wrote: "There are lies, damn lies, and statistics." In today's Russia, the State Statistical Commission, or *Goskomstat*, does not lie the way the old Soviet agencies did, but it does have its biases.

Ian Hague, writing in the September 1996 issue of *Chudo*, the newsletter of Firebird Management, notes that *Goskomstat* ". . . remains to a large extent unreformed in its methodological obsession with physical indices of gross output from particular sectors—for the most part industry, especially the heavy kind. *Goskomstat* GDP statistics are therefore biased toward products and sectors that are in decline and fail to capture the shift to new activities . . ." For example, statisticians will account for a catastrophic decline in production at a tank factory but not for the fact that its half-empty buildings and machinery are being rented by small enterprises, operating in a cash economy.

Hague brings up a tool for correcting errors of the government's GDP statistics crafted by Dr. Istvan Dobozi, an economist at the World Bank. Dr. Dobozi pointed out that ". . . electric power pervades all aspects of modern life," and showed that ". . . in all market economies aggregate economic activity and electric power consumption are closely linked, with a correlation of almost 1:1." Tracking the consumption of electricity allows us to check the validity of the government's GDP statistics.

Goskomstat tells us that the Russian GDP fell 48.7% between 1990 and 1994, but the electric power consumption for the same period fell only 21.1%. That was a severe drop indeed, but not nearly as disastrous. It seems to indicate that the Russian industry is much more active than the statisticians would have us believe.

Hague writes, "*Goskomstat* has also failed to account for a large share of personal income among Russians. Here, they can probably be forgiven since most entrepreneurs avoid telling anyone about how they are actually making a living, for fear they will arouse the interest of tax collectors and other shakedown artists." He is backed up by Layard and Parker who write in *The Coming Russian Boom* ". . . the official figures of industrial production exaggerate output before the 1991 coup (because managers needed to 'achieve their targets') and underestimate output now (because managers try to avoid taxes)." Russia is probably in better economic shape than the government statisticians tell us.[11]

THE SUBMACHINE GUN INDICATOR

The number of submachine guns in the streets is a good indicator of the economic and political state of any country. In the most prosperous and stable countries you'll see few if any submachine guns, while at the bottom of the scale the streets will be crowded by men carrying them. In the United States you almost never see a submachine gun, unless you go to the perimeter of a military base or the White House. You will not see submachine guns on the streets of Australia or New Zealand, but you'll see tons of them in Afghanistan or Somalia.

Singapore provides an example of how submachine guns reflect changes in a society. Singapore today is the Switzerland of Asia, its banks reaching into the sky, its dollar rock-solid, its hard-working people boasting the highest percentage of home ownership in the world. When I first went to Singapore in 1987, it was not yet as rich and you could still catch glimpses of the old textile economy. When you walked into a bank, you'd see a guard with a submachine gun in the lobby. I always felt those skinny young guards with big guns were more dangerous than any bank robbers.

The Singapore stock market, as measured by the Straights Times Index was near 900 then. These days when I travel to Singapore, I never see submachine guns. The country is richer, there is more to steal; and it had a huge financial boom—the Straights Times Index went up to above 2,000—and there is not a machine

---

[11] In June 1998, as this book was going to the printer, *The New York Times* reported that the president and several executives of *Goskomstat* had been arrested and accused of helping companies reduce taxes by underreporting their revenues. Over 1.5 million dollars was removed from the home of the arrested president and his associates whose official salaries were probably about $1,000 per month.

gun in sight. The country feels more secure and respects human life more than it does a bagful of dollars.

On my first visits to Moscow I saw submachine guns everywhere—in the airport, in my hotel lobby, in the banks, on the subway. During the Chechen War every bridge in Moscow had a pair of soldiers in bulletproof vests—with submachine guns, of course. Now the society is rapidly demilitarizing. In 1997 you see no submachine guns in the airport, and even cops in the subways carry only pistols.

In 1996 I went to a neighborhood bank in Moscow to exchange $200. The doors of a Stalin-era building reached up high like in a cathedral, with a dirty rag in front for wiping dirty boots. I pulled hard on the handle, and an elderly doorman scrutinized me from behind his shabby desk: "Whatdya want?" "Can I exchange dollars into rubles?" He pointed toward the door deep inside the cavernous lobby, made of heavy metal bars. Four men stared at me, three young ones with submachine guns, the officer with a pistol in a holster. Everybody wore a bulletproof vest. I told them why I came, speaking slowly, keeping my hands away from the body, conveying with my body language I meant no harm. They opened the door and the officer escorted me to the exchange room in the back.

The bank gave me a good rate, I chatted with the clerk, and by the time I walked out the guards paid little attention to me. They appeared relaxed and bored.

I hope those guards are learning new job skills. Their jobs will disappear soon, just as they did in Singapore. It is a dying craft, guarding a few hundred dollars with a submachine gun. By the time these guys lose their jobs, Russia will go through a financial boom. Going peaceful is good for the country.

WILD GROWTH IN THE RUBBLE

When the Mt. St. Helen's volcano erupted in the US in 1980, it blew the top off the mountain, burned out enormous forest acreage, and covered the entire Pacific Northwest with a layer of volcanic ash. After the smoke cleared, the area around Mt. St. Helen's looked like a moonscape; many environmentalists prophesied it would take two generations to recover from the catastrophe. But nature had a different schedule: in just a few years, the slopes were covered with lush young forests, teeming with wildlife. The ash served as a fertilizer, and the recovery was especially strong in areas not seeded by the Forest Service. Nature did its best when left to its own devices.

In 1945, Germany and Japan lay in ruins, their industrial might smashed by Allied bombings, their social systems shattered, American cigarettes taking the place of their debased currencies. Who could imagine that in a few years the world would witness "the German miracle," that the Japanese car makers would drive circles around their American competitors, and the value of the Japanese stock market would exceed that of the US!

Paradoxically, it is the depth of Russia's political and economic crisis that makes one optimistic about its future. Westerners in general and Americans in particular believe in progress by evolution and think that revolutions are destructive. In Russia today, the opposite is true.

The regime that collapsed in 1991 had been unworkable, rotten, evil. It killed, repressed, and exiled the country's best people. It destroyed its agriculture, polluted the land, commandeered resources for a mindless militaristic program, and built a vast net of labor camps. While ordinary people lacked basic consumer goods, the rulers launched aggressive wars against most of their neighbors—from Finland in the West to Afghanistan in the East. The KGB informers poisoned the nation with suspicion, while undercover squads of killers and kidnappers roamed Europe.

The Soviet regime could not be modernized, improved, or salvaged. It had been rotten to the core, and no reform could work. The communist regime had to be torn down and swept away so that a new system could be built in its rubble. The country needed a revolution to become a normal nation.

That's what most Russian people want today—to become a normal country. While politicians squabble in Moscow, most people have become intensely apolitical. They simply want to be left alone, make money, and improve their lives.

The Russian economy stopped growing in the 1980s, and then the revolution of the 1990s pushed it over the edge and the average per-capita income in Russia fell in half. Imagine what would happen in the US if the average per-capita income was sliced in half within five years! After the communist system collapsed, the empire built by the tsars and the communists fell apart. Imagine living in New York and suddenly having to get a visa and go through customs to visit your folks in Florida, which is now an independent republic with its own currency and nasty border guards looking for bribes.

Imagine living all your life in a cage, always looking over your shoulder and never being allowed to see what life is like on the outside. Suddenly, KGB eavesdroppers disappear, you can read and say anything you want, and, if you like, take a train, a plane, or a car and visit faraway lands. All you need is money, but no one is holding you back. Would you want to go back to the security of your cage?

Now that the economy has begun to improve, the national consensus is stronger than ever. There is no turning back. The nation has suffered too long and too hard. It will not turn back. It has elected the government whose stated goal is to build a liberal capitalist society.

The Russians got rid of the Communist Party's monopoly on power, they have a free press, and democratic elections. They have liberalized their banking system, cut subsidies to backward industrial firms, and stabilized the ruble. Military spending is being drastically cut, most recently another 20% in May 1997, on top of many previous cuts. The budget deficit has been reduced to less than 3% of the GDP in 1995.

With the economy still paying for the mistakes of central planning and the military out of gas, the Russians lost any imperial aspirations. They just want to be left alone, build up their economy, make money and enjoy life if they can.

Daniel Cloud remarked, ". . . often a serious threat to national survival precipitates deep reform. The more serious the threat, the deeper the reforms." Postwar Japan, Taiwan, Korea, and other East-Asian tigers have stayed the economic course during the Cold War. They ". . . organized and pursued a serious program of modernization for as long as they stayed worried. The Russians, of course, are still worried."

Fear saves countries from abandoning reforms, and the fear of sliding back propels Russia into the future. Russians are keenly aware of the risk of sliding to the status of a developing country, a mere supplier of raw commodities for the West and a market for its over-flow of industrial production. They are determined to avoid that dead end, and lift themselves to the level of a normal European country.

HOW FAST CAN RUSSIA CHANGE?

The Soviet government kept telling its people they lived in a workers' paradise. Why were they so far behind the West? That was a dangerous question. Opening your mouth could ruin your career or land you in jail.[12]

The government claimed the country had to build up its military against American aggression. It promised to industrialize the country first, and consumer goods would come later. It said they had to help brotherly communist parties in Africa, Asia, and Latin America. All the while, the standard of living in the Soviet Union kept falling farther behind the West.

Russia's economic backwardness did not start with the communists. The country had a six-hundred-year run of bad government.

The Mongol invaders, followed by the tsars and aristocrats, followed by communist *apparatchiki* all ruled Russia for the benefit of narrow elites. Ideologies changed, but as long as the ruling groups "got theirs," the rest of the nation could rot. The dictatorial regimes wanted to keep the population down; poverty prevented people from becoming uppity. The economic and political systems under the tsars and under the communists prevented most Russians from reaching the Western standard of living.

In the balancing act between guns and butter, Russians got plenty of guns but very little butter. Things we take for granted in the West—a comfortable pair of shoes, toilet paper, a car, a tele-

---

[12]My great uncle was arrested after he joked at a party, "The only permanent things about the USSR are our temporary difficulties." A *stukach* (an informer) turned him in. He was sent to a labor camp; then the war began, and the government threw inmates into the so-called punishment battalions. They were sent into the bloodiest battles, with their better-armed, better-fed guards in the rear, shooting at them if they did not advance. An inmate stayed in a punishment battalion until he was either killed or wounded, which earned him a transfer to the regular army and a chance to survive the war. My great uncle never returned. A sense of humor could be a life-threatening affliction in the USSR.

phone, a vacation abroad—seemed wildly extravagant and out of reach to most Soviets. People worked hard, often in dangerous conditions, for very little.

Soviet peasants were practically indentured on their collective farms. Deprived of any incentive to work, they grew apathetic and many drank themselves out of their minds. Well-fed bureaucrats presided over this centrally planned empire. They lived behind tall fences in guarded compounds, vacationed on special *dachas*, and shopped in special restricted shops. They controlled the media that sung the praises of this workers' paradise.

The repressive regime collapsed in 1991. It had tottered for several years and when old communists staged a reactionary coup, nobody anticipated the intensity of public backlash against them. The Communist Party was briefly outlawed and the reformers who came to power dismantled most vestiges of communism. Russia now has a free media, democratic politics, and a privatized economy. After spending decades as an international outcast, Russia is becoming fully integrated into the free world economy and its political bodies.

For the first time in Russia's history, the country has a freely elected government that is promoting political freedom and economic prosperity. For the first time in Russia's history, the nation has an opportunity to lift itself economically. Russia has unparalleled natural wealth, an educated and hard-working population with a world-class culture.

The old governments prevented Russians from improving their lives. Now, with the communists beaten both at the polls and on the barricades, Russia is free to move into the future. For the first time in Russia's history, its creative energy has been unleashed and directed toward rational economic goals.

The economic miracle among the Asian tigers, such as Hong Kong, Korea, Singapore, and Taiwan took some 20 years to gather steam, and another 20 years to lift them to their recent pinnacles. Russia has greater natural resources, a better educated population, and the benefit of the East Asian example. It is likely to rocket forward at a much faster rate. The Russian boom will amaze the world in the next two decades.

Russia's economy has stabilized and started to grow while this book was being written. People want to save and invest, auguring well for Russia's financial markets. Even "black capital" that sneaked out of Russia may be viewed as a reserve that will flow back once the economic conditions and investment climate improve. Russian capital in the West is restless. Its owners are not satisfied with Western rates of return. They vividly remember earning 100% annually on US dollar deposits in Moscow just two years ago. Returning capital will help fuel an investment boom, similar to what overseas Chinese money did in China. The time to start positioning yourself in Russia's financial markets is now.

5

MOSKVA BANDITSKAYA

My Moscow publisher is not in a happy mood when I visit his spacious office in December 1996. He just heard that an acquaintance, a 47-year-old executive in the richest publishing house in Russia, had been murdered—seven bullets in the head and not a single miss while getting out of the car in front of his house. Nothing was taken from the body, no witnesses came forward, and there was no doubt that the killer and those who sent him will ever be caught.

"*Chechentsy* (the Chechens)," sighs my friend. "The worst *bandity* of all. Russian bandits—when they come up against them, they just piss in their pants." The dead man used to be the third in command at the publishing house, which always paid protection money to the Chechen mafia. After Russia went to war with Chechnya in 1995, most Chechens were run out of Moscow, and the Russian bandits used that golden opportunity to take over their protection rackets. After the peace agreement with Chechnya was signed, the Chechen gangsters returned.

"They probably came to the man and told him his company hadn't paid in a while and owed them money. And he probably said he had paid the Russians and the Chechens should take it up with them. And the Chechens probably said, "Aha, uhu, so that's what you want us to do," and left. You can haggle with Russian bandits, and plead poverty, and drink vodka with them, and beg for a break, and they will yell at you and threaten you, but they will deal. The Chechens—they do not yell or threaten.

"They get some 16- or 17-year-old kid that just came from the mountains. His second or third uncle is already in the mob, both came from the same *teip* (clan), the kid looks up to him like he was God. And this uncle says, here, look at this photo, this man disrespected us, he insulted us like we are not men, go kill him. And the kid takes a gun, and goes—he's like a guided missile. You can't stop him. He's probably a nice kid if you ever chat with him, even though not too bright, but his uncle sent him to kill and you can't stop him. It's all clan and pride."

What's going to happen next, I ask. "The kid will take a break from Moscow, cool off in the mountains for a while. Other Chechens will go visit the number-two man in that publishing house. If he doesn't pay, they'll kill him too (which is exactly what happened in 1997, as reported in *The Wall Street Journal*). After that, they'll go to the head man. By that time, he'll pay."

My friend's secretary comes in and sets up his table for lunch—borscht, cold cuts, salad, wonderful black bread, an icy bottle of vodka. A printing plant owner and his assistant join us for the Russian version of a business lunch: two hours of good food, good drink, and rambling conversation about history and politics. You can't get a lunch like that in America. The dead man is mentioned just once. I eat, drink, talk, and hope that my friend is fully paid up—I want him alive, to enjoy his company for years to come.

THIEVES-IN-LAW

Anyone operating in Russia today must be alert to its crime situation. I would not worry too much about the street crime; you are safer on the streets of Moscow than in New York. Just avoid a few slum areas, just as you would stay out of American slums, especially after dark. There are areas on the outskirts of many Russian cities full of *khruschovki*—shoddy four and five story tenements, built during the Khruschev era, often in factory areas. People joke that some *khruschovki* have only four stories because the fifth was stolen and sold for vodka. Those areas tend to be populated by a pretty rough crowd, and a foreigner has no business walking there.

While driving with friends in Russia, I sometimes become lost and pull up to pedestrians to ask for directions. Nobody seems afraid of a car with several men in it, not even women. Try pulling up in a car to a sidewalk in New York and talking to a woman—she'll probably recoil in terror. Moscow appears generally safer than New York.

The real risks in Russia come from organized crime. It is more vicious and pervasive there than in America. Like almost everything in Russia, its background is in politics, with its roots in the Stalin era.

When Stalin began to pursue his monopoly of power after Lenin's death in 1924, he ruthlessly repressed criminals—professional thieves who had long existed in Russia, along with "criminals" Stalin created himself—political prisoners, called *politicheskiye*. Those men carried their political disagreements into prisons and labor camps, while professional thieves were tightly organized. They had several "guilds"—pickpockets, house thieves, and so on—with a rigid code of behavior, a strong system of mutual support, their own informal court, and even their own language. *Phenya*, the spoken language of criminals, sounds Russian, has the same grammatical structure, but most of its words are so odd, a noncriminal Russian cannot understand them. Two thieves can talk in front of you about how they are going to rob you, and you will not know what they are talking about.

The thieves' "code of honor" forbade them to be employed, to engage in business, to serve the state, to own property, or to marry. They could only steal—from outsiders, never from their own. They supported one another with food, money, fists, and knives. Like any men's club, the thieves were preoccupied not just with money, but with status, prestige, and internal power structure (when a pirated translation of *The Godfather* by Mario Puzo first appeared in Russia, it quickly became a "must read" among those thieves who could read). Their leaders were called *vory v zakone*, or "thieves-in-law." Those Russian godfathers, anointed at meetings of top thieves, held the power of life and death over ordinary thieves.

The Soviet Union built a huge network of prisons and forced labor camps—an archipelago of islands circled by barbed wire had spread across the country. Most inmates were *politicheskiye*. The government used them to cut timber, dig mines, and work on grandiose construction projects. Initially the regime set out to repress thieves in camps, starving them for refusing to work and shooting them for defying authorities (Russian career criminals tend to be heavily tattooed, but getting a tattoo "Slave of the CPSU"—Communist Party of the Soviet Union—on the forehead earned an automatic death sentence.) Soon camp commanders realized that instead of fighting the thieves, they would be better off using them to help run the camps.

The thieves formed cohesive violent clans, and found it easy to intimidate the disorganized political prisoners who came to dread them more than their guards. The thieves forced the *politicheskiye* to work, maintained discipline within camps, and lived off the political prisoners whose hard labor fed the entire system.

Thieves suffered after Khruschev freed most political prisoners in the early 1960s. Camp commanders had little use for the thieves and went back to repressing them. They put large groups of thieves into small holding units where only those who agreed to work could survive. Those who refused were literally starved to death, but those who went to work risked death from thieves-in-law for breaking their code. Thieves had a stark choice.

When the shadow economy of the Soviet Union began to perk up in the 1970s, the thieves who survived the camps profited from shaking down Russia's emerging businessmen. Underground entrepreneurs built secret factories for making shoes, clothes, and other scarce consumer goods. They earned enormous profits, but risked their lives for defying the State. Thieves could rob them with impunity, knowing that underground businessmen could never go to the police. Later they moved up from outright robberies and kidnappings to selling protection to underground businessmen. Thieves provided an early warning system about impending raids, thanks to their contacts with corrupt politicians and the police. They protected businesses from petty criminals and helped them collect debts. Soon thieves-in-law began mediating their disputes which could never be taken to courts.

After the Soviet system collapsed in 1991, thieves-in-law made out like bandits. The government largely ceased to function, and the Soviet legal system—crude, inefficient, and communist-driven—ground to a halt. New businesses sprouted like mushrooms. Who was going to enforce their contracts and mediate their disputes? Thieves-in-law stepped into the vacuum left by the state. Within two or three years they became a major quasi-legal force in Russia.

Gangs of *bandity,* controlled by thieves-in-law, collected pay-offs. The hoodlums provided several services to their victims. For example, they helped collect bills and enforce contracts.

If someone cheated a businessman who was making payoffs to the *bandity,* he would complain to them. They would intervene on his behalf, and go to the other businessman's *bandity.* They'd get together in a restaurant or some other hangout, where each would advocate for *his* businessman. In this, they were similar to lawyers. A higher fee often bought better justice. Their stock in trade was the knowledge of the unwritten rules, capacity to gab, and readiness to use fists and guns. If they couldn't resolve a dispute, they referred it to their gang boss, and, if necessary, all the way up to the thief-in-law. That man's word was final—he decided who was right or wrong, who had to pay and who got the money, who lived and who died. He was the supreme judge in the area under his control.

After the Soviet state collapsed, some businesspeople found those services indispensable and went looking for *bandity* themselves. Many Russian businesses today make monthly payments, either a percentage of gross or a flat rate—to *bandity.* This is called having a *krysha*; literally, a roof. This roof protects them from petty thugs, unpaid bills, and broken contracts. *Bandity* play a quasi-legal, contract enforcement role in postcommunist Russia.

The glamour of being a *bandit* appeals to many young men—driving big cars, having pockets bulging with cash, getting a lot of respect from everyone. The occupation has a high mortality rate—it is something of a dead end. Plenty of spare time and easy access to guns lead to drinking, violence, and shootings. And then there are deadly turf battles between neighboring groups. The discipline of *bandity,* like everyone else's, has weakened after the collapse of the Soviet Union.

As the economy grows, the stakes become bigger, and the number of gangsters trying to muscle in on each other's turf and getting shot also increases. Rivalries between groups of thieves run along geographic, ethnic, and even age lines. According to Russian police, the number of thieves-in-law went up from 660 in 1990 to 740 in 1995. Only one third of them are ethnic Russians. Another third are Georgians (from the Caucasus mountains, the Russian Sicily), and one third other minorities, also primarily from the Caucasus, such as the Chechens.

KRYSHA OVER YOUR HEAD

Sometimes a businessman goes looking for a *krysha* (protection), but usually a *krysha* comes looking for him. The *bandity* keep an eye out for cash. Whenever they see a building that used to house a sleepy failing state enterprise teeming with new tenants, they smell money, like bears smell honey.

For example, an old government enterprise in central Moscow is privatized, and each worker invests his voucher and receives several shares. It looks like people's capitalism, but soon the director gets hold of most of the shares, buying them up for pennies, especially when his workers are hard up before paydays (which he can easily delay). He proceeds to run his enterprise into the ground, throws most workers out and sublets the empty space to other businesses. On paper, he is the director of a failing privatized enterprise, begging the government for subsidies. In reality, he is a rich landlord being paid in cash. Between 10 and 20 percent of his take goes to the *bandity*. This man needs all the protection he can get.

Bandity have tentacles out, alerting them to profit opportunities. Some of their information comes from clerks at government agencies, such as customs and taxation. This is why many Russians are doubly shy about reporting their income to the government. One of my early warnings about the bandits' intelligence gathering came in 1995 after I asked the woman who worked for me in Moscow to install a second phone line in her apartment. "No way," said her husband, a very savvy man. "If we put it in, a week later *bandity* will

come to extort us for a *krysha*. We're better off with a single line."
To install a second line would have cost over $1,000, about ten
months' average salary at that time. Clerks at the phone company
knew that only businesspeople could afford a second line, and that
information would have been sold to the *bandity*.

Thieves-in-law usually begin by paying you a friendly visit—but
things can quickly escalate to beatings, maimings, and murders.
Russian businesses can be extremely profitable, but risks are com-
mensurate with rewards. Moscow has half the population of New
York but about the same number of murders—about six per day—
making its murder rate about twice as high. Some of those killings are
family and friends going at each other with knives or axes in drunken
rages. But a large share of murders are "business related," hits by organized crime. Such murders are almost never solved. Some professional
killers are said to have graduated from the Special Forces. Witnesses
are afraid to cooperate; the police are not too keen to pursue gangsters who have bigger guns, better cars, and often pay them off.

Whenever I get a postcard enticing me with frequent flyer miles
to stay in Moscow's Radisson Slavyanskaya Hotel, I think of Paul
Tatum, an American who owned 40% of that hotel and was killed in
November 1996 by a man who waited for him with a submachine
gun in an underground passage in the Moscow subway. Tatum had
been one of the first Westerners to venture into the Soviet Union. As
a pioneer of Russian capitalism, he got himself a sweet "early bird"
deal. He paid less than $3 million for a 40% interest in a new hotel
in downtown Moscow. The Radisson Corporation of Minnesota put
up the bulk of the money for the project and received 10% of equity,
while the Moscow city government, famous for its business savvy,
took 50%. By the mid-1990s the hotel, with a Chechen chief executive, was grossing about $60 million per year, but the partners
squabbled about slicing their growing pie.

Tatum was a hard-boiled small businessman (*The New York
Times* had called him "loutish"), who was sued repeatedly in the US
before he discovered Russia. In the chaos of the disintegrating USSR,
his lawyers wrote an ironclad agreement in English that was highly
favorable to him, and he dug in his heels when his partners wanted
to change it. At one point he barricaded himself in a hotel room with

armed guards. He sued his partners, including the Moscow City government, and took out large ads in Moscow papers ridiculing them. Later, the magazine *Den'gi* (Money) referred to Tatum as "the man who was in everybody's way." Only in Russia, instead of a lawyer, he wound up facing the business end of an AK-47 assault rifle.

Who did him in? The killer was never found. You wonder who would shoot a man so brazenly—with a submachine gun at 4 P.M. in a busy subway station. The killer must have been either very stupid or very well protected. Who sent him? Who profited from Tatum's death?

My Russian friends keep saying Tatum was stupid. He should have taken what money he could get and clear out of Moscow a long time ago. He had plenty of warning, much more than any Russian would have received. The Russians are surprised when I tell them that Tatum's murder was big news in America where it shocked people and set back the cause of investing in Russia.[13] In a civil society people do not kill their partners if they do not like their contracts. The Russians appear wistful and say that someday they too will get to that point.

People who get shot in the course of business disputes know they are going to be shot. It is rare for a bullet to come as a surprise. Players know the rules of the game. This is similar to getting sued in the US. You are not likely to be surprised by a process server bringing you a summons to appear in court. First you are going to get several calls or letters from the attorney for someone with whom you are having a dispute. When they give you an ultimatum, you know that negotiation has run its course and a process server will be arriving. Why do people sit around waiting to be shot? The smart ones don't; they make themselves scarce and go abroad. Those who remain fall into two groups. Some think that their own *krysha* will protect them, while others shrug their shoulders with the famous Russian *avos*—maybe this will blow over.

Ragged thieves of Stalin's era could not own property—just steal and live hand to mouth. Today they drive expensive cars, have

---

[13] On the day of Tatum's death a prominent Ukrainian businessman was also gunned down. He had given Tatum $80,000 to support his lawsuit against his partners. When he returned home in a private plane with his wife, a car full of bandits drove onto the landing strip and raked them with submachine gun fire. That news made scarcely a ripple in the Russian media.

bodyguards, live in big houses, and stash money away in the West. Thieves-in-law are turning into prosperous godfathers, connected with corrupt politicians. Nikolai Modestov in his best-selling book *Moskva Banditskaya,* from which the title of this chapter was borrowed, describes how a top Moscow police official got back his stolen BMW, outfitted with the latest police gear. He simply called one of Moscow's top thieves-in-law, and a few hours later was told where to find his car (it was parked in a quiet yard without a scratch).

The temptation to use *bandity* can be very high. A businessman who had been cheated by a partner, swindled by a big customer or squeezed by the government knows he can solve his problems if he calls them for help. A *krysha* will help you collect overdue bills, intimidate competitors, and even lend you money. People under pressure often forget that when you sup with the devil, you need a very long spoon—and still can wind up with burned fingers. *Krysha* is a Faustian bargain that more and more businesspeople choose to do without.

A LEAKY ROOF

In 1994, a banker friend of mine ran into a problem in Moscow. His bank used to make commercial loans, but many customers did not like to repay them. The bank retained a team of loan workout specialists. If a customer was tardy, the team would visit his premises to explain the importance of paying on time. They would underscore their message by breaking his furniture and smashing office equipment. If that didn't fully sink in, they returned, beat up the debtor and promised to shoot him the next time. By then anyone with half a brain knew he had to pay back his loan.

The business was profitable—the bank kept making loans, while the workout team made sure they got repaid. Profits rolled in, and my friend, busy with other ventures and a new wife, left his bank in care of a manager and seldom came to visit. Then the chief of the workout team—a big, tough, violent, heavily tattooed, abusive man who spent most of his life in prisons and was heavily armed—came to the bank manager. "We're doing a great job for you," he said. The manager agreed. "We're doing such a great job for you, I feel like we are partners." The gangster demanded a share in the bank. The manager's heavily armed guards threw the man out, but it was too late. The gang had been inside the bank for too long and knew where everybody lived. When they came to the manager's house rather than his office, he called my friend for help.

My friend had a very serious problem. If he gave in, he'd lose not only a great deal of money but even more prestige. The word would get out that he could be extorted, sending an open invitation to other criminals. He could not afford to settle with his workout team—but the team was not going to go away.

Soon after my banker friend became involved in this problem, the chief of the workout team was driving at night on Circle Road, a beltway that surrounds Moscow. Two traffic cops pulled him over for a routine document check. They were not polite, and he became menacing and abusive. He was big and armed. It looked as if the traffic cops were in big trouble. It just so happened that a detachment of OMON—antiterrorist police—drove by in a van on the same deserted stretch of road. They got out to help—and two days later the chief of the workout team died in a prison hospital from the injuries he suffered while resisting arrest. The rest of his team disappeared. My friend no longer had a problem.

He told me his story over a dinner of local trout, fresh from the ponds and brooks dug by Molotov for Stalin in the 1940s. We sat in a heavily guarded former government *dacha* on the outskirts of Moscow in the middle of the woods, my friend's beautiful naked wife splashing in a private swimming pool next door. Warm and clean after a sauna, eating trout and gulping vodka, I realized I was sitting across the table from a killer. The banker, a mild and highly educated man, did what he had to do to survive in business in Russia in the early 1990s.

THE CRIMINAL LANDSCAPE

Russian criminals, like their peers all over the world, operate in all the usual areas—prostitution, drugs, and guns. Gangsters control many of Moscow's clubs and casinos. They skim profits and supply security;

they sweep visitors with metal detectors; and they provide enough burly guards to give second thoughts to any potential troublemaker.

Criminals control prostitutes. A whore on Tverskaya (formerly Gorky) Street, just off Red Square, costs $100 for the night, but a girl would be lucky to receive $20. She doesn't even get to hold the money; a gangster collects it before she goes on a call.

Petty hoodlums sometimes stake out a city block and collect money from anyone who wants to park there. Russians call such illegal charges *na ozeleneniye*, literally "a greens fee," meaning its purpose is to get some "grin," a slang term for dollars.

Moscow's Sheremetyevo airport, like most airports in Eastern Europe, is tightly controlled by gangsters who prey on arriving passengers. A taxi from downtown Moscow to the airport costs about $15, but if you take a taxi at the airport into the city, it will cost you over $50. Most of that money goes to the *bandity*. This is a common problem these days in airports of Eastern Europe, something with which I had to deal with in Kiev, Ukraine and Warsaw, Poland.

The driver who took me to the Sheremetyevo in December 1996 began to shake as we neared the international terminal. He knew he was not supposed to pick up any passengers there, but a few weeks earlier had offered a free ride to a woman with a child. She needed to go just a quarter mile to the airport hotel, but the mob-controlled drivers wanted to charge her a high price. He took pity on her, a typical Russian trait. As she was getting into his car, several *bandity* ran up and slashed his tires. The airport police could not have cared less. Now he was really afraid. He had learned his lesson.[14]

Some industries are more vulnerable to criminals than others. This applies not only to Russia but to many other countries. Businesses such as stores, restaurants, and gas stations are visible, open, deal in cash, and cannot move. If *bandity* come to your gas

---

[14] Speaking of Eastern European airports, a more dangerous problem than overcharging is the lack of assurance that you and your luggage will safely make it in a taxi downtown. If someone on the plane sees you flash cash or valuables and alerts the airport bandits, your taxi may get stopped in a secluded spot before you reach your destination. I had been warned of this danger repeatedly—most recently in 1997 during my stopover in Warsaw by a Russian whom I met in a transit lounge. He told me of getting robbed a few months earlier in a taxi he took at a Ukrainian airport. You may use a taxi to go to the airport, but do not take a taxi into the city. Arrange for someone to come and meet you. If gangsters stop your car, try not to look in their faces to assure them you'll not be a witness against them.

station you'll have to deal with them—out alone at night with valuable property that could be torched. On the other hand, if you run an Internet shop or market cellular phones, your chances of coming into contact with criminals are much lower.

As I drafted this chapter in New York, I got a call from my friend, a money manager in Hawaii. A friend of his had opened an American fast-food franchise in Moscow, but when he went to visit his business, the Russian partner brought in several enforcers and told him to clear out of town. That American dashed to the airport and is now trying to sue his Russian ex-partner in one of the European courts.

I told my Hawaiian friend that most cultures take advantage of foreigners and see them as fair game for locals. Perhaps America is the only country in the world where it's different, where foreigners get a fair shake. "Naah, it's the same here," laughed my friend. "I watched the Japanese come into Hawaii. We ripped them off right and left, sold them the worst junk at the most ridiculous prices and most of them lost money."

You need trustworthy local guides in any country. People all over the world are not eager to send you their money simply because you had a clever idea and brought in some capital. You have to choose what business to get into. If profits in a food franchise seem very attractive, you have to ask yourself how come the Russians are not taking them. Finally, few businesses can be run via remote control. It pays to be on the spot and speak the local language.

WESTERN PERCEPTIONS

Most Westerners see the Russian crime situation as much darker than it really is. Mass media can take a lot of credit for that. Crime sells newspapers. If a man walks down the street and a dog bites him, there is something to write about. If a dog doesn't bite, there's no "news that's fit to print." An editor of a US newspaper can send a reporter to Moscow and tell him, get me a fresh crime story every day, and he'd get it and sell newspapers. He could get a new crime story each day in New York or Berlin, but that's old hat and less colorful. Russia is fresher, and more exotic.

Each society has its criminals and many have organized crime. We have John Gotti in the US, and for every mafioso behind bars we have more on the street. Just try to deliver cement to a construction site in New York City without paying off gangsters—your truck will be vandalized, and if you still do not understand, they'll teach you a more physical lesson. Commercial garbage hauling in many American cities is controlled by organized crime. You can get your legs broken right here, in New York or Boston. We have organized crime in the US even after 200 years of developing our legal system. A huge country like Russia, emerging from a great political upheaval, needs time to get a better handle on its criminals. We can expect Russians to put more pressure on their *bandity* each year, and gradually drive them into narrow niches, similar to what has happened in the US.

Magazine editors who keep publishing scary stories about crime in Russia are trafficking in yesterday's news. Organized crime was a huge story in the early '90s, but it took years for most US journalists to wake up to it. Now Russian society is becoming increasingly legal and transparent. The economy is growing bigger and more complex; it is expanding from under the criminals' grasp. This is the story that most newspapers and magazines miss.

Successful investing and trading requires us to act on information not obvious to the majority. For example, as recently as mid-1996, Russian government bonds sold for about 50 cents on the dollar as most international investors feared Russia's slide into political instability. Six months and one presidential election later, Russian bonds were rated just a notch below investment grade, sharply driving up prices. Savvy Russians and farsighted foreigners who bought those bonds on the cheap because of their confidence in the Russian system earned superprofits. Those who hung back and waited to see what would happen missed the boat.

Prices of Russian stocks today reflect a huge "risk discount." The misperception of the crime situation in Russia is a part of that discount—the more people are afraid, the deeper it is. Being able to see the reality behind the media smokescreen allows you to act. If you want to make sensible and profitable investment decisions, you need to look deeper than the mass media.

GROWING FROM UNDER A *KRYSHA*

Bandity reached the pinnacle of their power and influence in Russia in 1994–1995. They had a few fantastically good years thanks to an accident of history. In a country whose government collapsed, whose legal system ground to a halt, and whose military sat in the barracks, thieves-in-law emerged as the only organized force with guns and a rough system of justice.

Bandity became a major force in society because they did more than prey on businesses and individuals. They provided quasi-legal services that many found indispensable and were willing to pay for. Thieves-in-law helped keep petty criminals under control, enforced business contracts, and collected bills. Their power grew when society needed them. Now the democratic government of Russia is growing stronger, and people find its emerging system of justice both fairer and cheaper than that of thieves-in-law. *Bandity* began to slide from the top in 1996, after becoming less of a necessity and more of a hindrance. As the democratic system of justice keeps maturing, *bandity* are slipping into an early stage of what is likely to be a long slow decline.

After the Soviet government fell apart, assets of the entire state—factories, banks, mines, and so forth—were left without a clear owner. What wasn't nailed down got privatized. Organized crime became a major player in the vast transfer of wealth. The initial accumulation of capital is seldom a pretty sight in any country. If you wanted to walk into a bank and privatize it, money alone was not enough; you had to have guns to ward off competitors. Organized crime in the early 90s had more work and more money than it could handle, but that process was completed by the mid-1990s.

Easy money had been stolen—assets now have new owners. It became hard in the mid-90s to accumulate major new capital using guns. Now it is more important to manage your assets. Whether you've acquired them legally or not, you want a legal system to protect what you have.

Six years ago Russia had no legal businesspeople. A businessman was a criminal by definition. Today, whenever Russian businesspeople gather for any trade conference, they pass resolutions calling on the government to provide them with a better legal framework. People want laws, and the democratic system is going to give them what they demand. Law-giving is a messy process. It may even turn out to be as messy in Russia as in the United States, but this process cuts the *bandity* out of the economic mainstream. The fight against the *bandity* will be long, it may never fully succeed, as it never fully succeeded in the US, but the smart money in Russia today bets on legality.

Smart criminals are rapidly going legal. They are investing in businesses, especially simpler ones they can easily understand, such as import-export, banks, and retail. They are becoming respectable and concerned with legalities. People who acquired great wealth in a few short years, whether by legal means or not, want to protect what they've got. In another generation or two many of them may look similar to the founders of some of the great American dynasties who made their fortunes by robbing Indians, buying land from corrupt legislatures, or bootlegging. Let another generation pass in Russia before its new rich learn social graces and start endowing charities.

The more stupid gangsters are starting to go broke. Many of them acquired crazy spending habits in recent years and cannot adjust to the new economic realities. Many are getting shot during increasingly vicious turf battles. Working-class mothers are said to discourage their daughters from marrying *bandity*—"BMW today, graveyard tomorrow."

Russian businesses are growing so fast that organized crime cannot keep up with them. Businesses are expanding from under the *krysha*, into the open. As they become more and more complex, it becomes harder for the *bandity* to size them up and shake them down.

It is becoming increasingly common for businesspeople to operate without a *krysha*. People are starting to take their disputes to arbitrage courts. The temptation to call *bandity* for help is still there, but more and more people resist it. When I visited the man who ran the Russian branch of a Fortune 500 company, he bitterly complained about locals who owed his firm $15 million in unpaid bills. Some of them laughed in his face, but he recoiled from the idea of calling in *bandity* to help collect bills. He planned to work with the system, write off his losses, be more careful in the future about extending credit.

Bandity are very interested in banks, which they see as piles of cash waiting to be picked up. A favorite game used to be to take control of a bank, collect deposits, give friends credit, and bankrupt the bank. That used to be an easy game, but it is becoming harder and harder to play, as the Ministry of Finance is becoming more savvy about regulating the banks. The Soviet Union, with a population of a quarter billion people, used to have only one consumer bank and a handful of industry-related banks. Regulating them was easy and most officials were party hacks. Today, Moscow alone has over 1,500 banks! As new banks mushroomed in the country, *bandity* and their helpers could run circles around the regulators. The new financial professionals, many of whom were recently educated in the West, are just starting to come in to regulate the system. They make it harder and harder to run swindles, reducing opportunities for *bandity*.

Russian securities firms have always been largely free of *bandity*. Criminals are not the smartest people in the world, and few if any can follow the complexities of initial and secondary offerings, ordinary and preferred shares, short-term and medium-term government paper, to say nothing of derivatives and arbitrage. As a result, most brokerage firms in Russia operate without a *krysha*. This makes life easier for an international investor.

Moskva banditskaya is becoming *Moskva biznesmenskaya*.

6

BATTLING THE "NEW SOVIET MAN"

The Iron Curtain cut off the communist empire from the rest of the world. Behind its protective cover the totalitarian regime went to work, spinning its web, entrenching itself in power. For 74 years the rulers of the USSR pursued a sinister plan called "breeding the New Soviet Man." Not only would they build a new economy to bury capitalists, as Khruschev once promised Nixon, they would change the very human nature. Some of the ugly sights you see in Russia today are there because the Soviets partly succeeded. Some of the most hopeful developments are there because the Soviets partly—and with some people wholly—failed.

The New Soviet Man, nicknamed *homo soveticus* in the West, was to be a selfless social bee. He would give up his individuality, privacy, and the pursuit of private goals for the advancement of the socialist society. He would work wherever the party sent him, sacrificing his time and health, never asking questions or complaining. He would monitor his co-workers and neighbors, pressure them to work hard and live just like him, be vigilant in class struggle and report any suspicions to authorities. A New Soviet Man would be a hard-working human ant, with zero independence, paranoid of his neighbors, and wildly proud of his country. Needless to say, he would bring up his children the same way—to ensure that several generations later the entire country would be populated by the New Soviet Men.

And women. The Soviets sent almost all women to work, famously staffing road repair crews with them. They paid lip service to the equality of the sexes, but women in the USSR were rarely allowed to advance ahead of men, except for a few show cases. The glass ceiling had been set somewhere at knee level. Women were considered a lesser form of life. A common saying in the Soviet Union was "A chicken is not a bird, a woman is not a person." Even today, the Russian media remains full of casual derogatory remarks about women. The result was brought home to me in a stark incident 14 years ago. My ex–sister-in-law, then recently arrived from the USSR, congratulated me on the birth of my son (I already had two daughters) and added, "Now you are no longer a junk maker (*brakodel*)." I shuddered. She was speaking in front of her own daughter—continuing to breed a New Soviet Person in the West.

RUSSKIY AND *ROSSIYANIN*

When you refer to people in Russia, be aware of an important distinction—whether a person is a *russkiy* (ethnic Russian) or a *rossiyanin* (a citizen of Russia). A large number—81.5%—of Russia's 150 million people are ethnic Russians, and the rest are minorities, practically all of whom speak Russian. The word *russkiy* reflects ethnicity, membership in Russia's native ethnic group, whether that person lives in Russia or not. The word *rossiyanin* reflects citizenship or residency in Russia, whether that person is an ethnic Russian or not. For example, Georgians or Ukrainians who permanently live in Russia are *rossiyane* but not *russkiy*, and so are the Jews. The distinction between a *russkiy* and a *rossiyanin* is totally lost on foreigners—there are no words for it in English—while most Russians (whether *russkiy* or *rossiyanin*) are keenly aware of it.

An American who refers to a Jewish émigré from Russia as a Russian simply advertises that he is just another dense foreigner. A more correct way to phrase a question would be "Are you from Russia?" (*rossiyanin*) rather than "Are you Russian?" (*russkiy*).

The tsarist Empire, like most countries of its era, was plagued with bigotry, racism, and anti-Semitism. Still, Russians proudly claim today that they never had *pogroms*—those murderous anti-Semitic riots in the Russian empire occurred in the areas of the Ukraine and Poland.

Stalin, who, as a native of Georgia in the Caucasus, was a *rossiyanin* but not a *russkiy*, did more than anyone to stir up ethnic divisions and hatreds after World War II, and they persisted long after he died. The Soviets waved the flag of internationalism abroad, taking a holier-than-thou attitude against the US, while conducting vicious mass deportations of entire ethnic groups at home. The Volga Germans, the Crimean Tatars, the Chechens, and several other ethnic groups were uprooted and exiled to Siberia and Central Asia where millions perished from hunger and cold.

A distant relative of mine described how, as a teenage draftee in the 1940s, he guarded the trains with deported Tatars. Their villages were surrounded at night; men, women, and children were given 15 minutes to take what they could carry and get into waiting trucks. Those trucks, escorted by motorcyclists with machine guns mounted on sidecars, took them to waiting trains and from there to Central Asia. Anyone who resisted or tried to run away or hide was shot on the spot. In 1953 Stalin ordered his henchmen to prepare camps and trains again, this time for a mass deportation of Jews. My grandfather, one of the men to whom this book is dedicated, was an orthopedic surgeon and a department chairman at a medical school in Leningrad at that time. He described to me how people would use any pretext to visit Jews' apartments that winter, to case them out, expecting huge vacancies to occur any week. And then the Jews got lucky—Stalin died, and in the ensuing power struggle nobody had the time or the drive to carry out his plan.

The Soviet Union suffered from virulent anti-Semitism. Several career paths had been off-limits to Jews: the government, international affairs, top management. Most universities had "numerical clauses," which limited the admissions of Jews to 2% or less of any incoming class. A person could be accosted and insulted on the street simply for looking Jewish.

After the communist system collapsed, there was a striking decrease in ethnic bigotry, particularly anti-Semitism. Today's

Russians, whether *russkiy* or *rossiyane*, tend to be apolitical, busy getting on with their lives and trying to make money. Nobody seems to care whether a person is Jewish or not. Jews serve at the highest levels of government and run some of the top businesses and banks. The numerical quotas in colleges are just a memory.

The country still has a strong prejudice against blacks, of whom there are very few, mostly visitors from Africa. There is a nasty ethnic prejudice against olive-skinned people from the Caucasus. Many Soviets long envied small businessmen from the Caucasus who sold flowers and fruit during Russian winters and always seemed to have money. Now the caucasians (men from the Caucasus) get blamed for crime in the capital. During the Chechen War every olive-skinned and curly haired caucasian was seen as a possible terrorist, and to this day police harass them. The country seems to want a scapegoat, and the media helps whip up the hysteria. I have two Georgian friends in Moscow who are currency dealers. The darker one is forever being stopped by the police and hauled in for questioning, and the other, blond and Aryan-looking, has to go and get him out.

The brutality of life in the Soviet Union, paradoxically, led to a much greater mutual loyalty among people than in the West. Diamonds come from coal harshly compressed in the bowels of the earth. Back in the Soviet days an Armenian friend of mine visited his Georgian buddy in a provincial prison. Both had been running underground businesses, and the Georgian got caught. My friend traveled on dirty trains to the faraway prison city, which was unsafe, considering he was under the gun himself. He brought his buddy two sticks of salami, but when the guards escorted the inmate back into the cell they patted him down and found it. They took away the salami and beat the man mercilessly, screaming, "You blackasses, you take care of your own—you eat better in prison than we do outside." They threw the Georgian into solitary and told my friend to clear out of town. He was highly vulnerable in a faraway city where he had no contacts, but instead of leaving for the relative safety of Moscow he stayed. Each morning he went to the prison office to ask about his buddy until they let him out of the solitary. He may have saved his life. The guards could have killed him if they knew no one kept an eye on him.

The Soviet intolerance went far beyond ethnicity. People would stare, point, and jeer at anyone with unusual clothes. Soon after winning World War II, they passed a law prohibiting people with "offensive disabilities" from entering public places, such as restaurants. Veterans who had a few years earlier saved the country from Nazism were being kept out of eating places, lest their ugly scars upset other diners! In the mid-70s in New York I asked a friend, a Russian Orthodox priest, whether he planned to visit Russia. "I will not," he answered, "until I can walk down the street in my cassock and collar without people throwing stones at me or insulting my church." It sounded like an impossible dream. Now people walk the streets in their religious garb—Christian, Jewish, or Moslem—and nobody pays any attention. New churches and synagogues are being built all over the country. Father Cyril died too soon.

RUSSIAN FRIENDS

One of the most attractive aspects of Russia is the intensity of its friendships. Russians tend to have much stronger friendships than most Westerners. They are more generous, loyal, giving, and prone to spend long and intensely pleasant hours in each other's company, often behind heavily laden tables in each other's apartments. The thin walls of those cramped apartments seem to spread wide as the conversation, music, and vodka flow late into the Russian night. There may not be enough food tomorrow, but today the guests are in and the table is full. Life is hard and sometimes downright brutal outside, but as Andrey Voznesensky, a modern Russian poet wrote, "Our backs are like the halves of a shell. The greater the pressure, the closer it brings us together."

Life in Russia has been brutally hard for generations, and good friends remained the only source of support for most people. The totalitarian regime set out to destroy, subvert, or control all informal social structures we take for granted in the West, such as churches, clubs, and even the neighborhood taverns. The only structures it could not destroy or subvert, even though it tried, were family and friends. Your freedom and your life depended on your friends. The net of KGB informers reached far and wide. A casual political joke could end your career or condemn you to a labor camp. They said during Khruschev's era: "What's a 'reduced' joke? It's a joke that used to get you five years in prison, but now only gets you two." When you trusted someone, you often trusted them with your life—but then you had a real friend. Dangers rarely broke Russian friendships; they usually made them stronger.

In a country where few people had any savings, businesses were illegal, and state-owned banks made no loans to individuals, who could you borrow from when you needed money? If you wanted to buy a car, an apartment, meet an emergency, or simply buy food when money ran out before payday, to whom could you turn? Friends loaned to friends without interest, on a handshake, usually without a promissory note. Tight informal networks kept people afloat, from workers borrowing five rubles before payday to underground businessmen borrowing to finance inventory.

Relationships between people in Russia tend to be warmer than in the US, and mutual support is greater. When Russians ask, how do you do, they actually wait for an answer (the downside is the lack of American ease and casualness in social life). Russians are open people, not rigid; they are trusting, not greedy or calculating. They feel that the law of friendship is above the law of competition.

When Russians accept you as a friend, they do great favors for you, above and beyond any Western expectations. They put their own work aside and take you where you have to go, introduce you to those you need to meet, push your agenda, without watching the clock or calculating a payback. On other hand, Russian friends will ask you for favors that may seem extraordinary to a Westerner—and if you hesitate, they will cut you off for good.

As I am writing this chapter on a Tuesday afternoon in New York, my phone rings. A Moscow friend's younger sister just received a US visa for an internship I arranged for her on Wall Street. My friend bought her a ticket to New York for the coming Saturday, giving me 3 days to find her an apartment, meet her at Kennedy Airport, and get her settled. My friend takes it for granted that I will put my own business aside and do everything for his sister—which is precisely what he did for me in Moscow. Three days later, on a freezing rainy day, the girl arrives—with a bottle of duty-free vodka for me but no winter clothes for herself. She thought New York was warm. To save her money, I take her to local Russian friends who have a daughter her age, and sure enough, they find her a warm coat, cook us a big meal, and insist that both of us come for a weekend with them in the country.

If you do business in Russia, I hope you make friends there. It is one of the most intense and rewarding experiences a person can have.

SUSPICIOUSNESS AND PASSIVITY

After seventy years of "breeding the New Soviet Man," little wonder that there are quite a few specimens still walking around. You know you've run into one when you encounter dull laziness or unprovoked rudeness and suspicion. Modern Russian slang for this is *sovok*—derived from *Soviet*, meaning a leftover of the old system. Those traits are rapidly becoming less common, to the point where a Moscow financial weekly named *Kapital* instituted a "*sovok* award" for readers who sent in examples of such encounters. Still, the low-grade *sovok* is more widespread than Russians like to think.

Many Russians consider openness and trust, the qualities we value so highly in the US, as silly and childish. In the old repressive society a trusting person was a fool. To this day in Russia you keep running into secretiveness and suspicion, even duplicity inherited from the communist years. When you sense those traits in a person do not waste your time trying to build mutual trust, American style. People who viscerally and illogically distrust you have been damaged—leave them alone. In general, you'll find younger people more Western in this regard.

The repressive Soviet regime burrowed deep into people's lives. The KGB informers watched everyone, and the system punished deviants. People were fired from jobs for listening to jazz and sent to labor camps for telling politically incorrect jokes. You always had to watch yourself—always on guard, ready for trouble. It was better to maintain an impassive face. A person who looked upbeat was more likely to come under suspicion. "What are you smiling about—you have more than others?" was a common refrain.

After years of living under such pressure, many Soviets acquired a sullen, suspicious look. It became indelibly impressed on their faces; it showed in their posture—tense shoulders, rigid neck, and perpetually darting eyes. The look became so ingrained that even today I often recognize people from the Soviet Union on the streets of America. I see them from half a block away. Even if they have lived here for years and wear Western clothes, you can't miss that tense and hypervigilant look.

The stiff Soviet look has begun to fade in recent years, especially among the young. Russians not only dress better; their body language is changing. It used to be that only foreigners held their heads high or smiled riding Moscow's palatial subway. Many Russians today look very Western; they carry themselves as free people, in a manner that would look perfectly normal in New York, Paris, or London.

You hear Russian speech more and more often in the West. During the Easter school break in 1997, I was standing at the base of a ski lift in California's Mammoth Lakes, waiting for my son to ski down, when I heard a cheerful group of college kids speaking Russian and taking photos of each other. I turned to them, offering to snap their picture. We continued to chat on a long chairlift ride to the top. The casualness of this scene forcefully brought home the magnitude of change in Russia. After I jumped a Soviet ship in 1974, it was very rare to hear Russian spoken in the US. When you did, it came from either embassy people, often KGB, or Jews who had emigrated via Israel. The novelty of that scene—three Russian kids from moderately well-to-do families skiing in California on spring break—is amazing because it is so normal.

Still, rigidity and passivity remain common in Russia. As an investor, you will be reading annual reports and other documents composed by people whose personalities were formed during the Soviet era. Their first impulse, taken in with their mother's milk, is to lie, cover up, and look out for trouble. Try to pull an informative annual report out of a man who had been hiding information all his life!

Russian businesses have to slog through a thick net of rules and regulations, forcing them to generate tons of paperwork—or move into a cash economy. They must document each step several times. Russians are amazed at how much Westerners accept on trust. Russians have a saying, "Without a paper you are a bug, with it you are human."

A bookkeeper has to fill out nine forms before cutting a check. Most business letters or documents must be stamped with a *pechat*, (a company seal), or better yet, several *pechati* by several officials. Whenever you do business in Russia, your counterparts will pull out their *pechati* from special holders, hold them close to their lips, forcefully exhale at them to freshen the ink, and slam them onto documents, making the desks shake. It is a hypnotic process. After a few days in Moscow, I start asking people to imprint a *pechat* on any paper they give me and even plan to get myself one of those. I forget that idea immediately after buckling into a plane seat on my way from Moscow.

Suspiciousness in Russia is often combined with passivity, and a low level of initiative. The Soviet system trained people to cover their butts, to point accusing fingers, to assign blame. The system did little to reward people for taking risks but was harshly inventive in punishing them. Being active got you in trouble, while being passive kept you out of it. Many Russians to this day operate defensively, with a grossly stunted sense of initiative.

Russians haven't always been this way. Before the communist regime clamped down, people had more enterprise and initiative. The history of Russia's eastward expansion into Siberia has many similarities to the westward expansion of the United States. Before the communists took over in 1917, the Russian Empire was developing an industrial base and opening itself up to the West. The Soviets deliberately set out to repress the independent initiative in order to breed their New Soviet Men.

To this day, Russians are less likely to follow through on plans than Westerners. You want something done, you talk to a person who agrees to take the next step. This does not mean it will get done. Maybe it will and maybe it won't. And why not? Perhaps out of a great Russian sense of futility; nothing is going to be accomplished anyway.

Many Russians are afraid to lose face by showing they want something. Deep in their hearts they expect to be frustrated, and hold back to avoid disappointments. You talk to a businessperson, discuss a project—and they don't call you back. If you call them again, you often find they're still interested, but afraid to show it by making a phone call. This lack of initiative and follow-through can be very frustrating. You need to counteract it by carefully choosing who you deal with and being relentless about your business plans.

When I had started a business in New York in the 1980s, I told myself I was not going to hire any people from the USSR. I knew all too well how the system maimed its people. To my surprise I kept running into more and more survivors who kept their energy alive. I wound up hiring several Russian émigrés, people who had managed to survive as normal, honest, and hard-working even under the Soviet system. We cannot tar and feather the entire population of a country, but we must be alert to problems and avoid dealing with those who have them.

THE *AVOS* ATTITUDE AND
THE MAVRODI SYNDROME

Russian suspiciousness has a flip side—a vague belief that things are somehow going to work out by themselves. The great Russian word *avos* expresses that. There is no equivalent to it in English. The closest may be "hopefully it will work out by itself." The Russian pilot who let his teenage son fly a passenger airliner in the 1990s until they hit the ground in Siberia had an *avos* attitude. A stock trader who buys a block of shares on a vague gut feeling that those shares may actually be good has an *avos* attitude. *Avos* is part and parcel of imprecision, fuzziness, and *oblomovschina* (empty daydreaming).

The *avos* attitude is the exact opposite of the approach of a Westerner with his checklist, who goes by the book, sticks to the rules, and aims to leave as little as possible to chance. Russians have a grudging admiration for Western efficiency, but find it cold and heartless. *Avos* to some is another indication of their great Russian soul.

Watching the *avos* attitude of cabin crews on domestic flights in Russia makes me wonder whether their mechanics are just as lax (I have no qualms taking Aeroflot flights between New York and Moscow which use Boeings and conform to the more rigid American rules). On the last flight I took from Moscow to Kiev people sat in unlatched folding seats facing each other across domino tables while overhead open shelves overflowed with heavy luggage. Suitcases clogged the aisle, while cute stewardesses in ethnic dresses maneuvered between them pouring piping hot tea from 2-gallon iron pots painted with red flowers. It was a joy to step out of the airplane and walk on the ground knowing you've arrived unhurt.

The Russian saying, "The Lord takes care of drunks, children, and idiots" is another expression of the *avos* attitude. When you do business in Russia or buy stocks there, make sure you do not belong to any of the above groups. You need to have something more solid than *avos* working in your favor.

The paradoxical flip side of Russian suspiciousness leads to occasional spasms of incredible gullibility. I call it the Mavrodi syndrome after the promoter who bilked millions of Russians out of their money (see Chapter 3). Mavrodi built an investment organization called MMM, with offices throughout the country. His clever advertising on TV promised enormous and safe returns. He used some of the new money to pay off his early investors, enhancing his reputation and attracting more customers. The Russians later called it a pyramid; we call it a Ponzi scheme in the US.

Several other pyramids imitated Mavrodi, and for a brief happy moment almost everyone in Russia seemed to be making money. Once investors started withdrawing their supposed profits out of MMM, the pyramid collapsed and Mavrodi was arrested. Locked in a Moscow prison awaiting trial, Mavrodi, genius that he was, campaigned for a seat in the *Duma* (the Russian Parliament), making exorbitant promises to his suburban district. He was elected and then released from prison thanks to his parliamentary immunity.

My Moscow friends keep giving me MMM certificates as souvenirs. They look like Russian currency, only the paper and printing are better and the picture shows not the Kremlin but a pudgy young man with bushy hair. How could a pauperized nation entrust its money to Mavrodi, how could it vote for him after he had been disgraced? It is sometimes easier to cheat those who do not trust.

Russians have a fascination with successful crooks. They condemn murderers and other violent criminals—unless they were drunk at the time of their crime and "did not know what they were doing"—but have a very forgiving attitude toward financial criminals. It is probably rooted in Russia's long and still-fresh memory of serfdom. A serf owned practically nothing, was robbed by landowners and merchants, and could never improve his lot. He felt entertained by successful thieves who managed to beat the system.

The daily parade of scandals in Russia—busted banks, corrupt politicians, looted companies—can make a Westerner's hair stand on end. Russians condemn those crimes, but at the same time many seem amused by the carnival of theft.

SERFS AND NOBLES

The roots of Russian suspiciousness and passivity reach far into the past, beyond communism, into the dark centuries of serfdom. While Western Europe had been free of feudalism for hundreds of years and America had a relatively brief though violent brush with slavery, the long centuries of serfdom in Russia officially ended only in 1861, but their shadows linger to this day.

Serfs were peasants who toiled on nobles' land, and were prohibited from leaving. They could be bought and sold, and their families broken up. Almost everyone in Russia had been a serf, except for small numbers of nobility and clergy, merchants and craftsmen. Nobles could do whatever they wanted with their serfs, short of killing them. They could flog men and women, and some even claimed the "right of the first night"—taking their serfs' daughters before giving them permission to marry.

For centuries serfs had been taught it did not pay to strive because most of what they produced would be taken away by nobles. Nobles did not strive too hard either, knowing they were going to get theirs by "natural right." The nobles, whether feudal or communist, felt free to grab what they believed was naturally theirs, and the serfs felt free to steal what they believed the nobles looted from them anyway. The thieving and laziness of serfs, combined with the grabbing and laziness of nobles, did Russia little good. Its medieval class system undermined the initiative of its people and the cohesiveness of society.

The people at the top changed after the communists overthrew the monarchy, but class divisions became stiffer than before. It would be unthinkable to many status-conscious Soviets to do what we do so casually in the more democratic America: say thank you to a limo driver, shake hands with a waiter, and so on. The party/government/KGB elite enjoyed special housing, fleets of chauffeured cars, even special food stores that ordinary mortals could not enter. People called the best buildings in Moscow "servants' housing"—that's where the top officials lived, whom the media called "servants of the people."

Even speech patterns in the supposedly classless USSR reflected profound class divisions. To this day, after hearing a Russian speak for about 15 seconds I can tell what class he or she comes from. I was amused after arriving in New York in 1974 to see how shocked the old-style pro-Soviet liberals were after hearing that my family had maids or that we owned a house. In the workers' paradise from which I came, members of the ruling elite had several maids and often a chauffeur for good measure. At least in our house, in a style that was considered wildly liberal by many, the maid sat at the table with the guests after serving dinner and before leaving to wash the dishes.

The class system in the USSR was designed to keep cheap labor on the farm and at the factory. The Soviets used their propaganda machine to instill a prejudice against personal service—rulers did not want to lose cheap labor to the private sector. Women who pushed brooms on factory floors considered it demeaning to clean house for a private family. My parents got their maids from villages, by offering those young women new passports to replace the originals locked away by their collective farm chiefs. A new passport meant liberation from servitude on a collective farm. My mother had many patients from the police and the KGB. The world moves in amazing ways. Some communist chief's gonorrhea or syphilis, cured and covered up by my mother, would in due course translate into a maid for our family who'd cook, clean, and do laundry. All of that is history now. Humbled by the Depression of the 1990s, Russians for the most part lost their prejudice against personal service.

Upper classes in the USSR were full of pseudo-aristocratic pretensions, complete with the kissing of ladies' hands. When I wanted to get a summer job in high school, my parents were shocked: What will the neighbors say? You do not need to work. We can afford to support you. The system of nobles and serfs pigeonholed people. It made those at the top and at the bottom feel it did not pay to try, and there hadn't been any middle class to speak of.

There always had been exceptions, people who escaped the system and built their own lives—independent peasants, creative nobles, enterprising craftsmen. One of the great changes in recent years, following the communist collapse, is that the official class system has gone out the window. For the first time in the nation's history, serfdom is out and individual achievement is in.

The old class differences based on power are being ground down by the new money culture in Russia. Russian money is much younger and more brash than in the West. Spending is in and counting is out. Russians consider it poor taste to check their restaurant bills, even though they understand that Westerners do it.

This is a stressful change for people whose minds had been formed under the old system. Even the language has begun to change, primarily among the young, and class differences are blurring and becoming harder to detect. The generation that came of age after the collapse of communism is naturally egalitarian. The fact that the young are among the main beneficiaries of the anticommunist revolution augurs well for Russia's future.

RED DIRECTORS—*SOVOK* IN HIGH PLACES

Russia never had a bill of rights or a charter of freedoms. The closest thing it had to the declaration of human rights came in the 1980s from the West—the Helsinki agreement, signed by the old communist government in its last decade. The Russians suffered for centuries from too much central government and not enough local control. "After Russia freed itself from the Tatars it kept their method of administration. Local representatives of the central authority ran their areas at will, unconstrained by any laws or rights of the governed, only by occasional orders from the center or local passive resistance," sighs Maxim Sokolov, a philosopher turned journalist in Moscow.

Everything people owned ultimately belonged to the monarch. Communists deposed and eventually murdered the tsar but adopted his operating methods, making them more brutal and efficient.

The communist government owned everything in the USSR, but the rulers in the Kremlin felt their grasp slipping as they tried to control every aspect of the increasingly complex economy. Their price-setting committees and hordes of functionaries could not run public baths, traffic lights, and tractor factories all at the same time. Eventually the government retreated, without ever making it explicit, to the position of tightly running a few key military industries, but elsewhere delegating a great deal of responsibility to local managers.

The central government never delegated enough—its control of prices and production quotas kept gumming up the economy. Still, it tended to leave managers alone, as long as their enterprises came close to fulfilling quotas and they did not get caught stealing too much. Most managers treated state enterprises as their own. Those who controlled scarce goods, such as food or clothing, could get rich. The government could sack any manager, and every year or two it would catch a handful who were getting too rich too quickly and shoot them after a show trial. The Russians were philosophical about those trials. "The government cannot arrest a thousand guys and give each 15 days in prison," my grandfather said, "so they catch one and give him 15 years."

The privatization of the 1990s liberated old managers from government control. "The talk of people's privatization makes me laugh," says Maxim Sokolov. "The government didn't control the property in the first place. It was in the hands of directors and bosses. The privatization simply legalized their positions." The public benefited from privatization because it removed obstacles to private ownership. People could go out and create new businesses, but most existing ones were grabbed by their managers.

Privatization created a new class of "Red Directors"—Soviet holdovers, operating by the old book, only much more brazen than before. Red Directors are giving capitalism a bad name, stripping enterprises of assets and banking their loot abroad, throwing workers out and not paying salaries. They would not have dared to do this in Soviet times, under the watchful eye of the district committee of the communist party. Now they have all the rights and none of the responsibilities. This is what Garik Superfin, an historian and one of the men to whom this book is dedicated, called "smoke-brained *sovok* kapitalizm."

Many top positions in the new economy are held by men who used to be communist party bosses. Their titles have changed, but many of the people who ran the economy under the communists are still running it today, especially in the provinces.

"Red Directors" tend to be reactionary and anti-Western. Says Maxim Sokolov: "The first freedom is the freedom to steal. In privatization corporations went broke, but 'Red Directors' became millionaires. They no longer have to report to the ministry. The passion for theft is no longer contained by a measure of fear. Thieves do not want to be found out—a strategic investor may audit their company, they may lose control, even their jobs. They want investments—but without disclosure of old theft or interference with the new."

Harvey Sawikin, a New York money manager, distinguishes between stealing *from* the company and stealing *part* of the company. "Petty larceny was particularly easy to commit during the early stages of privatization, when ownership was unclear and regulatory oversight nonexistent." Oil, metals, and anything worth stealing was diverted, sold, and the money hidden abroad.

"Petty larceny still goes on in the murk of trading arrangements and barter deals. For example, one steel company distributes most of its product through an 'independent' entity owned by the son of the general director." Larcenous insiders will either bankrupt the company or receive a government bailout. They are unconcerned with share values since they have no intention of going to the capital markets.

Grand theft, in Sawikin's definition, is "the use of money and political clout to achieve, in a more or less lawful manner, a large-scale shift of corporate control." The best example is the use of "loans-for-shares" in which banks bid for the right to lend money to the government, receiving large ownership stakes in blue-chip companies as security. The government had been widely expected not to repay those loans, allowing well-connected bidders to acquire large quantities of shares well below market value.

Where does this leave minority shareholders? Petty larceny is bad for them because it strips the company of assets and often signals that the insiders do not see their firm as viable. There is a vicious cycle at work. The company becomes less and less attractive as it is being robbed, prompting the insiders to tear at its flesh before the expected collapse or a government bailout.

Grand theft, on the other hand, is often accompanied by a virtuous circle. In Sawikin's words, "The insiders of a viable company, having accumulated shares in a legal or quasi-legal way, find themselves with greater incentives to promote the shares' value. This in turn sparks enthusiasm from outsiders and a rising share price, which reinforces management's view that wealth can be created, safely, through the overall enhancement of shareholder value."

GETTING TOSSED

The government of the Soviet Union corrupted its citizens. Its net of informers made people distrustful, passive, and sullen. The government trained people to steal from their jobs by keeping wages so ridiculously low that workers used to say, "They pretend to pay us, and we pretend to work." It was common in the USSR to supplement meager incomes by "carrying things home." People felt morally justified stealing from their jobs. If you called a worker a thief, he'd punch you, because he did not consider what he did stealing.

The government, understandably, took a sharply different view. It prosecuted crimes against state property much more harshly than those against individual property. A thief who stole 10,000 rubles from a private person could get a couple of years in prison, but stealing the same amount from the state could cost him his life.

After the Soviet Union collapsed, people realized they could steal with impunity. The police became demoralized, the legal system ground to a halt, and thieves-in-law emerged as a major power in the land (see Chapter 5). People who grew up as economic slaves of the state lost the ability to distinguish between freedom and free-for-all. A new ugly word became common in Russia—*kinut*.

Kinut—literally "to toss"—means to swindle or cheat. After the repressive mechanism of the Soviet state crumbled, and before the principles of a free economy began to crystallize, the country was thrown wide open to cheats and swindlers. Every person in Russia—high or low, rich or poor, clever or slow—had been tossed. In all my travels throughout Russia I never met a single person who hadn't been tossed. Most Russians had been tossed repeatedly, by different people, in different ways—until the atmosphere of distrust became pervasive.

It is hard for a Westerner to comprehend just how badly Russians have been bruised in recent years. Everybody has been hurt, and most people are on their guard. I helped several Russians open brokerage accounts in the US. Their biggest worry is always the same—that the broker may steal their money. I keep explaining how the system is different in the US, how our rules of segregating funds protect customers. While we go over the same ground again and again, most US brokers become exasperated. The Russians keep feeling them out and do things like closing their accounts prior to going on vacation just to make sure they can get their money back.

Two visiting Russian bankers ask me whether they could rent a car in New York. I tell them it is not going to be easy, as neither has a credit card.

"Can we rent a car without a credit card?" "Yes, but then a rental company will demand a deposit." "How much?" "Oh, I don't know—maybe $500 or $1,000." The bankers laugh. "So, the price of a car in America is $1,000!" They tell me that back home many people would plunk down a deposit and disappear with the car. When I try to explain to them the value of operating for the long term, building up a credit history, they laugh. "You Americans are so naive!"

After starting to work with Russian businesspeople, I got into the habit of giving what I called my "20-second sermon." I would tell them honesty is profitable; it is better to have a steady client who pays you $10 a month than to toss him once for $1,000. People look up, move their lips, count, stay silent for a moment, and then say in amazement, "You know, you're right . . . we haven't thought of that." Then they tell me no one else would understand this concept.

I think they are underestimating their countrymen. Today I sense less need for those sermons. By 1997 the climate of honesty has taken a sharp turn for the better. People are much more prone to deliver as promised and are less preoccupied with documentation and paperwork. Russian businesspeople are moving closer to the American model, where massive amounts of business is done on the strength of verbal agreements. One still needs to be extra careful in Russia, but a free economy has proven to be a good teacher—and Russians are very fast learners.

BENDING THE RULES

Whenever you deal with Russian officials, you run into a myriad of bewildering rules. Those rules, laws and *ukases* may seem insurmountable, but take heart and get a trusted local guide because most regulations are not much of an obstacle to those who know their way through the system. As president of a large investment bank in Moscow said to me, "The law is like a telegraph pole—you can't jump over it but it is easy to go around it." Russians have schemes for getting around most of the laws with which the government tries to hem them in.

For example, in mid-1996 Russian Treasury Bills (GKOs) were paying over 80% annual interest to domestic investors, but the government capped the rate for foreigners at 23%. Many Russian brokers offered a scheme whereby a foreigner would "lend" them funds at 60+%, they would use his money to buy GKOs, and then at maturity repay him and pocket the difference. Russians thought it was the most natural thing to do—run a curve around the government—but most Westerners to whom I mentioned this scheme thought it was too brazen and missed a great opportunity.

It is a fundamental principle of Western law that everything is permitted except for what is prohibited. Individuals are free to do anything, except for what is specifically illegal. For centuries in

Russia the opposite was true—everything was forbidden except for what had been expressly allowed. People had to find a law stating that what they wanted to do was legal—imagine what it did to their sense of initiative!

Americans tend to respect laws written by their elected representatives; they feel they have a stake in the government. Things had been very different in Russia until the last few years. For centuries, the laws, regulations, and the power had been absolutely external, dangerous, and exploitative. If people could cheat the government or other rule makers, they felt proud rather than ashamed or embarrassed.

To an American, the words "local power" reflect community involvement and self-determination, but to a Russian they have a sinister and dangerous ring. They remind him of personal insecurity. "Local power" meant killings by the Mongols, whippings by the nobles, forced labor for the communists. If you hoped for justice, you looked to the faraway center—to Moscow. Russians had a saying: "God is high above, the tsar is far away, and honor is a flexible concept." Little wonder they put more stock in personal relationships than in laws.

The authorities in Russia can be brutal, but you can bargain with them. Russians expect much more accommodation than Westerners from their officials. Whenever they face government or corporate authorities, they expect their personal circumstances to be taken into account to a degree unthinkable in the West. Pleading with a traffic cop, carrying an extra suitcase onto an airplane, rescheduling a test in college are all quite normal, as far as most Russians are concerned. They have a saying—"The severity of our laws is mitigated by the laxness of their application."

The enforcement of rules in Russia is nothing like the cold efficiency in the West. The longer you beg an official, asking him again and again to please appreciate your situation, the better your chances of getting what you want. Simple, if unpleasant, transactions between a citizen and his government in the West, such as receiving a traffic ticket or paying customs duties, are subject to long and heated discussions in Russia. The outcome of haggling can sometimes be influenced by a judicious application of cash.

When law-avoidance does not work, and begging fails, a bribe can carry a great deal of weight. Bribery, unfortunately, has become a big problem in Russia after the communist collapse, since most officials are grossly underpaid, and have lost their fear of higher authorities. The government is broke; it cannot afford to pay civil servants even halfway decent salaries and demand accountability. The underpaid officials look at bribes as a heaven-sent opportunity to supplement their meager incomes. This situation will improve only after the economy improves.

Traffic cops are the most visible examples of this new corruption. Moscow today has an informal scale of bribes, depending on the severity of offenses. For example, being stopped for driving with a broken tail light costs $10, while drunk driving weighs in at $300—and those are prices for locals! It may be cheaper to pay a ticket, but it would kill several days, as tickets have to be paid in person and require standing in never-ending lines. If you don't want to be stopped too often, better drive a beat-up domestic car rather than a flashy import.[15] The fastest way to get a driver's license in Moscow is to buy one for a few hundred dollars. It is more than a month's pay for many people, but you save a great deal of time and aggravation. The wife of one of my associates was too principled to pay, so she spent three weeks of her summer vacation taking the required courses and classes, which were not cheap either.

Many Russian stockbrokers buy their professional licenses. A friend in a securities brokerage firm told me that 21 out of 24 brokers in her company, including herself, paid for their licenses. The remaining three were too principled or stubborn, which cost them just as much because they had to pay fees to retake the exams several times. Those exams are so mindlessly detail-oriented and include many questions that can be answered this way or that way, so that clerks who grade them can pass or fail whomever they want. It is more efficient to pay a few hundred dollars and move on. At one point in 1996 the authorities tried to introduce a computerized exam

---

[15] The situation is even worse in the provinces and the former Soviet republics. Driving a sports car in Kiev was like driving an obstacle course. When we parked, the cops removed our license plates and harangued us for alleged infractions before allowing us to buy the plates back. I still carry in my wallet a receipt for paying a ticket—3 million Ukrainian *karbovantsi*.

system, similar to those in the US. Local bureaucrats killed that experiment in two months—it was easier to squeeze out cash without a computer.

Bribes start at a few dollars and go all the way up to what a banker friend calls "a governor's unit." That "unit" is an attaché case full of $100 bills. According to my friend, it holds 1.5 million dollars. After he delivered one, his company could operate in that provincial region without being hemmed in by laws. Russians have an old saying—"Even a priest may feed himself from his parish."

Law-breaking and bribes do not mean that Russians do not know right from wrong. On the contrary, they have an unusually keen sense of what is right. They need a stronger inner gauge precisely because they often have to operate in the atmosphere of lawlessness. Russians are not as law-abiding as Americans but they have a strong moral sense. When my grandmother was a teenager in the 1920s, she and her mother had to cross vast stretches of countryside torn by the Civil War. After hiring some local peasant for the next leg of their perilous journey, the women would ask their driver to cross himself and promise to keep them safe. A direct personal promise, sealed by the sign of the cross worked better than any law, gun, or insurance.

THE AGE DIFFERENCE

A person's age played a key role in determining their success or decline in the great turmoil unleashed in 1991. Many young people saw amazing opportunities—new roads opened to them that their parents could not even dream about. Among the older generation, the party/government/KGB/industrial elite made out very well in privatization, as did businessmen, but the majority of the people over 30 got beaten up. The older they were, the worse beating they received.

Most Russians in their late 50s, 60s, and older are hurting badly. They toiled all their lives for the Soviet state which sold them a bill of goods, promising to take care of them from the cradle to the grave. Now the USSR is gone and they have nothing. Their savings have been wiped out by inflation, their jobs pay little or no salaries, while the old age pensions are worse than meager. Communists keep trying to exploit the older people's discontent in their election campaigns, but the majority still vote for reform.

The well-dressed 50- and 60-year-old Russians who wear Rolexes and drive flashy imports tend to be the former Communist Party officials, KGB officers, and Soviet government functionaries. They used to run the old USSR and managed to privatize a big enough chunk of the new Russian economy. When I meet them in the course of business, I sometimes ask what they did "before the revolution" and watch their reactions as much as their replies. You need to be extra vigilant with the former Soviet bosses. If you work with them and your project runs into difficulties, they are likely to give you the full Soviet treatment—sink you and run.

People under 30 entered their formative postadolescent years after the Soviet Union began to crumble. The grandiose program for breeding the New Soviet Man had ran out of steam by then, and people began to grab their own slices of the economic pie. Young people who grew up in the emerging market economy saw free enterprise as something perfectly natural rather than demonic, the way older Soviets had been trained to view it. Foreigners who teach economics in Russia are surprised that Russian students tend to score higher than their professors on tests of market economics.

Advancement in the old Soviet Union depended upon party loyalty and age. In today's Russia, it is based primarily on merit and the ability to generate results. It is amazing how many important positions are held by people under 30. The young quickly adjusted to new economic realities: they run banks and businesses, serve as executives of large companies and head government departments.

The young are much more open toward the West. They consider themselves just as good as Westerners and compete as equals. They are materialists, with an eye for quality. They do seem to have less interest in culture than older Russians, but are more open, spontaneous, and energetic.

Just a few years' difference in age can make a huge difference in Russia, placing people on either side of the great divide. That line between being modern or rooted in the New Soviet Man era was at

30 years of age in 1996, 31 in 1997, and 32 in 1998. Another great divide is geography. People who live and work in Moscow and a few other major cities had more exposure to the West and better opportunities than people in the provinces, where the old lifestyles linger.

It would be absurd to pigeonhole all people based on age. There are plenty of people in their 30s, 40s and 50s who are vibrantly active and successful in the new Russia. I keep meeting people in their 60s, 70s, and even 80s who have risen in recent years thanks to their savvy and energy. The "30-year divide" is merely a reminder for Westerners working with Russians to treat those under 30 in a more casual, Western way, and to be a bit more careful with people whose age is typical of Western executives.

THE FANTASTIC WESTERNIZATION

The Soviet Union had a schizophrenic attitude toward the West. The media, totally controlled by the government, kept pouring buckets of filth on the Western way of life. It kept trying to convince people that life in the West was miserable for all except a few millionaires in the military-industrial complex. At the same time, the Russian rumor mill made the West seem like a fairy tale land.

The Soviet media reported major crimes, plane crashes, and natural disasters in the West, while the same calamities were kept secret when they occurred in the USSR. My brother-in-law's father went on a business trip in the 1970s and disappeared. The family was going crazy with worry. Two weeks later they were called into the KGB, given 300 rubles, and made to sign a pledge of secrecy. The man had perished in an airplane crash. A crash in the West would have made the front pages of Soviet newspapers, which tried to create an impression there were no murders, collapsed bridges, or plane crashes in the workers' paradise—such things happened only in the West, which was dirty, rough, and dangerous.

Forbidden fruit is sweet, and many Soviets kept glorifying the West. People wove snippets of foreign broadcasts and glimpses of foreign tourists into a Disneyland picture of the West. After the Iron

Curtain came down and foreigners started coming in, Russians reacted to them at first as if they came from another, more advanced planet. For a few brief years in the early 90s foreigners occupied a place halfway between experts and demi-gods.

A flood of imports rushed in; Western brands quickly made inroads in Russia. Russians switched to foreign brands of everything—cars, food, even vodka. Soviets used to wear dark, shapeless clothes, buttoned up to the neck, but today summer office dress in Moscow often runs to slit skirts and see-through blouses.

People who owned nothing just a few years ago often boost their self-confidence with brand names—from $1,000 Versace ties to $25,000 Cartier watches. The country has acquired a class of the new rich, sarcastically called the New Russians. They rose, as the saying goes, "from dirt to princedom" in just a few years. They tend to have more money than taste and none of the subtlety of Western moneyed elite. Many think that the more they pay, the better the product. Two New Russians run into each other wearing identical Versace ties. "How much have you paid for yours?" asks one. "A thousand *buks* (dollars)," says the other. "That's shabby," says the first man. "I paid two thousand *buks* for mine in that shop around the corner!"

Life imitates art. In August 1996 I was admiring $500 sweaters in a gift shop in the tiny New Zealand ski village of Methven when the owner told me that Russians were very rich. "They always buy several thousand dollars worth. The first time a Russian bought $2,000 worth of sweaters, I offered him a discount, but he got angry—'I am not poor, I can afford to pay full price.' I then gave him a free pair of wool socks, and he was very happy. I never offered Russians a discount again."

Both unrealistic views of the West—loathing or worship—are rapidly fading away. Now Russians can travel and have free access to uncensored media, and they are becoming liberated both from the Soviet false sense of superiority (which used to be based on the military might and the space race) and from the sick sense of inferiority (stemming from a low standard of living). Russians are emerging with a realistic image of themselves, quick to see that they are just as good as Westerners. They know they are behind economically but view themselves as more practical and clever. Russians, with their deep competitive streak, are eager to beat the West at its own game.

Throughout centuries of relative isolation, Russia had several brief periods of openness to the West, which did the country good, until reactionaries stepped in and slammed the door shut. Back at the dawn of Russia's recorded history there had been an episode when the nobles said, *"Strana nasha obilna, poryadka zhe v ney net"* ("our country is rich but it ain't got no order"), and invited the Vikings in. Then there was Peter the Great, Russia's 17th century pro-Western tsar. Not only did he found St. Petersburg (which communists later renamed Leningrad) and moved Russia's capital closer to the West, this physically huge man got a job as a worker in a Dutch shipyard, learned to build wooden ships, and upon returning to Russia, founded the Russian Navy. For much of the rest of Russia's history, the country had been isolated from the West. Communists did not invent restrictions on travel—going abroad without permission was considered treason and people were jumping Russian ships two centuries ago.

Communists considered Western-style clothes as a possible first step toward developing anti-Soviet tendencies. They were right. The totalitarian regime needed to exercise total control over its people in order to survive. Long hair, jazz, colorful clothes, sexuality, exotic food all dented the Iron Curtain. My buddy at the university in the USSR found an American girlfriend who came to Moscow as a nanny for an embassy family in 1972. When that girl slept with him and hung out with his hippie friends, she was as subversive of the system as another friend of mine who arranged clandestine shipments of political books from New York into Moscow. People who slept with whom they wanted and read what they wanted could no longer be trained as New Soviet Men.

Most of the USSR was off limits to foreigners who were allowed to live in only 25 of the largest cities and needed special permits to travel more than 30 miles from their centers. The Soviets issued very few visas, prohibited free travel, and forced foreigners to live in special compounds. After the communist collapse, Moscow's foreign population swelled to between 25,000 and 50,000 people. The city now has two English-language dailies, and foreigners live anywhere they want—from luxury buildings facing the Kremlin to cheap apartments on the outskirts. They are thoroughly intermixed with the Russians, who for the first time have a daily opportunity to mingle with foreigners.

At first, foreign companies establishing offices in Moscow brought in their own staffs. Many expats (expatriate workers) earned more in a day than local employees in a month, and got free apartments and chauffeured cars. Russians are very fast learners. By 1997 they took over most of the expats' jobs, at comparable pay but with fewer benefits. The first thing one used to hear after landing in Moscow was an Irish brogue—a Dublin firm used to run duty-free shops. Moscow still has a St. Patrick's Day parade—an amazing sign of Westernization and normalcy—but Russians now run their airport duty-free shops. Brokerage firms and investment companies still use expats but most of their staffs are local. This trend toward using locals is likely to accelerate as young people return from the West with freshly minted degrees.

The West has a higher standard of living, but Russia has great future prospects. Under communists, the country was at a dead end, and an opportunity to work or study abroad was a rare and eagerly pursued prize. Not any more. A top fixed-income analyst at a local brokerage tells me he is turning down invitations to work in New York—he loves living in Moscow. He likes Europe and may go to work in London for a year, but New York holds no attraction for him. Ten years ago, a job in New York would have been the sweetest carrot you could wave in front of anyone's face. As I worked on this chapter in New York, my assistant manager received a letter from her girlfriend in St. Petersburg. The woman's daughter had an opportunity to study at the Sorbonne, but preferred to stay in St. Petersburg, expecting to get a better education at home. This is a sign of change in the country.

Russians are patriotic but they are extremely low-key talking about it. Communists played the patriotism card to the hilt, pushing people to backbreaking sacrifices in the name of patriotism. After seven decades of that, people have grown too cynical. The love of the country has not disappeared; it only runs deeper and quieter than before.

The more Russians see the West, the less they worship foreigners. Many are starting to look at them with a tinge of superiority. I spoke at an investment conference in Moscow in 1997 where three American experts strutted in front of the audience and later, at a dinner at *Aragvi,* one of the city's famous restaurants, congratulated each other for bringing enlightenment to the needy. I kept my mouth shut. Earlier in the day I asked several attendees, in Russian, what they thought of the conference. "Very simplistic," they said, "very unidimensional."

Russians tend to feel that they possess a soul most foreigners do not have. They can't quite explain what the soul is, but they know they have it. It has to do with intuition, human values rather than money, capacity for grand acts rather than petty accounting. Maybe it has to do with the size of the country. They know that their country is rich and have a peculiar sense of superiority toward smaller nations. They see that Switzerland or Holland have higher standards of living and it galls them. What have they got that we haven't? Now, for the first time in centuries, they can actually do something about it—go out and compete on equal terms.

One of the unpleasant leftovers of the Soviet regime is the system of charging foreigners higher prices than locals for the same service. You will pay higher rates for hotels and domestic plane and train fares if you do not have a Russian passport. The two-tier system of prices is annoyingly widespread. In May 1997 I stood on line to the Pushkin Art Museum in Moscow speaking English with two local girls when we reached the window and a cashier demanded 50,000 rubles (about $9) per ticket. I couldn't believe the price and protested, in Russian. "Aren't you a foreigner?" she asked. "Do I sound like a foreigner?" I retorted, and she charged me the Russian rate, 15,000 rubles (less than $3) each.

A similar system operates informally in Russian securities markets. They are still quite inefficient, with wide bid/ask spreads. Quite a bit of trading is done privately, crossing the buy and the sell off the computer screens. Foreigners are presumed to be rich and fair game for clever locals. Make sure you do not come into the market as some self-important *dvoryanin* (noble), ready to have your pockets picked by clever serfs. Insist on being quoted the local price for the shares you plan to buy or sell.

Losing False Pride

The streak of smug superiority over foreigners has been a part of the Russian national character for centuries, according to V. O. Klyuchevskiy, old Russia's great historian. The Soviet propaganda machine spent decades pumping up a sense of false pride in the New Soviet Man. The mass media, pop culture, songs—all controlled by the state—kept drumming into people's heads that they lived in the most advanced nation on earth. Soviets even rewrote history to score propaganda points.

Who invented the electric bulb? Not Edison but Yablochkin. Who invented the radio? Not Marconi but Popov (although when I worked aboard Russian ships the common nickname for radio operators was Marconi). Who built and flew the first airplane? Not the Wright brothers but the Russian inventor Mozhaisky. The rewriting of history went far back; the first printer in the history of the world was not Gutenberg in Germany but Fedorov in Russia. Today, when I deal with a commercial printer in Moscow, I say to him, "Man, you are great, the best since Fedorov!"

Just a decade ago the Soviet government had people beating their chests, shouting that they were the most advanced nation on earth. When Khruschev pounded his aide's boot on the table at the United Nations and arrogantly promised Nixon that Russia would bury America, Westerners laughed, but many Soviets, deprived of objective information, believed their leaders. The pain and suffering of the Depression of the 1990s deflated that false grandiose self-image.

Just like relentless American bombings and the bloody push of Soviet infantry in World War II cured Germans of their delusion of being Aryan supermen, the blackouts, the hunger, the unemployment and squalor of the Depression of the 1990s, and the disintegration of the centuries-old empire finally convinced Russians that they were not supermen. They were hungry and poor, and they had to work extra hard to rise from the depths to which their grandiose leaders sank them.

Russians have changed in recent years—they work much harder now. The last time they worked so hard was during World War II, when the nation's survival was at stake. People are poor, but for the first time in their history they have a chance of bootstrapping themselves. They no longer look down upon business. Free enterprise is no longer a dirty word—people are trying to figure out what consumers want, provide a service, and get paid.

The old pseudo-aristocratic pretensions are disappearing. Unemployed Russian Ph.Ds wash floors in Moscow and finagle the US or Canadian visitor visas to work as baby sitters. People take on any work that pays.

Russian media honestly reports problems in the country: obsolete factories, mismanaged farms, corruption, and crime. Those problems will not disappear overnight, but admitting them is revolutionary—and healthy. Living with eyes open and being willing to work hard puts people in a position to succeed.

One of the most positive results of the Depression of the 1990s was the loss of false pride, putting the nation in a position to work hard and compete as equals in world markets.

Where the Money Is

7

THE RUSSIAN FIXED-INCOME MARKET

People lend money only to those they trust. Lenders demand an interest rate that reflects their opinion of the borrower. When you buy a fixed-income instrument, such as a bond, you lend money to the government or the company that issued it. The Russian fixed-income market exists today because more and more people worldwide trust the Russian government, and want to buy its bonds. Their buying has pushed bond prices up and interest rates down from their fantastic early peaks.

The history of the Soviet Union was a history of theft. People who ran the country stole from foreigners, stole from their own citizens, stole even from each other. "Fixed income" meant fixing to rob a bank—the founders of the Russian Communist Party had armed a group of bank robbers to raise money for the revolution. Their murderous heists, called "expropriations," laid the groundwork for their future relationship with the banking industry. The man in charge of the gang of robbers was Soso Dzhugashvili, better known by his party name—Stalin.

The first financial act of the communist government in 1917 was to repudiate Russia's sovereign debt. French, English, and other Western banks and individuals who bought hundreds of millions of dollars worth of Russian bonds during the tsarist era were left holding the bag—and the nation's credit was destroyed in one fell swoop.

Having stiffed foreigners, the Soviets directed their sticky fingers toward the property of their own citizens. They nationalized the economy, including real estate, with zero compensation to former owners. The government simply took everything that wasn't nailed down—and many things that were, including gold- and silver-plated icons from churches.[16] It forced people to give free labor on weekends—*subbotniki*. This was just a trial run for putting millions of political prisoners into labor camps, the largest exercise in forced labor since the Pharaohs built the pyramids.

After the Soviet government stole what it could, it "borrowed" the rest, developing a scheme for forcing people to hand over their savings. Each worker had to spend a percentage of his or her salary buying *obligatsii vnutrennego zaima*, or internal loan bonds. The party said they needed the money for the nation's defense and industrial development. They used the money mostly for current expenses, and had neither the inclination nor the ability to repay. The *obligatsii* were sold on paydays wherever people worked. Each workplace had a quota, and those who refused to buy the bonds were labeled political enemies, which could bring disastrous consequences.[17]

---

[16] The government confiscated essentially all church property: first gold, silver, and gems accumulated over the centuries, then the land, buildings, and even bronze bells. Plunderers took gem-encrusted frames from the icons but did not recognize the monetary value of icons themselves. They were often trashed or used as lumber, destroying a national treasure.

The history of the church under the Soviets deserves its own book. The Russian Orthodox Church grew fat and lazy in its incestuous bond with the monarchy, and offered little resistance to the communist onslaught. Over 20,000 priests were killed, countless churches destroyed or converted to industrial use. After Lenin died in 1924, the Soviets mummified his body and built a mausoleum for it by the Kremlin wall. Digging the earth for the foundation during one of the coldest winters in history, construction workers accidentally severed a sewage pipe which immediately froze. It thawed in spring, and raw sewage flooded the mausoleum. Tichon, the patriarch of the Russian church, quipped "Holy water fits the relic." He was shot, and for the next 20 years Stalin would not permit a new patriarch to be elected. He relented only after he decided to use the church in World War II. The new patriarch was a KGB officer—the joke was on the believers.

The church seems to have learned precious little from its near-annihilation, and after the collapse of the USSR has been doing its best to cozy up to the new government. Freed from most taxes and customs duties, it is rapidly growing rich. To maintain its position, it lobbies for legislation to exclude foreign missionaries.

[17] Controlling people through their workplaces was highly effective. The USSR gave everybody a job, no matter how menial. Unemployment was a crime. Most social benefits—housing, medical care, retirement, and so on—were distributed through the workplaces, keeping the people on a short leash. The great Russian poet Joseph Brodsky, who won the Nobel Prize in literature, had been sentenced to manual labor in a northern village for "parasitism," since he did not hold a job and was not a member of the writers' union.

As a child I saw stacks of *obligatsii* in my parents' and grand-parents' homes. I can still see their silvery designs and hear my parents' bitter jokes about having to buy them to keep their jobs. The government gave people a consolation prize—the *obligatsii* were numbered and doubled up as lottery tickets. They held drawings each quarter, creating an incentive to hold *obligatsii* rather than use them as shelf liners.

The Soviet government was a kleptocracy that stole even from its own. The property of men and women shot and imprisoned during Stalin's purges was confiscated and given to party loyalists. After Stalin's death, his chief of security, Lavrenty Beria, was shot by Khruschev, and his own huge stock of *obligatsii*, stolen from his victims, was looted and sold cheaply throughout Moscow. Families of Beria's victims traced their serial numbers, which led to a scandal, described by Pavel Sudoplatov in his explosive memoir, *Razvedka i Kreml.*

REFORM OR PERISH

After the reformers threw the communists out of the Kremlin in 1991, the new Russian government had to overcome a horrible financial reputation inherited from the Soviets. The reformers earned the trust of domestic and international financial markets by scrupulously keeping their promises. The Russian government paid interest on its obligations to the penny and on time, and never tried to change the rules of the game retroactively. The creation of a liquid Russian fixed-income market and the fact that the interest rates are down from 200% to 30% prove the reformers' success.

The Russian government sent a powerful message of responsibility when it negotiated with the London and Paris Clubs of creditors to assume the Soviet Union's debts and the debts of the tsarist government prior to the 1917 communist plot.

At the end of 1996 the Russian government had about $17 billion of foreign debt, plus the old Soviet debt (called *Vnesh* on the international markets) of about $100 billion. Russia's biggest lender was Germany, to which it owed $23 billion, far more than $4 billion owed to the US. The Russian government budgeted $9.2 billion toward paying its foreign debts in 1997. As Layard and Parker wrote in 1996 in *The Coming Russian Boom*, ". . .never underestimate the power of Russia's Ministry of Finance, which is as dry and tough as many of its counterparts in the West."

The reformers know they have to stay on the path of financial integrity because any step back to the old Soviet style of misconduct would lead to a flight of capital, financial panic, and economic collapse. The government keeps bending over backwards to prove it is a reliable financial partner. It has shrugged off the grandiose Soviet posturing and acts more and more like a reliable corporate state. Just like a recovering alcoholic finds support in Alcoholics Anonymous (AA), the Russian government has joined the International Monetary Fund (IMF) and accepted its discipline.

THE RUBLE IN A CORRIDOR

The Russian government signaled it meant business—in the best sense of the word—when it stabilized the ruble in 1995. Early in the Depression of the 1990s the government debased the nation's currency by printing tons of rubles. It printed to pay salaries, reward loyalists, buy off segments of the opposition; it printed simply to stay afloat. The markets reacted by devaluing the ruble 99.9%. It sank from 5 to a dollar in 1991 to nearly 5,000 to a dollar in 1995.

The annual inflation rate in Russia reached 2,510% in 1992, declining to 840% in 1993, 220% in 1994, 130% in 1995, 21.8% in 1996, and below 12% in 1997. Inflation was even worse in many other ex-Soviet republics—in 1992 it reached 10,155% in the Ukraine.[18] As the

---

[18] By 1996 a million rubles was worth less than $200, while a million Ukrainian *karbovantsi* was less than $5. A Moscow banker told me a local joke:

A man walks into a travel agency and says he'd like to spend a million on his vacation. "Oh, for a million dollars we'll send you on a first-class cruise around the world, fully escorted, with side trips by private jet," gushes the agent.

"I've got a million, but not dollars!"

"Oh, a million rubles. Well, I can suggest a very nice rest home outside of Moscow. You get two meals a day, and I hear they have pretty good fishing in a nearby lake."

"I haven't got a million rubles, I have a million *karbovantsi*."

"Gee, that's tough. The only trip you can take today for a million *karbovantsi* is erotic tourism."

"Oh, this sounds interesting, tell me more!"

"Go sexually abuse yourself."

ruble lost most of its value, most Russians lost their savings. When I jumped ship in 1974, I left behind a little over 400 rubles in the bank—about three months' salary. When I returned 20 years later, the bank was gone, but even if it hadn't disappeared, that money wouldn't buy me a cup of coffee. For a visitor from America it was a joke, but for most locals it was a tragedy.

Many Russians expected the ruble to go into a free fall, plunging the country into hyperinflation. That view became widespread after Black Tuesday (October 1994), when the ruble crashed from 3,081 to a dollar to 3,926, wiping out 30% of the value of the nation's currency in a single day.

In May 1995 the Russian government declared a "ruble corridor." It promised to support its currency and not let it drop below 4,900 or rise above 4,300 to a US dollar. Cynics jeered and told smutty jokes about things people do in corridors, but the government delivered. It slowed down its currency printing presses, brought in fresh loans from the IMF, and kept the ruble in its corridor. It even made that corridor narrower than promised—between 4,400 and 4,600 rubles to a dollar.

After stabilizing the ruble at R4,500/$1 in the autumn of 1995, the government extended its peg through the end of that year. On December 1, 1995 it announced new boundaries for the peg for the next six months—between R4,5550/$1 and R5,150/$1. It would allow the ruble to decline very slowly, at a rate that would limit the maximum currency loss for ruble holders to 14% per year. Investors and businessespeople could plan ahead based on those parameters.

In July 1996 the government extended the ruble corridor, gradually moving its boundaries to R5,550-6,000/$1 by January 1, 1997, aiming to keep the ruble depreciation below 1.5% per month for the year. The ruble was strong and ended the year near R5,550/$1. In December 1996 the government announced the ruble boundaries for 1997—between R5,750 and R6,350 to the dollar.

I was in Moscow in December 1996 at the time of that announcement. Locals greeted the news with a yawn—a stable ruble had become a given. The communist deputies in the Duma complained about the austere budget for 1997 and campaigned for printing more money "to take care of the people." Their proposals were rejected, thanks to a firm public consensus in favor of the steady ruble.

The ruble is a firm currency today. The government pegs it against the US dollar, allowing it to sink very slowly, at a rate announced a year in advance. The ruble is declining slower than the current inflation rate, which means it is appreciating in real terms. A steady ruble allows businesses and individuals to plan ahead, but it has ended the wild ride in the ruble/dollar and ruble/mark futures. People use futures to hedge against uncertainties, but there is very little uncertainty left in the ruble which is now firm and predictable. Some traders anticipate a bullish play on the ruble in the near future. The CBR (Central Bank of Russia) is working to fulfill the requirements of Article 8 of the Charter of the IMF (International Monetary Fund), calling for a full current account convertibility. Once the ruble becomes fully convertible, traders expect it to strengthen. They plan to profit at that time by going long the ruble against Western currencies.

In August 1997 the Russian government announced a long-expected ruble reform. It went into effect on January 1, 1998, when new rubles were issued, lopping three zeros off the old ones. Instead of 6,000 rubles to a dollar, the exchange rate became 6 rubles to a dollar. Russia had a long history of robbing people during currency exchanges. The current government waited a long time until it could build up the public's trust before introducing this reform. Its terms were straightforward and honest—people had a year to convert old rubles into new ones, without any limitations.

FIXING THE FIXED-INCOME MARKET

The Depression of the 1990s left the Russian government financially strapped. By the spring of 1993 it had run out of reserves, its tax collections became very low, while IMF credits were sparse. The government needed to borrow money, but was tarred with the old Soviet reputation which precluded it from borrowing in the international markets. It had to raise money inside the country, by offering extremely attractive terms and scrupulously paying its creditors.

On May 18, 1993, the new Russian government floated its first domestic loan. It sold GKOs—a Russian acronym for *Gosudarstvenniye Kratkosrochniye Obligatsii* (State Short-Term Obligations). They were short-term zero-coupon paperless bonds, modeled on US Treasury bills. The government had to pay a stiff price—the annualized interest on its 3-month bills was over 200%, nontaxable! That first GKO issue brought in less than a million dollars worth of rubles. From those humble beginnings the market grew to $40 billion at the end of 1996.

The Ministry of Finance paid off every single GKO at maturity. There has never been a default, a delay, or a dodge. The GKOs gradually became a symbol of financial reliability. Today, Russian companies and individuals park their funds in GKOs almost as freely as Americans park theirs in US Treasury bills.

Banks and savvy individuals made a great deal of money on GKOs. The one negative side effect of high interest rates was that they siphoned money from industry. Even payrolls were diverted into tax-free GKOs by unscrupulous managers. Their greed was partly to blame for the payroll crisis that gripped much of the country in 1996.

In 1996, in the runup to the first free Presidential elections in Russia's history, the threat of a communist victory was perceived as a huge risk factor for GKOs. Interest rates ticked up with every communist advance and ticked down whenever Yeltsin rose in public opinion polls. The reformers, running against the communist opposition, used their power of incumbency to the fullest and spent money on vote-getting projects.

With interest rates shooting up into triple digits, some accused Yeltsin of paying off bankers who almost unanimously backed him and who benefited from high GKO rates. Critics said the government was issuing GKOs it could not afford to redeem, that interest payments would soon overwhelm its budget. The gloom-and-doomers extrapolated trends before the election and concluded that the government was building a huge financial pyramid. It would have to borrow more and more simply to pay interest. Soon it would suck in all available money and the pyramid would collapse. Russia had had enough "pyramids" in recent years.

The naysayers, with their linear predictions, were wrong. As the government's credibility increased, it was able to reduce interest rates on fresh GKOs. Rallying from Yeltsin's landslide victory in July 1996, the government announced it would lower the rates on new GKOs. The Ministry of Finance would not entertain any bids above 60% for 3-month paper and 80% for 6-month paper at its weekly auctions. The markets gulped—and swallowed.

GKOs were too good a deal to pass up, even at a reduced rate. The government was credible enough for people to want to hold its paper. It was the best rate available, and investors kept piling in.

To say that the decline in rates was dramatic is an understatement. For example, 3-month bills were issued to yield 154% in May 1996 before the election. Two months later, after the July election, new 3-month bills were issued to yield 76.5%. The 6-month bills issued one day before the first round of the election yielded 212.8%. The 6-month bills that were issued a week after the second round of the election in July yielded 131%, a week later 93%, and 74% in August.

It didn't take too long for canny foreigners to wake up to GKO opportunities. At first, the Government sold GKOs only to Russian residents in order to keep the interest inside the country and reserve the gravy train for domestic banks. It slowly relaxed this rule, allowing foreigners to buy up to 10% and later 20% of every GKO issue, but capped the interest rates available to foreigners by forcing them to hedge their ruble risk at the government-designated rate. The result was a foreign currency ceiling—first at 25%, then at 16%, and later at 12.5%.

The Russians are very inventive at playing games with government rules. In 1996 several Russian banks and financial firms offered schemes for foreigners wishing to invest in GKOs at a "Russian" rate. A foreign entity would give them a "loan" at a rate several percentage points below the GKO rate for the duration equal to the maturity of the GKO. They would invest the "loan" in the GKOs, hold them to maturity, and then "repay the loan," keeping several percentage points as their fee. I brought those offers to several money managers in the US and Australia, but all had been too fearful. Things change very fast in Russia, and a few months later domestic interest rates fell deeply enough to make the whole game uninteresting.

Paying the Tsars' Debts

After the communists grabbed power in 1917 they repudiated all debts of the tsarist government, stiffing European bondholders. Those investors formed vocal organizations, which prevented the Soviet Union from selling its bonds abroad. The modern Russian government knew it had to settle with international bondholders before it could tap into Western debt markets.

Several factors worked in Russia's favor. Most of the original bondholders had died in the 80 years since the last tsarist bonds had been issued. Many bonds disappeared in the wars that swept Europe in the 20th century. Few people expected to be paid, and Russian bonds were traded in flea markets as decorations, and many were lost or destroyed. The Russian government claimed damages from bondholders' nations for intervening in its civil war in the 1920s and grabbing parts of the tsarist gold reserve. The financial elites of creditor countries wanted the debt issue settled in order to earn fresh fees from lending to Russia.

Accepting responsibility for tsarist debts earned the Russian government a great deal of international goodwill at a relatively low cost. Russians are canny negotiators. They dealt with one country at a time and negotiated with governments, which were more interested in cutting deals than individual bondholders.

First, the British and Russian negotiators agreed to cancel their "mutual debts." These were the tsarist bonds against damages from the British intervention in Russia's civil war in the 1920s. The British even returned the small portion of the tsarist gold reserve that they held. Now the Russian government could borrow in the UK, but the biggest and most vocal bondholders' lobby remained active in France.

In November 1996, the former Russian prime minister Victor Chernomyrdin flew to Paris and signed an historic agreement on repaying French holders of the tsarist bonds. The agreement was somewhat of a fudge: The French agreed to forgive Russia 80 years worth of interest. Russia promised to pay the principal, after deducting damages for France's intervention in Russia's civil war and the value of the tsarist gold reserve kept by France. The final tally came to approximately $400 million, to be paid over several years. Many French called that a token payment, while nationalist press in Russia protested paying hundreds of millions to France at a time when Russian workers were going unpaid. But the principle of national responsibility was upheld.

Having re-established its credit at home and abroad, the Russian Government could start raising money in the Eurobond market. It received nice surprises from the rating agencies—Moody's rated Russia's sovereign debt Ba2, and Standard & Poor's rated it BB–. Both were just a notch below investment grade. In November 1996 Russia sold $1 billion of 5-year notes, its first external sovereign debt since 1917.

Russia's first Eurobond issue, paying 9.36%, was oversubscribed, with about half taken by Korean investors. It was priced 445 basis points higher than the US 5-year Treasury notes, equal to the rate on Argentine notes of the same maturity. The Argentines had been selling their government paper for years—the fact that Russia was rated at the same level for its very first Eurobond issue was a remarkable achievement.

"Da! or duh?" asked Alan Abelson in *Barron's*. "On the one hand, they're getting a better yield—9.36%—for sure than they would have had they bought Uncle Sam's five-year paper. And, of course, they also get the incalculable psychic income of helping make Karl Marx whirl in his grave." He added, "The bull case on Russia is that inflation has come down from 130% a year to 20%, and GDP growth has stabilized at a negative 4% annual rate. That's the bear case also. . . . There is, apparently, something of an inverted yield curve in Russia: that 9.36% on the five-year bonds contrasts with 40% short-term interest rates."

Fresh from the success of its first Eurobond issue, the government is preparing larger new flotations. Various government agencies and municipalities are also getting ready to sell their paper abroad. In 1997 the Moscow city government became the first municipality in Russia to float its bonds abroad. Russia's ability to enter world capital markets marked the end of the extraordinary rates on domestic GKOs. The government keeps lowering GKO rates. The speed of the decline is limited only by its concern for weaker domestic banks that need time to adjust and learn to live without that extraordinary income.

RUSSIAN FIXED-INCOME INSTRUMENTS

Germany and Japan built powerful industries on the rubble of World War II, and Russia's financial industry is springing up on the rubble of communism. The speed with which Russia's markets are developing defies imagination. A financial instrument can sprout, develop, become institutionalized, and be swept aside by a new financial instrument in a year or two.

The past is certain, but the future is fluid and fundamentally unknown. We can review Russia's fixed-income markets today, but they will be different tomorrow. They will become deeper, richer, with new opportunities in the years ahead. When you invest in Russia, make sure to get the latest information from reliable sources.

GKO (RUSSIAN GOVERNMENT TREASURY BILLS)

GKOs are paperless zero-coupon bonds with 3-, 6-, and 12- month maturities. The 3-month bills had been the most popular through 1996, but they have been essentially phased out in 1997, when the government decided to extend its loan maturities. The face value of a GKO is 1 million "old" rubles—under $200. The Russian Ministry of Finance conducts primary GKO auctions on Wednesdays and secondary auctions from 11 A.M. to 1 P.M. on all other weekdays at the Moscow Interbank Currency Exchange (MICEX).

Participation in primary auctions is limited to the dealers authorized by the Central Bank of Russia (CBR). Each is required to make a commitment to buy at least 1% of each GKO issue, and they are allowed to conduct repo operations with the CBR. Dealers can submit competitive or noncompetitive bids. A competitive bid specifies a purchase price—it is like a limit order. MICEX allocates GKOs to the dealers submitting the highest bids, and fills noncompetitive bids at the average price for the session. A canny dealer who can guess the lowest price for the session correctly and bid at that level earns an immediate profit. He buys near the low of the day while prices close higher—at the average for the session—where noncompetitive bids are filled.

Prior to each auction, dealers must transfer the funds they are planning to invest to the MICEX, fully eliminating any counterparty risk. On July 1, 1996 the CBR began announcing the volume of money reserved in the MICEX clearing and settlement system prior to each secondary auction, making the GKO market even more transparent.

MICEX utilizes a computer system of remote terminals, originally designed for trading securities in Singapore. Bids and offers are ranked first by price and then by the time of submission. All unfulfilled orders are canceled at the end of each session. MICEX charges a 0.05% fee for each side of each transaction. On an average day, between 1 and 2.5% of all outstanding GKOs are traded. There were approximately $44 billion worth of GKOs in existence at the beginning of 1997, and the average daily trading volume neared $600 million.

The yields on the GKOs fell from over 200% per year into the low 20s and teens in 1997. Those yields are almost certain to continue to fall, as the government shifts its borrowing to the less expensive Eurobond market. Back in 1993 the government was so desperate to borrow, it made GKO profits tax-free. After the Presidential election in 1996, the government announced it would start taxing profits on GKOs, starting with those issued after February 5, 1997.

The government was reluctant to allow foreigners to reap the high yields of the GKOs and only slowly gave them access to this market. In February 1996, it introduced a scheme allowing repatriation of GKO profits, but cut them down to 19–25% per annum through compulsory dollar hedging. The Russians at that time were earning 60–70% per annum, leaving them with about a 50% gain after converting rubles into dollars. Foreigners used to be allowed to buy up to 20% of every GKO issue, but their limit has been raised to 30%. Their profits are still being capped using the compulsory currency hedge. In February 1997, the rate on 3-month GKOs available to Russian residents was 16.3% in dollars, against 12.5% for foreigners. Russians could get 22.6% in dollars for 9-month paper, against 12.5% available to foreigners. Little wonder that most foreign investors interested in GKOs used the informal scheme described earlier.

Starting in August 1996, Western investors were allowed to trade GKOs in the secondary market. Previously, foreigners were restricted to buying GKOs at primary auctions and holding them in "T" accounts, which complicated profit repatriation, but now they can put them into "S" accounts, designed specifically for profit repatriation.[19] In 1997 the CBR allowed foreigners to trade GKOs directly through remote terminals. Demonstration terminals have already been installed in Luxembourg and Paris.

OFZ—FEDERAL LOAN BONDS

OFZ, or *Obligatsii Federalnogo Zaima* (Federal Loan Bonds), were introduced in 1995 to help finance the government's budget. The government prefers OFZs because of their longer maturities, but the market prefers GKOs, and the OFZ volume is only about 1/10 of the GKO volume. The value of each OFZ is a million "old" rubles (less than $200), the same as the GKO.

OFZs are 1- and 2-year paperless bonds that originally had a fluctuating coupon rate. OFZs with a permanent rate were issued for

---

[19] "T" accounts are opened in Russian banks for foreign legal entities with registered representation or subsidiaries in Russia. "T" accounts can be used only for transactions within Russia and are forbidden to operate with foreign currency. "I" accounts are ruble accounts that may be opened by any nonresident. A law, more often honored in the breach, is that all ruble investments and purchases of foreign currency for repatriation of capital and profits from those investments must be conducted by nonresidents through "I" accounts. The proceeds from investment activity in rubles are taxable, and rubles may be converted into dollars only after paying taxes. Banks holding "I" accounts are responsible for the collection of taxes.

the first time in 1997. Interest on fluctuating OFZs used to be paid quarterly, but now it is paid semiannually, with yields pegged to the GKO market a week prior to the payment date. OFZs with a fluctuating coupon rate are more volatile than GKOs and their yields are higher, because of the less predictable size of future coupon payments. New OFZs with a permanent coupon rate pay interest once a year. The interest on OFZs used to be tax free, as were capital gains on OFZs held to maturity. If sold prior to maturity, capital gains were taxed as ordinary income. The tax-free status was terminated for OFZs issued after February 5, 1997. The limitations on foreigners who buy OFZs are the same as in the GKO market.

OGSZ—FEDERAL SAVINGS BONDS

OGSZ, or *Obligatsii Gosudarstvennogo Sberegatelnogo Zaima* (Federal Savings Bonds), are designed to attract individual Russian savers. They are issued in bearer bond form with face values of either R100,000 or R500,000 (under $20 or under $100). OGSZs are floating-rate one-year bonds to which four quarterly coupons are attached. Coupon rates are pegged to the OFZ rates, which in turn are pegged to the GKO rates.

There are no restrictions on OGSZ ownership—the owner may be either Russian or foreign, either an individual or a corporation. Coupons are redeemed either in cash or through direct deposit. Bearer instruments are popular in Russia, due to their anonymity and also because in remote regions people do not have to wait for payment. Their coupon income is currently 21–25% in rubles.

MINFIN (MINISTRY OF FINANCE) 3% BONDS

This dollar-denominated debt, originally distributed to Russian banks and companies by *Vnesheconombank* (Foreign Trade Bank), is now held for the most part by foreign firms. MinFin bonds are less liquid than GKOs, owing in part to their large size; a standard lot is $2 million. Yields early in 1997 were 9–14%. While yields of GKOs keep falling, MinFins are likely to remain stable because they represent longer-term obligations. The next tranche (installment) of MinFin 3% bonds is scheduled for redemption in 1999 and the last in 2011.

The MinFins were widely dispersed throughout Russia, even though most of them are deposited at Vnesheconombank, where they are stored while changing owners in the course of trading, sometimes several times a day. The trouble with MinFins is that they are tainted by scandal, so that interest on them reflects a risk premium. There are occasional alarms when old holders of MinFins in the provinces report that their bonds have been stolen. For example, $7.8 million worth of MinFins were taken from a bank safe during the assault on the city of Grozny during the Chechen War in 1995 and sold to an unsuspecting investor. Another $105 million worth of MinFins were stolen by the president of a Moscow bank who pledged them as security for a loan, wired the proceeds to himself in the US, and disappeared. In each case, there were at least two victims—the original holder whose MinFins were stolen and the most recent buyer who paid good money for stolen merchandise. Stolen MinFins may have changed hands dozens of times since being put on the market. Any MinFin bond without a specific pedigree that traces every change of hands, carries the risk of plunging an investor into the financial game of "old maid."

When someone claims his MinFins have been stolen, a local prosecutor may freeze the bonds, pending an investigation. In June 1996 authorities "arrested" (froze) $24 million worth of MinFins and in August 1996 another $7 million worth. Those two freezes affected 0.33% of all MinFins. The actual amounts of stolen MinFins are much higher, but many victims do not go to the police, resorting to what Russians call "phone justice." Well-connected investors believe that phone calls from top government officials yield faster results than the legal system.

All freezes were lifted by prosecutors in the autumn of 1996 under pressure from the central government, which swept this problem under the rug to present the best picture of Russian finance prior to its first Eurobond issue. With freezes lifted, the original owners were robbed for the second time. The most recent holders of tainted MinFins cannot sell them either. So many clients lost money that Salomon Brothers, which traded $700 million of MinFins in 1994–1996, temporarily stopped trading them. The trouble with MinFins reflects a weakness in the Russian financial infrastructure. The problem could be fixed easily by an agency acting as a guarantor of MinFins, for a fee, spreading the risk among all market participants.

EUROBONDS

Russia's first issue of Eurobonds in 1996 was oversubscribed, and those bonds now trade steadily in the secondary market. Russia continued to sell Eurobonds in 1997, and this trend is likely to continue.

Two Russian municipalities came to the Eurobond market in 1997. The cities of Moscow and Nizhny Novgorod have been given the highest possible ratings by American bond-rating agencies. A slew of lesser municipal borrowers are lining up at the gate. The crowd is growing so fast that the federal government is becoming worried about competition for the funds. It is drafting a law that would limit the amount of municipal Eurobonds to a percentage of federal borrowings.

MUNICIPAL DEBT

St. Petersburg and Novosibirsk were the early issuers of municipal bonds, but the giant in the field of municipal finance is a relative latecomer—the city of Moscow. Moscow is to Russia what Hong Kong is to China—a dynamic, successful metropolis amidst a huge but impoverished countryside. To say that Moscow is the richest city in the country is an understatement. Two thirds of Russian banking capital is in Moscow. The city is an economic, political, cultural, and even industrial capital of Russia. It is run by a tough, business-minded mayor, re-elected in 1996 with over 80% of the popular vote in a 4-person race. Moscow is the city that works.

Americans are used to the idea of large poor cities, going hat in hand to the relatively rich federal government. The opposite is true in Moscow. The city is a hugely prosperous landlord with a hand in many businesses. It runs a balanced budget, while the country as a whole, with many poor regions, suffers from budget deficits. Moscow plans to borrow money in order to invest in its infrastructure and profit-making projects, while the federal government borrows to pay salaries on time. In November 1996 Mayor Luzhkov announced that the European Bank for Reconstruction and Development will issue a $135 million loan to the city for 5–7 years at LIBOR (London Interbank Offered Rate) +2.5%. Incidentally, listening to speeches of Russian politicians or reading Moscow newspapers, you will encounter plenty of criticism of the central government but not of the city mayor. It is safe to criticize the President or the Duma, but not the city which owns almost all the land in Moscow and acts as a benevolent but tough landlord to most political parties and media outfits.

An investor in the city of Moscow had a choice of three municipal bonds in 1997: Eurobonds, GKO-like bonds for domestic investors, and bearer bonds for the public. In February 1997 Moscow was awarded a Ba2 rating by Moody's and a BB– by Standard & Poor's. Both agencies implied that they would have rated Moscow's credit even higher, but were precluded from doing so by their own rules which do not permit them to give any city a higher rating than the country in which it is located. Moscow has a good shot at having a federal law passed that would make its Eurobonds free from Russian taxes.

Moscow issued its first domestic municipal bonds in 1997—a $2 million test issue, to be followed by much larger flotations. Those bonds are similar to the federal GKOs and yield slightly more. Their spread may narrow or even reverse if domestic markets rate Moscow's debt higher than that of the Federal government. Moscow bonds, just like the GKOs issued after February 5, 1997, are taxable.

As more Russian municipalities float their bonds, an investor should remember the unique financial position of Moscow. The city that runs a balanced budget of $7 billion per year and borrows $2 billion abroad for long-term investments in income-producing projects is in a great position to service its debt. Other cities, such as St. Petersburg, already saddled with heavy debt for which they pay interest at well above the GKO rate, are desperate to borrow just to pay off their old creditors. They owe so much inside the country that going to the Eurobond market looks like an attempted escape for them.

Both Moody's and Standard & Poor's gave only one other city in Russia a credit rating as high as Moscow's. It is Nizhny Novgorod (Lower New-City, often called Nizhny in Russia). It is the third largest city in European Russia, an industrial center on the Volga River, home to a successful auto company GAZ, as well as oil refining and river shipping industries. The old Russian Nizhny was renamed Gorky under the communists. The city had been off-limits to foreigners (the great Russian scientist and human rights activist Andrey Sakharov was exiled there). The city is the capital of an *Oblast* (region) ably run by a young, democratically elected Governor Boris Nemtsov, who was recently brought into Yeltsin's cabinet and is the favorite of many Russian political liberals for the next Presidential elections in the year 2000.

Those who want to invest in municipal paper need to consider one more point. The inefficiencies of the Russian financial infrastructure are such that collecting payments on bonds issued in faraway cities may take several weeks, filled with writing letters and making phone calls, while no interest is being earned. Obviously, this is not a problem in Moscow whose bonds will not suffer from lengthy settlements.

VEKSELS—PROMISSORY NOTES

The promissory notes of banks, corporations, and municipalities called veksels represent the "wild and woolly" segment of Russia's fixed-income market. Calling them "fixed income" is problematic for two reasons—first, you may never get any interest, and second, you may never get your principal back. For these reasons, *veksels* often sell at huge discounts, tempting investors. Only local experts with strong personal connections in Russia have any business buying them. *Veksels* issued by absolutely top-tier banks, such as Sberbank and Unexim are highly rated inside the country, but even the first-rate Tveruniversalbank, one of Russia's biggest issuers of *veksels*, went belly up in 1996.

Companies and municipalities issue *veksels* to suppliers when they have no money to pay their bills. A foundry delivering steel to a tractor plant may accept a *veksel* in payment as an alternative to being stuck with metal it cannot sell. It may unload that *veksel* at a discount, sending it on a journey from one semisolvent payer to another. Ultimately, a farm may buy that *veksel* at a steep discount and use it to pay for tractors delivered to it from the tractor plant. Personal relationships between *veksel* sellers and buyers matter a great deal. If two people present their *veksels* for payment, who do you think will get paid first—a clever foreign investor like yourself, or a local yokel who drinks vodka with the *veksel* issuer and greases his palm?

Russian *veksels* reflect the problem of nonpayments that gripped the land during the Depression of the 1990s. How bad is this problem? In 1997, nonpayments exceeded the M2 monetary aggregate, according to Alexey Samoukov, fixed-income analyst at RinacoPlus, an investment bank in Moscow. The corporate segment of the fixed-income market holds a huge potential for the future development, but only after Russia gets its economic house in better order.

8

THE RUSSIAN
STOCK MARKET

A stock certificate represents the ownership of a productive asset—
an oil company, a telephone network, or a restaurant chain. You can
vote your shares and collect dividends on them, buy and sell them
whenever you want. The freedom and fluidity of shares are the
opposites of Soviet rigidity and inefficiency.

I saw my first Russian stock certificate in 1989 in Taiwan. The
Soviets were still in power in Moscow, but here a single share of the
Far Eastern Railway, a beautiful century-old antique, was gracing the
wall of the dining room at the Bankers' Club. The railroad had been
built by the French at the turn of the 20th century and stolen by the
communists long before any of us in that club had been born. My
Chinese friends framed the antique stock certificate as a piece of art.
They chuckled at my encounter with this forgotten bit of Russian history. Little did we know that several thousand miles to the northwest, in Moscow, a storm was brewing that would in a few years
lead to the rebirth of the Russian stock market and put quite a few
stock certificates into my hands.

Tsarist Russia used to have a stock market. Even after the communists took over, a group of hardy brokers continued to congre-
gate, trading bits of this and that until in 1927 several vans of secret
police pulled up to the old exchange building and herded them in.

They disappeared into labor camps, never to be seen again. According to communist dogma, share ownership was worse than a crime—it was an offense against human nature.

The rebirth of the stock market reflects a rebirth of freedom and economic sanity in Russia. Its stock market is growing at breakneck speed. Russians are determined to catch up with the West, leaping in a single generation the distance they lost in 74 years of communism.

Childbirth, if you have ever seen one, is rarely a pretty sight. The screaming naked baby is covered with blood and mucus, with a stump of an umbilical cord dangling from its belly. Newborns may not look great, but they have a natural immunity against most diseases and their growth is fantastic. The Russian stock market today is like a newborn baby, with its combination of screams, bloody mucus, and fantastic profits.

A money manager in the West who earns his clients over 20% per year is considered a good performer. Russians expect much higher returns. At the same time, serious problems in Russia's stock market can make a money manager's hair stand on end, if he has any hair left after his experience.

You can start investing in Russia now, or wait a few years until the dust settles. Investing in Russia will become simpler and easier as time goes on, but the great early opportunities will be gone. This chapter will help orient you in the Russian stock market. Then you can decide whether and when to invest in it.

A CHAOTIC BIRTH

The first new exchanges in Russia sprang up in 1990, just prior to the collapse of the USSR. People had zero experience with securities; communist laws making commerce a crime were still on the books. State borders just opened up, and businesspeople traveling abroad saw a lot of money being made on Western stock markets. Some decided to get on the gravy train of the famous Russian *khalyava*—free money, something for nothing. A group could start an exchange by renting space and having their buddies in the industry print them some shares. If those sold well, they printed more and marked them up. The ruble was crashing in the early 90s, wiping out the savings of the nation. Many Russians were desperate to put their money into something—anything!—that held value or went up. People broke free from communism's leash, but were unsophisticated financially.

Many of those early exchanges—disorganized, unregulated, and often rigged—took in money from the public by unloading questionable securities, including MMM certificates (see Chapters 3 and 6). Organized crime tried to penetrate and control them. Some victims welcomed those intrusions, hoping to benefit from powerful *kryshas* (protection). Most exchanges that cooperated with criminals have closed—you cannot survive in business if your partner is a thief. Others kept their independence by creating sophisticated security departments, run by hand-picked former KGB officers.

Prices of exchange memberships soared, tempting con men to form their own exchanges with grand-sounding names, sell memberships, and disappear. Legitimate exchanges enjoyed the boom but had to struggle to survive the subsequent bust. The cost of a membership on the Russian Exchange, the first commodities exchange in the country, rose from near zero to $200,000 in about a year. "We figured, people wanted to give us money, we'll take it and use it to develop our business," grinned the exchange president when I interviewed him in 1997. By then the price of a seat on this leading exchange had slid below $3,000.

The early wild boom collapsed as Russia stumbled into its Depression of the 1990s. Fast-buck artists had moved on, and many stocks turned out to be worthless. Similar booms and busts took place in most Eastern European countries in the 90s, as financial innocents of the continent awoke from their communist slumber to a wild "frontier capitalism." In Poland, for instance, each citizen was given a privatization voucher, and newly created paper began to chase stocks. Many companies had initially been undervalued, but they did not stay that way for long, especially after foreign funds jumped in. In 1993-94, the Exchange's index, the WIG, rose 20-fold, from 1,000 to 20,000, and the entire country was swept up in a year-long boom. People sold their cars and apartments to buy more stocks. Then the Polish government stepped up privatizations and flooded the market with newly issued stocks. The bubble collapsed, searing the collective memory of Poles just as 1929 seared the collective memory of Americans.

The Russian exchange boom of the early 90s had several lasting consequences. Massive losses cured Russians of their financial virginity—people became much more cautious. Russia was left with too many stock exchanges—60 of them as recently as 1995, nearly 40% of the world total. A vigorous capitalist economy is better served by a small number of exchanges whose high concentration of buyers and sellers improves liquidity. There are seven stock exchanges in the US, eight in Japan and Germany, six in the United Kingdom. Only India, another country with a relatively undeveloped economy has 19 stock exchanges. Most small exchanges in Russia are bound to disappear, as stock traders move over to a few strong exchanges and the RTS, Russian Trading System.

This brief chronology of the Russian stock market is based to a large extent on a chapter in a book by Professor Y. M. Mirkin, a department chairman at the Finance Academy in Moscow and a member of the Duma, the Russian parliament:

1917—Communists take power in an armed coup and nationalize the economy.

1927—Last remaining brokers imprisoned.

1988—The government allows the creation of heavily controlled commercial banks; government-owned enterprises allowed to issue shares.

1989—Promstroibank introduces *veksels* (see Chapter 7).

1990—The first joint-stock society is formed; first brokerages created; the New York Stock Exchange organizes a seminar in Moscow; the first stock exchange is founded; the first sale of stocks to the public.

1991—An explosive stage of creating new exchanges (to this day, portfolios of many Russian firms are littered with illiquid stocks bought during the exchange boom of 1991–92); foreign investors allowed to buy Russian securities; foreign securities sold to Russian investors; first industrial holding company is formed.

1992—The boom ends and many exchanges switch to trading raw commodities and industrial merchandise in order to survive; first listing rules and broker licensure rules; Securities Commission is created; privatization campaign releases massive quantities of vouchers to the population; the first trust companies are formed.

1993—The Central Bank floats GKOs for the first time; computerized system for continuous trading and clearing of GKOs is established; bookkeeping rules for securities; the creation of a network of securities registrars.

1994—Investment pools and pyramids start self-quoting their own shares; the MMM bubble; increased foreign demand for shares of privatized companies, especially oils and telecoms; *veksels* become more widespread, GKO volume overshadows stocks; the MMM crash; PAUFOR, the first professional association, is formed.

1995—First ADRs (American Depositary Receipts); first, albeit unsuccessful, hostile takeover attempt (Red October).

1996—Lexington Troika Dialog Russia Fund registered by the SEC and launched with $10 million under management, becoming the first open-ended SEC registered mutual fund focused entirely on Russian equities and fixed income; the government allows the creation of domestic mutual funds.

PECULIARITIES OF THE RUSSIAN MARKETS[20]

Western traders find it easy to navigate in the Russian stock market, built largely on the American model. Still, there are differences, and you must know the stripes on the tiger you are trying to catch.

The bulk of stock trading in Russia takes place not on the exchange floors; instead, traders use a system of computer terminals

---

[20]With apologies to Russian filmmakers whose 1996 movie *Peculiarities of Russian Hunting* was a hit in Russia.

linking independent dealers. The Russian Trading System (RTS) is based on the American system called PORTAL which was used in the US prior to the current NASDAQ. A group of international agencies brought old American equipment to Russia in the early '90s, and with it, the Russians found themselves only 20 years behind the US. That was a lot better than their previous 74-year lag! An inexpensive gift can do a great deal of good in the hour of need.

As the use of PORTAL spread, its ownership became russified and its name changed to RTS, the Russian Trading System. The name is something of a misnomer—RTS is not a trading system, but a quotation system. Brokers can display their quotes on RTS terminals but have to make a phone call in order to buy or sell.

At first, RTS was widely abused, as brokers walked away from agreed-upon trades, or put "indicative" prices on the screen, instead of firm bids and offers. As recently as 1995, you could see many bizarre quotes, put up only to test the market, with no intention of backing them up with real trades. In 1994, ten prominent Moscow brokerages formed a club to clean up the system. They named themselves the Professional Association of Market Participants, better known by its Russian acronym PAUFOR. Now you have to join them and follow their code of conduct, which includes making firm quotes, in order to get an RTS terminal.

The change from indicative pricing to firm quotes led to greater competition and increased market depth and liquidity. RTS promoted a greater transparency in Russian stock prices and narrower bid/ask spreads. Trading volumes skyrocketed, and RTS prices became the benchmark not just for Moscow dealers, but for regional brokerages.

The broad indexes of the Russian stock market doubled in 1996 and more than doubled in the first half of 1997, with many stocks rising by even greater percentages. Many stocks had price/earnings ratios of 1 or 2 in 1996, and even after the recent bull moves P/E ratios for most stocks remain well below Western standards. The daily volume on the RTS averaged $70 million in 1997. Most stocks are quoted in dollars and cents, even though the system allows traders to indicate whether they want to trade in dollars, rubles, or either. A few steps from the Kremlin where communist bosses used to preside over "the Evil Empire," where Stalin is buried, and Lenin's mummy still lies in its mausoleum, Russian brokers are trading Russian stocks using American equipment and quoting prices in American dollars. What a great sight for a returning refugee!

RTS is a trading system for professionals. Its minimum lot is between $30,000 and $50,000, depending on the stock. Almost all activity on the RTS is institutional, with a smattering of purchases and sales by wealthy individuals ($30,000 is more than most Russians earn in a lifetime). Forward-looking brokers are starting to say that people with $5,000 or $10,000 accounts should not be shut out—small accounts can add up to substantial volume. Today, those who do not have enough capital for the RTS go to smaller exchanges or retail shops that buy and sell shares at much wider spreads. Mutual funds are just being introduced to Russia.

Who trades Russian stocks? Reliable statistics are hard to come by, but Fred Berliner, the American director of trading at Troika Dialog, a leading investment bank in Moscow, estimates that 80–90% of the shares are owned by Russians. Most of those shares seldom see the light of day—they are put away for the long haul. Only 10-20% of shares are being traded, and at least half of RTS volume comes from foreigners who are the key players in the Russian stock market. "Moscow sucks in stocks from Russia," says Fred. "Prior to 1997, 90% used to go to the West, now only two thirds go to the West and the rest stays in Moscow."

The largest shareholders in Russia are the insiders (managers and employees of publicly held firms), banks and other early investors, both foreign and domestic, and the federal and local governments. Russian executives are of two minds regarding the stock market. The "Red Directors," holdovers from the old regime, hate the market, which they see as a dangerous force that can wrestle away control of "their" enterprises. Modern executives see the stock market as a tool for increasing shareholder value and raising low-cost funds. While the epic struggle between the two camps is raging, the sizzling volume on the RTS indicates that the pro-market forces are winning.

Russian banks are much more active in the stock market than US banks. The US government had forced banks to split into savings and investment banks after the Crash of 1929, reducing their overall involvement in the stock market. In Russia, all banks are free to trade stocks, which is similar to how banks in Germany operate. They may raise money from all sources, including the public, and invest directly in industry or buy shares in order to create and control large financial-industrial groups. Leading Russian banks like the German model, which promises them large profits and a secure central position in the economy. The rapidly developing stock market serves as a counterweight to bankers' power. It remains to be seen how much financing in Russia will be done by floating stocks (the American model) or bank loans (the German model).[21] We will have the answer in a few years, but at the moment the American model is the way to bet.

Fred Berliner points out that the stock market is one of the most advanced industries in the most advanced city in the country. He says in his New York staccato: "Moscow is not Russia—it's Disneyland. And the stock market is a Disneyland within Disneyland." He introduced me to one of his institutional traders, a bilingual Russian in his 20s, wearing a white shirt and tie, with a telephone in each ear, hands dancing over two keyboards: "I just got him a raise to $100,000 a year. Five years ago he was a sailor in the Soviet Navy, scrubbing whatever they scrub on those ships. Today he is getting more than 20 times the average salary in Moscow—and he is underpaid!" Brokers in Russia charge no commissions in order to escape value-added taxes; their compensation comes from the bid-ask spreads.

The RTS Index is a capitalization-weighted market index, similar to the Standard & Poor's 500. It was inaugurated in November 1995 with 13 Russian blue chips, grew to 21 stocks in 1996, and 24 in the early part of 1997. There are many other indexes in Russia— AK&M, Moscow Times, RosBusinessConsulting, and others—but most of them are based on some average of bid and ask prices. The RTS Index wins by being based on actual transactions. In March 1997 the Russian Exchange listed a futures contract on the RTS Index (see Chapter 9).

---

[21] I thank Dr. Andrew Spicer of the Wharton Business School for bringing this point to my attention.

The cost of entry into the Russian brokerage industry remains low. In 1996 and 1997 I was offered several small Moscow brokerage firms that had all the necessary licenses and were eligible to join PAUFOR for less that $100,000. Russia's financial industry is remarkably open, with no restrictions on foreign ownership. It reminded me how, when I first started coming to Russia in 1994, one could pick up a fully licensed bank for $50,000. Today, the price of a well-run second-tier bank is in the millions of dollars. The low cost of entering Russia's brokerage industry presents a great opportunity to enterprising Westerners. Now is the time to establish brokerage firms in virgin territory in the anticipation of the day when the Merrill Lynches and the Nomuras start coming in buying well-run local brokerages.

WAITING FOR THE DUST TO SETTLE

A serious problem in the Russian stock market is the settlement of trades. Clearing trades of even the most liquid shares used to take 14 days in 1995. That was cut in half in 1996, and down to a few days in 1997. Still, clearing a trade in an obscure stock as recently as 1997 could take up to 35 days and involve flying a clerk carrying certificates and cash to a registrar in a remote provincial city!

Having your shares registered after buying them is a simple routine in the West, but few things in Russia involving documents are ever simple. In the early 90s there were incidents when companies sold their shares to the public and then crossed the new purchasers' names out of their registry. Many registrars in Russia are owned by the companies whose shares they register. These "pocket registrars" make it easy to wipe the names of troublesome shareholders from the records or issue unannounced extra shares. Such "dirty issuing" used to be a common problem until the authorities cracked down on it in recent years.

Some investors in the early years of privatization arrived at firms in which they bought a packet of shares, only to be told they owned nothing. Their names were not in the little black book kept by the director and, if they wanted to argue, there was a group of thugs ready to take the complaint.

Sometimes the process worked in reverse—shareholders hijacked companies. As I write this chapter in a Moscow library, I see an article in today's newspaper naming a Western company that had shareholders vote it a major chunk of shares in a huge remote smelter at a meeting surrounded by an armed military group hired by those "investors." After Russia's attorney general canceled their shares, they took out protest ads in the Western media; but the evidence against them appeared pretty solid.

Early investors usually bought up shares as a means of gaining control over companies. This is why preferred shares trade at a discount to ordinary shares in Russia. Preferred shares do not vote (unless dividends were skipped) and cannot be used to control the company.

Registrations are more orderly today but investors continue to scrutinize their stock certificates to make sure every *t* is crossed and every *i* is dotted. The new law requires companies with more than 500 shareholders to appoint an independent registrar who must be licensed and maintain a minimum number of accounts. The government wants to see a few large independent operators rather than many little shops, each beholden to a single company.

Russia still has no centralized depository of stocks. A group of large institutions created a Depository Clearing Corporation (DCC) in order to register shares in a single day, against the usual five to seven days with company registrars. Using the DCC as the nominee holder of stocks enabled them to avoid paying registrars, some of whom charge high fees for each transaction. The registrars combined forces to defeat the DCC, which can no longer provide delivery of shares against cash, pushing traders back to the registrars.

The Russian law requires stocks to be registered to their owners, just like in the US. The only exception is that shares may be registered by brokerage houses and banks under "street names." Such nominee holding is becoming increasingly popular in Russia, helping to bypass the cumbersome and expensive registration process. Bearer shares, so popular in Germany and Switzerland, are not permitted in Russia.

CHECKS AND BALANCES

An industry group called NAUFOR is the most effective regulatory body in today's Russian stock market. Created as a club of ten brokerages in Moscow in 1995, it became a national professional organization of Russian brokers with over 200 members in Moscow, St. Petersburg, Novosibirsk, Ekaterinburg, and other cities. In June 1996 the group changed its name from PAUFOR to NAUFOR (P in its name used to stand for *Professionalnaya*—Professional, N stands for *Natsionalnaya*—National).

The group derives its power from controlling access to the RTS. Any firm that wants to get an RTS terminal must become a member of NAUFOR and obey its rules. It has to meet minimum capital requirements and be recommended by four existing members. NAUFOR's main objective is to promote the Russian stock market by developing and enforcing a uniform code of conduct. NAUFOR determines the rules of trading, registration, and payment for securities, subject to the applicable Russian laws. It can levy penalties ranging from fines (which go to NAUFOR's treasury), to a suspension from the RTS, to expulsion.

Any NAUFOR member can connect to the RTS in a "view only" mode, but must pass extra muster to gain access as a trader. RTS traders must honor all quotes they put up on the screen, quote at least two blue chips on a continuous basis, not quote more than 10% away from the best price, and not trade any lots smaller than the prescribed minimum. Any firm wishing to qualify as a market maker must quote even more stocks and maintain even larger minimum lot sizes.

Russian brokers have learned a simple truth, long accepted in the West—it pays to be honest. Everybody is better off if everyone plays by the rules. On my recent visits to Moscow brokerages and investment banks I could see that NAUFOR members enjoyed working in the atmosphere of straight dealing. They gladly give up the ability to cheat others in return for their own safety from rip-offs.

Russian and American stock market professionals tend to have different outlooks on government regulation of their industry. Americans want less regulation, while Russians want more. Wall Street was essentially free from government control until the Crash of 1929. That debacle made the nation angry enough to push Congress into creating the Securities and Exchange Commission. The watchdog agency forced Wall Street to clean up its act, increase fiduciary responsibility and reduce manipulation and stealing. Better compliance helped bring the public back into the market, increasing profits, but rules have become costly and cumbersome, making American stock market professionals complain about being overregulated.

Russian professionals, on the other hand, keep asking for tighter government regulations. Memories of massive scams of the early 90s left most Russians with a strong distrust of financial markets. Stock market professionals believe that stronger securities laws will reassure the public and bring more money to the markets.

Many Russians still keep their savings "under the mattress,"—in cash, usually in dollars. The Russian word *bank* means a bank, but the word *banka* means a jar. When people tell you they keep their savings *v banke*, you have to guess which of the two they mean. Ordinary folks keep about $20 billion in those jars, according to Russian statisticians. When that money comes out of hiding, it will fuel an investment boom. Professionals are asking for stronger laws for protecting the public in order to encourage people to invest.

The Russian Securities Commission, created in 1994, is still too young, weak, and disorganized to offer much help to the public. The Russian government has more pressing problems than regulating securities markets. Striking coal miners who haven't been paid for six months receive more attention than a group of financial traders asking for better regulations. Governments in most parts of the world tend to react to crises rather than plan for the future. It will be a while before Russia has US-style securities legislation. Meanwhile, deal only with brokers and bankers you know and trust. Russia is not America, where you can pull a broker's name out of a newspaper and do business with him or her, knowing your account is insured. In Russia you have to be extremely diligent when choosing people to deal with, because no one will protect you if a broker cheats you. An investor who has a conflict with a financial company faces it alone—and the little guy usually gets the short end of a stick.

Two problems in the Russian stock market are crying for clean-up. One is the collusion between traders at big firms. They all vehemently deny it exists, but it does! I was sitting in the office of the head trader at a Moscow brokerage, interviewing him for this book when one of his traders burst in. He was trying to sell a block of shares for a client when he noticed that another big local brokerage popped up on the RTS screen offering the same stock half a penny cheaper. It appeared they too had a large block to sell. The man I was interviewing ordered his trader to call the competitor and ask him ". . . not to press the market. Tell him to take the lowest offer, we'll take the second, but let's lift both!" Then he remembered I was in his office, turned to me, and said, "This is not collusion, we just do favors for each other."

Today large players in the Russian markets find it more difficult to hustle a selected issue up and down than in the old days, but they still can lean on a stock or nudge it up. They collude (or cooperate, depending on your point of view) because the growing size of the market reduces the importance of any one player, no matter how big.

Another system-wide problem in Russia is the corruption of brokerage exams. The Ministry of Finance requires market participants, such as traders and brokers, to pass mindlessly complex tests, graded by underpaid clerks. These clerks go out of their way to fail anyone who attempts to pass without paying them. A brief attempt to use computers was scuttled after about a month because it interfered with the clerks' extortion. One of these days MinFin is going to wake up and appoint someone capable of cleaning up and streamlining the licensing process.

FOREIGN AFFAIRS AND ADRs

The collapse of the Soviet system opened up the country to the West. People who grew up in isolation rushed to embrace Western ideas, styles, and products. Today, Westerners who come to Russia to work or visit freely mix with the locals who welcome them with open arms. (Unfortunately, bureaucrats saw growing Western interest in Russia and recognized a *khalyava*—a chance to get something for nothing. They jacked up prices on entry visas, which are now among the most expensive in the world).

Russia has virtually no restrictions on foreign businesspeople and investors. They have the same rights as Russians (and have to slog through similar bureaucratic mazes) in almost all lines of business, except for defense, energy, and banking. A few companies, such as Gazprom (see Chapter 10) restrict foreign ownership, but investors who bump into those restrictions find them easy to circumvent.

It is harder to do fundamental research in Russia than in the US. What we call research in the US used to be called spying in the Soviet Union. A few firms talk to analysts, but many cling to the old Soviet notions of secrecy. Adding to the confusion, the RAS (Russian Accounting Standards) are in flux, changing from the old Soviet to the Western model. The change is so drastic that the 1995 annual reports prepared in accordance with RAS for that year are not comparable with the 1994 RAS reports. Russian share prices are driven by political developments to a much greater degree than Western stocks. A president's illness may impact a company more than its earnings report. This is rapidly changing, as markets are normalizing and increasingly taking their cues from economic fundamentals.

Executives of many publicly traded Russian firms are eager to attract Western investments, but quickly discover that foreigners expect something a lot more substantial than a verbal promise of a bright future. Foreign investors find the RAS (Russian Accounting Standards) too vague for making investment decisions, forcing companies to hire Western accountants and perform GAAP or IAS audits.

GAAP is an acronym for Generally Accepted Accounting Principles, which are standard in the US. Europeans tend to follow another widely accepted set of rules called IAS, or International Accounting Standards. In 1995 Russian businesses began flying in planeloads of American accountants to audit them according to GAAP. Whenever I went to a club, a restaurant, or a hockey game in Moscow where foreigners congregated, half of them were young American accountants flown in by the Big Six accounting firms to audit Russian companies. (You can often tell what changes are brewing in Moscow by observing what professions predominate on flights into Moscow).

The trend towards the GAAP audits accelerated after Mosenergo—the Moscow utility company—issued its ADRs in New York in 1995. Everybody saw how much hard currency a company could raise by selling a small part of itself to Western investors. Russians move fast. Only two years later, in the beginning of 1997, over a dozen Russian companies had their ADRs listed in New York and London, Frankfurt and Luxembourg, while dozens more were in various stages of preparing to issue ADRs. ADRs have become a powerful force for better corporate governance among Russian publicly traded firms, while providing Western investors with a hassle-free entry into the Russian stock market.

ADRs are negotiable certificates representing the ownership of shares of a foreign corporation traded outside of the country in which those shares were issued. These securities have many names. The term American Depositary Receipts was coined years ago at the request of a Korean company that wanted the word "American" in its name. These instruments are also called ADS (American Depositary Shares), GDS (Global Depositary Shares), and GDRs (Global Depositary Receipts).

Some of the world's leading companies, such as Honda, British Airways, and Unilever had their ADRs traded in the US for years. ADRs of South African gold stocks used to be popular when the UN embargo coincided with a bull market in gold. The Bank of New York, the leading global custodian bank, has two thirds of the world's ADR market. It was the fastest on its feet in Russia, and now owns 100% of the ADR market there. One of the reasons for this remarkable feat is that the Bank of New York positions itself strictly as custodian, while its competitors also offer underwriting services.

Over 1,500 companies worldwide have issued ADRs for a variety of reasons: to obtain better access to capital markets, to broaden their shareholder base, and to heighten their corporate profile. From an investor's point of view, ADRs offer the convenience of trading foreign securities as if they were local stocks. ADRs follow the US clearing and settlement procedures and pay dividends in US dollars.

ADRs can be issued at the behest of the company itself or at the initiative of a foreign investment bank or a brokerage firm that believes its clients would want to own that foreign company. A bank serves as a custodian of foreign shares. It does not buy those shares for itself; it holds them on behalf of a foreign brokerage and issues ADRs, which are, in effect, receipts that certify that the actual shares are being held in the bank.

ADRs convert a local share into a global security after a custodian bank adds (for a fee) its own credibility to the process. It assures traders that if 5 million in ADRs are being traded, then the equivalent number of shares is being held by the custodian. Sometimes an ADR represents less than a full share, sometimes more. For example, an ADR of Vimpelcom represents ¾ of a share, while an ADR of Gazprom represents 10 shares. Those levels are set so that the initial public offering of an ADR is priced "in the teens"—between $10 and $20.

Here's an example: John Doe in San Francisco may call his Merrill Lynch broker and give him an order to buy Lukoil. Merrill Lynch will pass the order to a brokerage in Moscow, which will either buy the specified number of shares on the open market on behalf of Merrill Lynch or sell it shares from its own inventory and deliver them to the custodian (in this case, the Bank of New York). That bank will inform Merrill Lynch that it has Russian shares in its custody, and send the ADRs representing their number. The whole process is done electronically. Merrill Lynch will in turn credit John Doe's account with those ADRs. When Lukoil pays dividends, it delivers rubles to the Bank of New York in Moscow, which converts them into dollars and remits them to Merrill Lynch, which in turn credits John Doe's account in San Francisco. As the volume of an ADR rises, more trades get "crossed" in the US, matching local buyers and sellers, but there is always an option of going to Moscow for more shares. I have seen professional traders in Moscow watch local prices and ADR quotes on terminals side by side, looking for arbitrage opportunities (simultaneously buying the undervalued and selling the overvalued trading vehicle).

There are four types, or levels, of ADRs, that differ in their disclosure requirements, the ability to raise capital in the US, and availability to the general public. When a foreign company first issues ADRs, it often begins at the level called "144A Private." That's the level at which ADRs of Mosenergo are trading at the time of this writing. These securities are not reviewed by the SEC and may be sold only to "qualified investors,"—primarily large institutions that are considered savvy enough to fend for themselves and do not need the SEC protection. Actually, the process is safe enough even without the SEC because investment banks that sell those ADRs value their reputations. They tend to be very diligent about investigating foreign companies whose 144A Private ADRs they sell to their clients. A similar security in Europe is called Regulation S ADS. These securities help foreign corporations raise capital, but they do not provide as much visibility as other levels of ADRs.

Level 1 ADRs usually trade over the counter; they provide a convenient trading vehicle, but do not bring in new capital. Most ADRs issued by Russian firms through 1997 have been Level 1 ADRs. To offer them, a company must provide the same documentation in the US in English as it does at home in Russian. It does not even have to have a GAAP audit—an RAS (Russian Accounting Standards) audit will do, even though most firms issuing Level 1 ADRs get themselves audited according to GAAP. Level 2 ADRs are generally listed on one of the exchanges and may raise capital later on, after meeting more stringent disclosure rules.

The most useful and prestigious ADRs are Level 3—they are generally listed on one of the exchanges and allow companies to raise fresh equity in the US. A company that wants to issue Level 3 ADRs must meet rigorous disclosure requirements, including three years of GAAP or IAS audits. By mid-1997 only one Russian company, Vimpelcom (see Chapter 12), floated Level 3 ADRs, which became a huge success from the first day of trading on the New York Stock Exchange.

The main advantage of ADRs to investors is convenience; you can pick up a phone or punch a few keys linking you to an Internet broker to buy or sell them. Some ADRs are more liquid than the Russian shares they represent. They also allow you to trade in a smaller size. You can easily buy $10,000 or even $5,000 worth of Lukoil ADRs, but if you come to an RTS broker in Moscow with less than $50,000 to buy Lukoil, he'll turn you away.

The main disadvantage of ADRs is the wide spread between their bid and ask prices. Those spreads tend to be very narrow on the blue chips traded on the RTS, but when you buy or sell ADRs over the counter in the US, you are likely to be hit with much wider spreads. If you are an active trader, those spreads can quickly chew up your profits. This problem is less significant for someone who wants to buy and hold.

It is easy to receive an updated list of Russian ADRs from the Bank of New York. Many of them trade in Western Europe rather than the US. Remember that at the end of the 1990s Russia had stronger economic links with Europe than with the US. At the time of this writing, the following Russian ADRs traded in the US: Mosenergo (see Chapter 11), Seversky Tube, Surgutneftegas (see Chapter 10), Tatneft, Chernogorneft, Inkombank, Irkutskenergo, and Vimpelcom (see Chapter 12). At the same time, Gazprom (see Chapter 10) traded in London and Frankfurt, which also traded GUM (a department store) and Lukoil (see Chapter 10), while Luxembourg traded AvtoVAZ (see Chapter 13), and FESCO (ocean shipping).

The selection of ADRs is more limited than shares on the RTS. ADRs are listed for a handful of top Russian stocks, but the most promising new stocks do not appear on the list until they have been "seasoned." By that time the massive early gains had been bagged by locals and savvy foreigners on the RTS. For example, today the hottest stocks in Russia are Aeroflot—the just-listed former state airline—and Ingosstrakh, a just-listed former state insurance firm. Russians are snapping them up, but neither is likely to issue ADRs any time soon. A professional with substantial funds to invest in Russia is better off buying actual stocks than ADRs.

Foreign investments in Russian equities are booming. On September 30, 1996, the International Finance Corporation (IFC), an agency of the World Bank, included Russia in its Global Index Series. The IFC Russia Index was inaugurated with 15 blue chips, and later expanded to 24 RTS-traded blue chips. On January 1, 1997, Russia was included in the IFC Composite Index. Investors are waiting for the day when IFC includes Russia in its IFC Investable Index. That will serve as an international seal of approval and lead to an inflow of funds into the Russian stock market. Institutional investors worldwide track the IFC Investable Index and many are required by their bylaws to invest in IFC component markets.

OWNING RUSSIAN SHARES

Russian society is in the midst of a historic transition. The change is palpable and more profound than most observers realize. To find another period with a similar degree of turmoil, you'd have to go back to the revolutions or foreign invasions. This time there is no blood in the streets, and life is rapidly changing for the better. A huge nation is going through a millennial change after throwing off leg-irons that held it down for six centuries. The country is eagerly reaching for political and economic normalcy. You can feel the excitement of change in the homes, streets, and offices of Russia.

If you believe that Russia is in an early stage of an economic boom, then Russian stocks provide a terrific vehicle for profiting from it.

Investments always seem the most risky when the economy is weak, near the bottom of a recession or a depression. Buying near the bottom, when stocks are cheap, is a lonely business. The negatives loom large when prices are low. Psychologically, it is easier to buy stocks after a prolonged bull market, when everyone seems to be making money and buyers have plenty of company. But the rewards of buying closer to the top are smaller, while price risks are much higher.

Should we wait for the situation in Russia to settle? All investments involve uncertainty. A recent research report from Troika Dialog, a leading investment bank in Moscow, lists the following systemic risks in Russia today:

Shares are volatile, spreads vary, and liquidity is low.

No GAAP accounting for many stocks, few Western audits.

Custodial and registration risk due to lack of registrar independence.

Crime and corruption—no antifraud or insider-trading legislation.

Risk of changes in legislation and policy.

Should we buy now or stay on the sidelines? I think of George Soros' tongue-in-cheek advice, "Buy first, investigate later." By taking a small position in the Russian stock market today, you become a participant in the grand economic change, rather than an observer on the sidelines. Having a position gives you an extra incentive to monitor the news from Russia, follow its politics, economy, and its stocks—the ones you own as well as those you may buy later.

Troika Dialog has designed a test to help define Russian blue chips. They measure the following eight factors on a scale from 1 (excellent) to 5 (poor) and average them out in order to come up with the desirability rating for any particular stock:

A large-cap sector with investor-driven corporate policies.

A sector that produces a good product in a traditional emerging market sector.

Growth—revenue growth and margin expansion expected.

Financial transparency—full accounting according to IAS or GAAP, including an appointment of a "Big 6" auditor.

Management—forward thinking and investor friendly.

Research—available from major brokers.

Liquidity—firm bids and offers available.

Valuation—trades at a discount to asset valuation.

Russians have a saying, "We are slow saddlers but fast riders," meaning it takes them a long time to get going, but when they do, they move very fast. They lived under the communist yoke longer than any other nation, but when reformers privatized the economy, they did it faster and more thoroughly than in any other country. The Russian government privatized over 100,000 enterprises— some through vouchers, others through cash sales, many by issuing shares. It was one of the greatest privatization campaigns in history. By the end of 1995, 70% of Russian GDP (Gross Domestic Product) was produced by the private sector of the economy. The government plans to privatize more than 10,000 enterprises still under state control.

The number of actively traded stocks in Russia is still minuscule. There are a few dozen reasonably liquid shares, led by such giants as Lukoil, Mosenergo, and Gazprom. There are probably twice as many semi-liquid shares, allowing limited investment and trading. Once you go outside of the top 100 stocks, trading volumes become so thin that the difference between the bid and the ask may reach 100%! Many stocks do not even trade each day. Those dormant stocks represent a huge supply of investment and trading vehicles that will become active in the coming years.

There is a market expression called "the opening roll." It means that not all trading vehicles open for trading at once, but rather one after another, usually at an interval of a few minutes. An opening roll allows traders to give their full attention to one trading vehicle at a time, followed by trading all of them. The Russian stock market today is on its opening roll. First the oil companies became active, then telecoms, then energy companies. There are thousands of companies that are still not traded actively, promising us a steady supply of new opportunities in the years ahead, as new stock groups and shares receive the attention they deserve.

9

THE RUSSIAN DERIVATIVES MARKETS

Walking through the Russian Exchange building in Moscow at the end of a trading day, as the lights are being turned down, you notice at least half a dozen chess games going on in cubicles that surround its trading floor. Russian players have been winning chess championships for decades—trading derivatives calls for similarly multilevel thinking. The Russians appear highly adept at both.

Derivatives, such as futures and options, are among the most complex trading vehicles. An option is a right but not an obligation to buy or sell a specific security at a specific price during a certain time. A person who buys an option is free to exercise it or walk away from it—a loss is limited to the price of that option. A future is a contract to deliver or accept delivery of a specific unit of merchandise at a certain price at a certain time. A futures trade that goes bad can lead to unlimited losses. All derivatives provide great leverage, allowing traders to control large investments with a small amount of capital. They promise large rewards, along with large risks—and many Russians find their lure irresistible.

When Americans trade derivatives, they prefer options whose volume in the US is much higher than that of futures. The opposite is true in Russia, where several exchanges actively trade futures, but very few trade options. The difference may be due to the huge

American stock market offering hundreds if not thousands of option-able stocks, while the Russian stock market is much thinner. But Russians show little interest even in options on active stocks, and prefer futures on stocks—which do not exist in the US. Perhaps the reason is psychological. Americans are willing to pay more for "softer" options, which promise to limit their risks, while Russians prefer to trade "firmer" futures, which usually offer better odds than options. Futures on shares are popular in several countries. For example, Sydney Futures Exchange in Australia actively trades futures on a growing number of shares.

Different futures go up and down in popularity worldwide as the economy changes, but those swings occur much faster in Russia than in America. Once a futures contract becomes popular in Chicago or New York—for example, soybeans, or currencies, or the S&P—it tends to trade at a high volume for years, reflecting the stability of the US economic system. In Russia, the economic situation changes so rapidly that a futures contract may be listed, become highly popular and wither away—all within two years. At first, currency futures were immensely popular, followed by futures on GKOs (Russian Treasury bills), and, by the middle of 1997, futures on stocks.

CURRENCY FUTURES

In the early 1990s, inflation had depressed the Russian ruble, which lost over 99.9% of its value within three years. As the ruble fell from near parity with the US dollar to below 5,000 rubles to a dollar, shorting it became a royal road to riches. Banks did it with cash; they took in ruble deposits, converted them into dollars, and later reconverted and repaid their obligations with depreciated rubles. When dollar/ruble and deutsche mark/ruble futures were introduced, many savvy Russians rushed to trade them.

All you had to do in those days was to sell rubles short and use the profits to pyramid (increase) your position. You could start with very little money because futures contracts are small in Russia. For example, the dollar/ruble contract is worth only $1,000 or about 1%

of the size of the currency futures in the US (the Deutsche mark contract on the Chicago IMM is worth approximately $90,000 at today's exchange rate). I have several trader friends in Moscow who started out as poor ex-Soviet scientists with not a dime to their name and pyramided a few hundred borrowed dollars into several million dollars in one or two years.

In the mid-1990s, five exchanges in Moscow traded dollar/ruble futures: the Moscow Commodities Exchange, the Moscow Central Securities Exchange, the Russian Exchange, Moscow Financial Futures Exchange, and the Central Russian Universal Exchange. You had to be careful choosing where to trade. By the time the ruble stopped falling, two out of those five exchanges went bust, wiping out their customers' accounts. The Central Russian Universal Exchange defaulted in 1994 and the Moscow Commodities Exchange in 1995. The Moscow Central Securities Exchange almost went off a cliff, but managed to pull back from the brink and reopened for trading. An exchange could go broke because of stealing by insiders or by accepting questionable securities as margin and becoming insolvent after they lost value. The two roads to ruin sometimes merged, as groups that ran exchanges accepted bad securities from friends.

Futures markets thrive on instability but shrivel in the atmosphere of certainty; it does not pay to bet on futures when the future is clear. The dollar/ruble market withered away after the Russian government stabilized the ruble. The volume of ruble futures in Moscow is near zero today even though ruble futures became listed in Chicago in 1998. In 1995, while traders were abandoning the dollar/ruble futures, another contract captured their attention—futures on GKOs, the Russian Treasury bills.

GKO FUTURES

GKOs, or *Gosudarstvenniye Kratkosrochniye Obligatsii*, are paperless zero-coupon bonds with 3-, 6-, and 12- month maturities (see Chapter 7). The Central Bank of Russia conducts primary auctions of GKOs each Wednesday, followed by secondary trading until maturity on the MICEX, often called the home exchange of the Central Bank. You can trade GKO futures on several exchanges, but the largest are the Russian Exchange (RE) and The Moscow Central Securities Exchange (MTsFB in Russian). Their contracts differ; the RE contract is based on the primary auctions for T-bills, while the MTsFB contract is based on secondary auctions. The RE contract is based on 10 GKOs with a total value of $10,000, while the MTsFB contract is based on a single GKO, ten times smaller.

MTsFB officials say that their contract is "more real" because it is based on GKOs that already exist and trade in the secondary market. The Russian Exchange officials counter by saying their contract does exactly what futures are supposed to do—anticipate future auctions. If the Chicago exchanges can trade futures on corn and wheat still in the ground, why shouldn't the Russian Exchange trade futures on GKOs still to be issued? Historically, banks and other financial institutions have favored MTsFB, while individuals tended to trade on the Russian Exchange. Many hedgers use both and take advantage of arbitrage opportunities.

GKO futures were listed in 1995 and became the most popular derivative in the country in 1996 due to the tremendous volatility of interest rates. In the runup to the July 1996 Presidential elections, short-term rates shot up to 200% before falling to nearly 60% by year-end. Traders poured money into GKO futures both to speculate and to hedge their GKO holdings.

By the end of 1996 the party was in full swing, and even the staid MICEX announced its plan to list its own GKO futures. The decision of the Central Bank to force down the GKO rates following the presidential elections threw ice water in the face of that market. As interest rates fell and volatility declined, private traders abandoned GKO futures in droves.

The MTsFB, which always catered more to institutions, saw an increase in its volume and open interest, thanks to the inflow of bankers hedging their cash holdings. The Russian Exchange, which always catered more to private traders, saw its volume of GKO futures fall about 80% between October 1996 and March 1997. But another active market beckoned; the stock market was in the midst of a wild bull run, and the Russian Exchange listed futures on shares.

FUTURES ON STOCKS

The Russian stock market is only a few years old, and many of its participants are still relatively unsophisticated. Major market moves anticipated by savvy Western money managers often take them by surprise. Many Russians were amazed after their stock market doubled in the runup to the 1996 presidential election, but sold off for several months on the good news of the victory of the anticommunist candidate. They have yet to learn the old Western adage "Buy on rumors, sell on news." Many were surprised when the stock market took off again in January 1997 to gain 80% in nine weeks—after interest rates on the GKOs fell from 200% to 50%. The idea of funds flowing out of bonds into stocks when interest rates fall is still new to most Russians. They are catching up fast, and many inefficiencies may disappear by the time you read this book.

The Russian Exchange created a trading vehicle for extracting leveraged profits from the stock market. In September 1996 it listed its first futures on shares, long before the competing exchanges did. It listed futures on Mosenergo, one of the top utility companies in the country (see Chapter 11) whose stock is among the most active issues on the RTS (Russian Trading System). Underlying each futures contract are 1,000 shares of Mosenergo. The contracts expire on the 15th of each month, with four of them trading at any given time—the depth of this futures market is four months. The contract trades in US dollars, just as the stock does, and the settlement is either in shares or rubles.

The spreads between different delivery months tends to be very steep, but few if any Russians take advantage of intramarket arbitrage. They are making too much profit from outright trading or spreading futures against spot to do anything else. Also, many Russian traders are capitalized too thinly to profit from capital-intensive arbitrage.

In October 1996, one month after the successful launch of Mosenergo futures, the Russian Exchange listed a futures contract on Lukoil. Underlying each contract were 100 shares of one of the world's largest oil firms (see Chapter 10). The Russian Exchange has since listed futures on other shares, such as Rostelecom (a giant long-distance phone company; see Chapter 12) and Gazprom (Russia's natural gas monopolist and the largest gas company in the world; see

Chapter 10). It stands ready to list more contracts after the volume of the existing ones rises. The number of shares underlying each contract is selected so that each contract is worth approximately $2,000.

Futures on Lukoil shares emerged as the most actively traded instrument. With Lukoil shares trading at about $20 at the time of this writing, the value of the futures contract is about $2,000. With daily volume above 60,000 contracts a day in mid-1997, the exchange traded an equivalent of over $100 million worth of shares per day. (In the US, stock volume is measured in shares, but in much of the world it is measured in dollars). Anyone who thinks of Russia as a financial backwater should take a good look at this number! The second most popular stock future is Rostelecom. It is considered the most "technical" market by traders—the one best suited for technical analysis, a skill for which many Russians seem to have a special aptitude. Mosenergo comes third, while the volume of Gazprom futures is negligible; freewheeling traders give a wide berth to the monopolist behemoth (see Chapter 10). Other exchanges are starting to list futures on shares, but their volumes are far behind the Russian Exchange.

The engine that drives these contracts is the steady decline of interest rates in Russia. Banks can no longer get easy high-double-digit returns by lending money to the government. They are driven to look for opportunities in the stock market, but the abundance of speculators makes it highly volatile. The futures market allows banks to hedge their stock market risks. Hedging can be highly profitable: for example, buying Lukoil shares on April 4, 1997 and selling May 15 futures locked in a 45.3% profit—annualized, in US dollars! The Russians are so busy with outright trading, that a Westerner with a knowledge of spreading and hedging has a decided advantage— until the Russians catch up.

STOCK INDEX FUTURES

In March 1997 the Russian Exchange introduced a future on the RTS Index (see Chapter 8). The RTS Index is a capitalization-weighted average of 24 Russian blue chips representing key sectors of the Russian economy, such as oil, electric power, telecoms, shipping, autos, and merchandising. The value of each contract is the RTS Index multiplied by 1,000 rubles. With the RTS Index at 3,000, the future is worth 3 million "old" rubles, or about $535 at the current exchange rate. This contract is tiny in comparison with the S&P 500 futures contract in Chicago, which stands at nearly 900 at the time of this writing, making it worth $225,000. All Russian futures contracts tend to be much smaller than American, so it's no wonder most people trade multiple contracts.

The RTS Index contracts expire on the 15th of each month, with four contracts slated to trade at any given time, allowing four different delivery dates. The opening margin for the RTS Index future is 200,000 "old" rubles, slightly over $60 at the current rate of exchange, and double that amount in the last two days before expiration. The Russian Exchange charges buyers and sellers a flat fee of Rbl 200 (approximately 3 cents) for every contract. It also charges a fee of 0.5% of margin (slightly above 30 cents) on contracts settled in cash at expiration.

The RTS Index futures continue to languish with minuscule volume because exchange members suspect that the underlying index is being manipulated by large stock traders on the futures expiration days. They avoid the RTS Index, even though they are eager to have a tradable stock index future. They keep hoping that more stocks will be traded on the floors of various exchanges rather than on the RTS, and that those will be less prone to manipulation.

All market participants agree that an index future would allow traders to speculate on the overall direction of the Russian stock market and offer opportunities for hedging, arbitrage, and other sophisticated market games. The Austrian Stock Exchange was planning to list its own future on the Russian stock market, based on its own basket of Russian stocks, but Russian traders were highly skeptical of that project.

OPTIONS

MTsFB (Moscow Central Securities Exchange) pioneered options in Russia in 1995. It remains the biggest options exchange in the country, as options volume on other exchanges is negligible. Most MTsFB options are based on GKO futures. Less than 1% of volume is generated by orders coming from the West.

Option trading on MTsFB began after six top traders met in the exchange dining room. They drank vodka together and each man pledged to "take on his chest" (a term derived from weightlifting) a certain volume of new option contracts. This is fairly typical of how new businesses get started in Russia these days.

The main buyers of GKO options are hedgers who use them to reduce their margin requirements on futures positions. The exchange members are on the other side of most trades, selling puts and calls. Many of them believe options to be underpriced. Their premiums are often smaller than bid/ask spreads on futures, making them suitable for scalping. Several fortunes have been made in recent months by members who loaded up on very cheap far-out-of-the-money calls or puts prior to their expiration and benefited from sharp market moves.

During my visit to the exchange in the middle of 1997, several traders said that options were underpriced because the crowd of sellers did not know how to value them. Anatoly Arzamastsev is a trader who owns a clearing firm. He has a Ph.D. in physics and used to work in a research institute until the nonpayment of salaries drove him to the market—a fairly common switch in today's Russia. He laughed, describing to me how earlier that day he bought calls for less than the price of futures. "Mathematically, it made no sense, but someone was giving them away, so I took them."

These are the early days of option trading in Russia. Mispricing is common, there are no options on stocks, there is virtually no one with Western experience, and a savvy trader from the West who speaks some Russian has an advantage over many locals. That advantage will fade away as the Russians catch up.

THE EXCHANGES IN RUSSIA

Russia has dozens of exchanges—and all over the country the weak ones are going out of business. A few strong ones are emerging as permanent fixtures on the economic landscape, similar to the leading exchanges in Chicago. Which exchanges will prosper and which will disappear? Can we predict which exchange will succeed and which will die? Since there are no exclusive contracts, no exchange can boast an exclusive product. Operating costs are also similar and none can afford to price itself out of business by sharply undercutting others. Innovative contracts and reasonable transaction costs do matter, but in the long run, other factors being equal, there is one factor that will determine whether an exchange will sink or swim.

That factor is its level of integrity.

Exchange members everywhere in the world have a tremendous temptation to steal. Millions of dollars pass through their hands each day. It is tempting to lick your fingers just a little before holding them out, so that some loose money sticks to them. In the short run, it is virtually impossible to detect when an exchange steals from you. The trouble with someone who steals and gets away with it, is that he or she will do it again, and again, and soon people will begin to notice. Any exchange that tolerates crookedness will, in the long run, go out of business. It will either flame out in a spectacular scandal or wither away as disappointed traders abandon it.

Honesty pays. This may be a simple homily, but any exchange that fiddles with this principle threatens its own survival. This applies not only to Russia. For example, here in New York, COMEX (the metals exchange) earned a rough reputation. When I arranged seminars for traders in the 1980s, one of the topics that came up often in conversations among attendees was their distrust of the COMEX. They felt the floor was taking advantage of them with bad fills, terrible slippage, dirty data, and changing quotes. We even had COMEX members at a few seminars gleefully describe their shenanigans. The exchange thought it was secure in its position as the premier metals marketplace in North America, but it was badly mistaken. Hedgers drifted to London and speculators went to trade other markets, so that when the metals business slowed in the 1990s, COMEX had no loyal core of customers to carry it through hard times. It could not survive as an independent entity and had to sell itself to a stronger and better-run exchange. Having a good product is important, but integrity comes first.

A vice-president of an exchange in Russia said to me at a dinner, "We are the boundary of civil society. The government wants to screw its citizens out of money, and the citizens want to screw the government—we are responsible for preventing robberies, we protect the interests of both parties.

"During the privatization in 1992 each citizen was given a voucher. The president said that a voucher was worth 100,000 rubles. His head of privatization said it was worth 500 rubles. The government needed money; they printed those candy wrappers and thought they could tell us what their price was. Our price, on our trading floor, was 4,500 rubles—and we've got volume! Our market found the social balance. We allowed the privatization to go on. We have three golden rules: fair price, guaranteed clean deals, and independence.

"We have a security checkpoint by the door. You can do your deal outside—any which way you like, or you can do it here—by our rules. Outside the checkpoint is the street—there the government plays its games, banks do not fulfill their obligations. Inside you lay down your money and get your merchandise, at a fair price. Look at our quotes—they are the reality, no one can argue with them, not even the Constitutional Court. You can do what you want on the street—inside we have our price, in our hall, based on our rules. Outside, on the street, your connections matter. Here we do not care about your connections, but you get a fair price. The banks on the street may have you wait for your money for two months— here we settle in one day.

"We are a few hundred men who decided to deal straight. That's why the Gazproms of the world are afraid of us. Those who hate us forget that the exchange reflects society. If you have a 40°C [104°F] fever, do not blame us for it. We are not the fever, we are the thermometer." In translating this monologue I had to delete a great many expletives—traders all over the world use profanities, and the Russian language has an especially rich cursing vocabulary.

Pearls in
the Dirt

10

THE RUSSIAN OIL AND GAS SECTOR

Russia is one of the largest oil and gas producers in the world. Its oil reserves amount to 50 billion barrels—more than twice as large as in the US. It has 1,467 trillion cubic feet of proven reserves of natural gas—nine times more than the US. A network of pipelines carries oil, gas, and their products from remote production regions into the industrial West of Russia and abroad. Russia's pipelines for crude oil extend 30,000 miles, pipelines for oil products 9,000 miles, and for natural gas 90,000 miles.

Russia consumes more than half of its oil and gas and sells the rest abroad. This industry is one of the biggest foreign currency earners in the country. Even when domestic demand for oil and gas shrunk during the Depression of the 1990s, these commodities found a ready market in the West. While many industries in Russia deteriorated during the Depression, oil and gas producers earned enough abroad to invest some money in their maintenance.

The oil and gas industry is a major taxpayer in Russia, with close ties to the government—an important factor in any country. Some oil companies act as proxies for Russia during international negotiations involving oil and pipelines. Victor Chernomyrdin, the former chairman of the gas monopoly Gazprom, has been the prime minister of Russia since 1992 through 1998, just a step below President Yeltsin. Rumor had it that his office was equipped with a direct phone line to his old company.

The monolithic Soviet oil and gas industry was broken into more manageable units and privatized in recent years, creating a group of giant firms that control vast natural and industrial resources.[22] Shares of privatized oil companies are among the top performers on the Russian stock market. Many firms are being absorbed into vertically integrated holding companies. To a great extent, this process is driven by the desire to reduce taxes. If an independent producer sells oil to an independent refinery, it incurs a tax liability, but if both belong to a holding, there is no tax on dealings within the firm. When a company is absorbed into a holding, its shares get exchanged for the holding company's shares.

LUKOIL

Lukoil is one of the largest vertically integrated oil companies in Russia and its stock is the quintessential Russian blue chip. Lukoil owns both upstream and downstream operations, has a unique, close relationship with federal and local governments, and is involved in an increasingly formalized alliance with Atlantic Richfield (ARCO) in the US. Lukoil's transparency of operations and the openness of investor relations make it stand out among Russian listed companies—which is why its shares tend to carry a premium over other oil and gas companies.

Formed in April 1993, Lukoil comprises seven oil extracting companies, two refineries, eleven wholesale and retail companies, and some 100 affiliate and joint venture companies. It employs over 100,000 people, and is headquartered in Moscow. Lukoil controls approximately 16% of Russia's oil reserves, pumps 21% of Russia's oil and refines 12% of the country's crude oil production. Lukoil has the largest proven reserves of any oil company in the world, and is

---

[22] Russian oil and gas company names usually start with the geographical name of their main operational area (Tomsk, Surgut, and so on) and end either with -neft (oil), -neftegas (oil and gas), or -prom (industry). NK stands for *Neftyanaya Kompania*, or Oil Company.

the fifth largest oil producer and the 18th largest oil refiner world-wide. Lukoil drills for oil and gas in Western Siberia, the Lower Volga river basin, the Baltic Shelf, and elsewhere, including Kazakhstan and other former Soviet Asian republics, as well as Tunisia and Egypt. It owns refineries in Perm and Volgograd and trades petroleum products both wholesale and retail.

Lukoil produced over 400 million barrels of crude in 1996 and refined about half of that. Russian oil companies typically produce more than they refine, in contrast to Western companies which tend to refine about 20% more than they produce thanks to outsourcing. Lukoil refineries are growing old, and the company plans to spend $1.1 billion on their modernization by the turn of the century.

Lukoil exports the Urals blend oil (the Urals are the mountains in Russia that separate Europe from Asia). The Urals blend is a mix of mainly Siberian and Volga-Urals oil. It is heavier and contains more sulfur than the European benchmark Brent blend. The Urals blend usually trades at a $1–$2 discount to the Brent blend.

An audit by the international firm of Miller & Lents in 1995 pegged Lukoil's proven and probable oil reserves at 1.8 billion tons of oil—the largest of any company worldwide. Those reserves can last for 35 years at its current production levels. Chevron, Mobil, Exxon, and Texaco have reserves amounting to only about 10 years at their current production levels. All major oil companies are actively exploring, looking for new reserves. Lukoil drilled nearly 200 miles of new wells in 1996 and discovered over 200 million barrels of fresh reserves.

Lukoil owns a chain of more than 700 gas stations that sell 83% of its petroleum, with the rest sold through independent dealers. The company has interests abroad. It not only exports about a third of its production, but also drills for oil outside of Russia and is setting up gas stations in other former Soviet republics and in Turkey. While this book was being completed, Lukoil announced an agreement to start building gas stations in the US that will sell gas in parking lots of American shopping malls!

Lukoil revenues increased from $1.7 billion in 1993 to $2 billion in 1994, then jumped to $4.6 billion in 1995 due to company acquisitions, and rose to nearly $10 billion in 1996. Lukoil is overburdened by too many employees—a legacy of the Soviet era. It produces 11 barrels of oil per day per employee, less than half the current international norm of 27 barrels per day per employee. Like almost all companies in Russia, Lukoil has the potential for major productivity gains in the years ahead.

Lukoil's price/earnings ratio was approximately 15 in 1996—higher than most domestic and even many international competitors. On that basis, Lukoil is fully valued, while on other comparison scales it is undervalued. Its price of $0.70 per barrel of reserves and $25 per barrel of production are sharply below the international norms of $6 and $81, respectively. While most international oil companies trade at a multiple of over 2 times net assets, Lukoil recently traded at a 40% discount.

As of August 1996, Lukoil issued 649,600 ordinary and 65,000 preferred shares which were held as follows:

HOLDERS	PERCENT OF TOTAL
Government	28%
Lukoil—Imperial Bank Consortium	5%
NIKoil	18%
Bank of New York	18%
Crawford Holdings	1%
Kinsel Investments	1%
CS First Boston	1%
Other non-Russian companies	5%
Other Russian companies	18%
Individuals	5%
Total	100%

Lukoil common shares (symbol LKOH) trade on the RTS. Its market capitalization is the second largest in Russia, after Gazprom. Lukoil preferred shares (symbol LKOHP) are also quoted on the

RTS, where at the beginning of 1997 they traded at a discount of almost 25% to ordinary shares.

In 1996 Lukoil became the first Russian company to issue Level 1 ADRs, and their holders now control over 10% of Lukoil shares. The company plans to place up to 15% of its shares on the New York Stock Exchange and the London Stock Exchange. In 1996 the Russian Exchange in Moscow began to trade futures on Lukoil shares. They became its most actively traded contract in 1997, trading at a much higher volume than the underlying stock (see Chapter 9).

SURGUTNEFTEGAS

Surgutneftegas (usually called Surgut) is Russia's sixth largest vertically integrated oil company in terms of reserves, third in production (after Lukoil and Yukos), and fifth in refining. Its operating style is starkly different from Lukoil's—a vertically integrated holding run with Western participation and a perennial favorite of Western investors. When you stand on the front steps of the Russian Exchange in Moscow, the word "Lukoil" in huge letters in English glows right above your head, crowning its headquarters in the financial district.

Surgutneftegas headquarters is almost 1,500 miles away in a provincial city of Surgut in the Tyumen Oblast in Western Siberia. The company is rich, secretive, and nationalistic; it likes to keep foreigners out. It prohibits foreign holders from owning more than 5% of its shares (although Russians have a scheme to circumvent almost any barrier, including this one). Foreign oil experts love to hate Surgut, which has little use for them. Its charismatic chairman, Vladimir Bogdanov, a man under 50, born in a local village, with an oil degree, who still lives with his wife in an ordinary apartment and walks to work, believes it does not pay to attract foreign capital because up to 82% of profit goes for taxes anyway. The foreigners get the company and the company gets very little.

Surgut can be secretive about releasing information at home as well as abroad. It still has not published a set of fully audited financials. Russian investors howled in October 1996 after Surgut issued new shares, watering down old ones by about 10%, and informed investors only two weeks after the fact. In response to complaints, Surgut formed an investor-relations department and committed itself to releasing quarterly financial and operating reports, but they are less complete than those of Lukoil and published only in Russian. Any investor who wants to buy more than 1% of equity has to be approved by the board of directors. The company charter was amended in 1996 to make those who hold more than 1% of equity to obtain management's permission before voting at any meeting. The company executives believe that they know what is best for Surgut—and they have the loyalty of their workers. While the Russian economy is plagued by nonpayment of salaries, and even the giant Gazprom is behind, all Surgut employees, more than 80,000 of them, are paid in full and on time.

Surgut, with 11% of Russia's total oil output, is the country's third largest oil producer and among the top ten in the world; it is also Russia's second largest gas producer, after Gazprom. The Russian State Committee for Geology estimates Surgut's oil reserves at 11.1 billion barrels, while Surgut pegs them at 22 billion barrels. No international audits have been conducted to resolve this discrepancy. The quality of Surgut's oil is average for Siberia, but its oil fields are particularly rich. According to the Ministry of Fuel and Energy, only 34.4% of Surgut's reserves have been exhausted, compared to the Russian average of 70–80%. Surgut has enough reserves to last 42 years at the current rate of production.

The company is actively exploring for oil and drilled 150 miles of exploratory wells in 1996. It actively recovers oil from existing fields by horizontal drilling. That technique is technologically demanding, but horizontal wells can be three to five times more productive than regular ones, according to Abzal Nurgazief, oil analyst at Troika Dialog, an investment bank in Moscow.

Surgut is one of Russia's top three oil exporters, accounting for more than 10% of the country's total oil exports. The company is building its own port on the Baltic Sea, not far from St. Petersburg on the Gulf of Finland. It wants to become self-sufficient and not pay for using the ports of newly independent Baltic nations of Estonia, Latvia, or Lithuania.

Surgut's refinery is located in the city of Kirishi in the Leningrad Oblast (region), not far from St. Petersburg.[23] The company controls wholesale and retail gasoline markets in the second most prosperous region in the European part of Russia, after Moscow. The firm is not above mixing up in local politics. After its well-publicized court battles surrounding Nefto-Kombi in St. Petersburg, it threw its weight to the opposition candidate and expressed public approval when the Leningrad Oblast elected a new governor in 1996.

It is taking Surgut a long time to vertically integrate its holding. NK Surgutneftegas is the holding company, while AO Surgutneftegas (AO stands for *Aktsionernoye Obschestvo* or joint stock company) is its oil-producing arm. The AO shares trade more actively than those of the corporate parent. A clutch of daughter companies are balking at integrating with a strong-willed parent—and Russian journalists keep joking about Surgut's "loose daughters." Now it looks like one of the girls is pregnant; it is trying to spin off its own subsidiary and list its shares.

Surgut has some 10 million shares outstanding, with 45% held by the state, 10% by employees, 5% by the management, and the rest is in the hands of investors—institutional and private, foreign and domestic. Surgut cleverly used its pension fund for privatization instead of attracting commercial banks as other oil companies did, and thus avoided giving away a piece of itself.

The Russian stock market, whose trading volume is dominated by foreign investors, always traded shares of pro-Western Lukoil at a premium and Surgut at a discount. It wasn't until 1996 that the stock market took a closer look at Surgut—and liked what it saw. Surgut shares have been outperforming Lukoil's since early 1996.

Mike Comerford, writing in *The Moscow Times*, was the first to point out publicly how undervalued Surgut was. Back in November 1995 he showed that while NK Surgut was valued at $170 million, the French-based oil giant Total—producing about the same amount

---

[23] Why is the city called St. Petersburg and its surrounding area the Leningrad Oblast? Russian Tsar Peter the Great founded the city in the 1700s and named it after his saint. The communists who grabbed power in 1917 dropped the "St." from the city's name and after Lenin's death in 1924 renamed it after him. After the collapse of the communist government in 1991, democrats gave the city its old name back, but communists still dominated the provincial government and did not change the name of the oblast.

of oil but with smaller reserves—was valued at $14 billion. That discrepancy narrowed after Surgut's shares rose in 1996 and 1997, but the company remains seriously undervalued by international standards and even by domestic ones.

Shares of AO Surgutneftegas trade on the RTS. The symbols are SNGS for the ordinary and SNGSP for the preferred. An ADR listing has been approved but no shares have been issued at the time of this writing, although by the time you read this they may well be traded.

GAZPROM

Gazprom is the world's largest natural gas company. It controls almost all of Russia's gas—22% of the world's reserves—and is responsible for 33% of world gas production. Gas is used mainly as fuel for generating electric power and heat. It is less expensive than oil and more environmentally friendly. The chemical industry is another major user of gas, primarily for making fertilizer.

Gazprom has a monopoly on exporting gas from Russia. It supplies much of Western Europe through its 90,000 mile network of pipelines. They run West from remote fields near the Arctic Ocean and in Western Siberia. Exports to Europe are currently the key source of Gazprom's income. In 1995 it supplied 21% of gas consumed in Western Europe and 55% in Eastern Europe. Gazprom's position allows it to tap into cheap secured loans in Western Europe, reducing its costs and increasing its competitive advantage in the struggle with Norwegian gas exporters, its chief European rivals. As Russia pulls out of the Depression of the 1990s, both the domestic demand for gas and the industry's ability to pay for it are likely to rise, boosting Gazprom's domestic revenues.

While Gazprom has a monopoly on exports, at home it deals only with the largest customers, representing about 20% of the country's demand. The rest are served by a company called Rosgazifikatsiya, which buys gas from Gazprom wholesale and resells it to industrial, municipal, and residential customers. The federal government owns 59.69% of Rosgazifikatsiya, the local governments 40%, and its employees 0.31%. Gazprom announced its intention to increase its share of the domestic market to 50%. Any company involved in the domestic markets will need to invest huge amounts to repair and replace aging leaky pipelines.

Gazprom's long-distance pipelines, built using European technologies, are quite efficient. The 1970s saw a rift between the US and several Western European nations over whether to sell the USSR the equipment for making large-diameter pipes (the US was against it, but the sale went through). The average transportation distance of Russian gas from a wellhead to a consumer is 1,600 miles. Gazprom consumes 10% of its own gas to power its pumping stations (US and Canada, with much shorter pipelines, consume 9% of their gas).

To increase the demand for gas, Gazprom encourages the transportation industry to use compressed and liquefied natural gas to fuel cars, trucks, planes, and trains. Rem Vyakhirev, the chairman of Gazprom's management committee, scored a publicity coup by converting his family car to natural gas. The country already has a network of 375 gas-fueling stations, enabling a properly equipped vehicle to travel from St. Petersburg to Moscow and on to the Ukraine. An airplane using natural gas is making flights between Moscow and Paris. Gazprom is trying to increase the demand for gas by helping construct gas-fired power stations abroad.

Gazprom owns an ocean shipping company, Gazflot, which is involved in platform drilling for gas. It owns a cargo airline, Gazpromavia, that serves its far-flung operations, and it also owns Gazprombank. Gazprom is likely to divest many of the operations in the future, allowing it to concentrate on its core business.

Gazprom is playing a large role in converting old Soviet military factories to civilian use. On the surface, the projects seem to make little economic sense. The military knows how to design and build things for short-term intensive use on the battlefield rather than long-term reliability needed by a gas company. Their costs are high and deliveries tardy. It would be more efficient to buy equipment abroad. Some military companies may become profitable in the future and be spun off for a profit, but Gazprom actually has more immediate reasons for using them. It does so as a part of "cooperation agreements" with local authorities in faraway regions. Gazprom boosts local economies by buying equipment and services from local companies (including underutilized defense factories) in exchange for the local authorities' help collecting receivables from Gazprom's local clients. Business can be very political during the transition from planned to market economy.

Gazprom has a major problem with bad receivables. They reached an astronomic sum of US$9.4 billion on July 1, 1996, and are probably higher as this chapter is being written. Gazprom, like all Russian oil and power companies, is being used by the government to soften the transition to a market economy by providing energy to industrial and residential customers at below world-market rates. The government sets prices low in order to avoid a collapse of industrial output and social unrest in the country famous for its long cold winters. In order to support agriculture, the government sets natural gas prices for the fertilizer industry at a 50% discount. As Russia pulls out of its Depression, both Gazprom's prices and collections are certain to rise, with a slingshot effect on company earnings.

Gazprom wields a great deal of political power in Russia. The recent Prime Minister Victor Chernomyrdin, Deputy Prime Minister Vladimir Babichev, and Fuel and Energy Minister Pyotr Rodionov are all former Gazprom executives. Gazprom is far behind on its tax payments, but the government prefers to direct its collection efforts at other offenders.

Gazprom's single largest debtor is the newly independent republic of the Ukraine. Gazprom is usually quick to cut off supplies to countries that fall behind on payments (as it recently did in Bosnia). It cannot afford to press the Ukraine for the simple reason that 95% of its pipelines to Western Europe pass through its territory and 50% of its gas storage facilities are on Ukrainian soil. The Ukraine taught Gazprom two expensive lessons in October 1992 and again in March 1993 by diverting enough gas to reduce Gazprom's European deliveries 20% below contracted levels. Gazprom is building a huge pipeline from the Yamal peninsula in the Arctic Ocean to Western Europe partly in order to bypass the Ukraine. The very first stages of that pipeline will allow Gazprom to pump half of its exports across Belarus—a former Soviet republic that is most interested in reuniting with Russia.

The highly ambitious Yamal-Europe pipeline for pumping gas from the Yamal peninsula in the Arctic to Europe is being built in stages, with the first slated for completion in 1997 and the last 15 or 20 years later. Each stretch of the new pipeline will be exploited as soon as it is completed, without waiting for the rest. Gazprom has to deal with an extremely difficult environment in the Far North: rivers, lakes, ice, floods, and permafrost. All infrastructure, including roads, has to be built from scratch. Most supplies have to be brought in by boat via the Arctic Ocean, where ice is so thick that icebreakers can cut through it only during the two summer months. The project will require an investment of US$36–40 billion.

Gazprom has a thousand accounting units run by six thousand accountants. To perform a GAAP audit, it retained Price Waterhouse, which committed a team of 70 accountants to the task. Gazprom's estimated net income in 1994 was US$1.6 billion on revenues of US$10.6 billion, rising to US$3.4 billion on revenues of US$15.9 billion in 1995. Gazprom issued 23.7 billion shares, with 40% held by the federal government, which plans to reduce its stake after 1999. Fifteen percent of shares were sold to workers and managers at preferential rates. Twenty-nine percent were sold at restricted auctions to residents of the regions where Gazprom operates. The remaining shares are held by investors. Foreign shareholders must obtain Gazprom's permission to buy its shares, and their total holdings are limited to 9% of the company's capitalization. Anyone who plans to acquire more than 3% of Gazprom's shares needs to get written permission from the company.

Gazprom cooked up an amazingly arrogant scheme—*chutzpah* is the financial term for it—whereby domestic investors wishing to sell their shares must first tender them to the company, which has 30 days to either buy them or allow the investor to sell on the open market. Imagine tendering your shares and waiting for 30 days, not knowing whether Gazprom will buy from you or permit you to sell to someone else, while prices fluctuate daily. Needless to say, Russians have a scheme for bypassing this requirement, but Gazprom keeps making ugly noises threatening to cancel shares sold without its participation, creating an added risk for many holders.

In October 1996 Gazprom became the first Russian company to be listed on the London Stock Exchange. Its American Depositary Shares (ADS) program sold slightly more than 1% of the firm to Western investors and raised more than $429 million. Each ADS represented ten domestic shares of Gazprom, and the company offered 27.25 million of them at $15.75 each. The London ADS issue was five times oversubscribed, and rose to the equivalent of $2.30 per share at the time when domestic shares were selling at $0.45. Foreigners were lining up to pay a premium of more than 400% to buy Gazprom shares!

Gazprom, with its roots in the monopolistic Gas Ministry of the Soviet Union, has been busily rebuilding a financial Iron Curtain. It does not allow foreigners to buy its domestic shares, only ADS in London. At a time when Gazprom's domestic shares sell for about 50 cents, its London ADS, each representing 10 shares, trade at $15, which comes to $1.50 a share, three times the domestic price. The giant Gazprom is straddling its homemade financial Iron Curtain, buying cheap domestic shares in enforced tenders and laughing at foreigners to whom it sells ADS in London at triple the domestic price.

Gazprom is a huge and successful corporation. It is a major player in Russia's economy and politics, as well as its financial markets. It is also the company that investors love to hate. They see it as a heavy-handed monopoly, crudely imposing its will on the financial markets—and the markets are fighting back.

A report from Salomon Brothers in 1996 stated there was a serious downside risk for any monopoly. As European gas markets become deregulated and Russians grow increasingly restive in their struggle to break up the few remaining monopolies, Gazprom is likely to face hard times. We should not underestimate its power, but this is a company where more bad news is likely in the future.

Gazprom trades on the RTS—the symbol for its ordinary shares is GAZP. Its ADS trade on the London Stock Exchange. Futures on Gazprom shares are listed, but their volume remains very low, as free-wheeling traders give a wide berth to this monopolist behemoth.

ANY TRADING TIPS?

This heading comes from a note written by a friend who reviewed an early draft of this chapter. "It's all very informative," she said, "but what should I buy?" It is a question I can answer today, as this chapter is being written, and hope to be able to answer again in the future, as the situation in Russia evolves. But since I do not know when you will open this book, the value of any specific advice may change drastically as time passes.

When a manuscript is delivered to the publisher, edited, and sent to a printer, the book, any book, freezes in time. Meanwhile, all around it life keeps changing, as new companies emerge in the spotlight and others fade away. I faced this problem, to a lesser extent, years ago, when I published a newsletter for traders. Markets can change drastically in the week between issues, to say nothing of the year or years since a book was written.

This and the subsequent three chapters are designed to show you how one investor goes about discovering fundamental values in the Russian market. The last two chapters of this book tell you how to structure an investment portfolio.

There is an old saying, "If you give a man a fish, you feed him for a day; but if you teach him how to fish, you feed him for life." Any fish I put on the table today may be stale and inedible by the time you open this book. On the other hand, good fishing rods and nets and instructions on how to use them may last a generation. Please keep this in mind as you read this and subsequent chapters.

11

THE RUSSIAN POWER SECTOR

Growing up in the Soviet Union, I kept seeing a painting—reproduced so often that, as Russians say, it rubbed your eyes to calluses. In the picture, a group of *muzhiki* (peasants) huddled in a dark country cabin around a young technician, their grimy, awestruck faces harshly lit by the glare of an electric bulb. That icon of Soviet realist art was called "Lenin's Bulb"; it celebrated the arrival of electric power in remote villages. As Lenin said, "The Soviet regime plus nationwide electricity equals socialism."

The Soviets did bring electricity to the entire country. They built a grid of hydroelectric, thermal, and nuclear power stations, including the one that blew up in Chernobyl, polluting vast territories and making them uninhabitable for generations to come. They accomplished a great deal in their ruthless push to industrialize, but had zero concern for the ecological and human cost of development. To this day, many Russian utilities keep damaging the environment and pay nothing for it. The growing green movement assures us they will be forced to pay after the economy improves.

After the communist regime collapsed, the new government privatized the nation's electrical power system. Russia now has 72 regional power utilities or "energos," regulated local monopolies providing electric power and heat to businesses and individuals. Almost all energos have some generating capacity, but some are net buyers, others net sellers of electricity. The giant Unified Energy System (UES) owns the largest thermal and hydroelectric power-generating stations, operates the nationwide high-voltage electricity grid, and manages the nationwide electricity wholesale market. It holds equity stakes of at least 49% in 69 out of 72 energos, making it the key player in the electric power industry. The government, in turn, owns more than half of UES shares. Stocks of energos and UES accounted for a third of the Russian stock market volume by early 1997. The third major component of the energy sector has no share ownership. It is Minatomenergo—in charge of Russia's nuclear power stations.

Russia's maximum electricity generating capacity of 205 GW (gigawatts) is second only to the US. UES controls almost half of that capacity, or 90 GW. The local energos own a third of total capacity, from the high of 13 GW for the largest to under 100 MW (megawatts) for the smallest, and the rest belong to Minatomenergo. Hydroelectric stations produce 20% of Russia's electrical power. It is the cheapest generating method, which gives a cost advantage to hydro-owning energos. The energos with the highest proportion of hydroelectric power are Dagenergo (99%), Kolenergo (86%), Krasnoyarskenergo (75%), and Irkutskenergo (70%). The first serves one of the poorest areas of the country, in Northern Caucasus, while Kolenergo serves Kola Peninsula north of St. Petersburg and the other two serve the richer areas of Siberia. Nuclear power stations generate 12% of Russia's power, and thermal stations produce the rest.

Russian utilities are suffering from a lack of maintenance, with the thermal power stations in the worst shape. The power industry, like much of the rest of the economy, is strapped for cash, but faces competition from the power industries of China and India when it tries to attract international lenders. Mosenergo and Lenenergo, serving the more prosperous areas of the country, have already lined up Western partners to help modernize their aging capacity.

All Russian energos produce and sell heat for industrial and residential use, along with electricity. Heat accounts for 30% to 70% of their sales. Companies use so-called cogenerating plants to catch heat that is a byproduct of generating electricity—a resource that is commonly wasted in the US. Central steam heating of factories and apartment buildings is much more prevalent in Russia than in the West. It is more efficient and less costly than local heating. The problem with the old Soviet technology is that it loses nearly 15% of heat in transit due to poor insulation.

Sellers of energy include UES-owned hydropower and thermal stations and Minatomenergo-owned nuclear stations. Twenty Russian energos are net producers of electricity, and seven of them sell it in the wholesale energy market. The Central Dispatching Unit of UES can refuse to buy power at high prices, forcing producers to reduce costs and boost efficiency.

UES is in charge of assuring a stable supply of electricity throughout Russia and equalizing prices. It combines local energos into seven regional grids, each with its own average purchase price. UES plans to reduce those grids to two—one for the European part of the country and the Urals region, the other for Siberia and the Far East.

In a huge country spread across 11 time zones, UES directs the flow of electricity between regions, as their demands shift throughout the day and night. The demand for power changes around the clock, while production is relatively constant. A nuclear station cannot turn down volume when people turn off their lights at night. UES allows the industry to operate more efficiently by switching electricity between time zones. Only 4% of Russian electricity is stored on the grid at any given time—more efficient than the US where the comparable figure is 25%.

The Soviet Union used to have a rapist's approach to natural resources, and its energy use was wildly inefficient. Russia has inherited old technology, and to this day consumes 1.8 kilowatt-hours of electric power for every dollar of GDP, compared to 0.90 kWh/$ in Canada, 0.45 kWh/$ in the US, and only 0.24 kWh/$ in Germany. Russia loses 8% of its electric energy in transmission. These inefficiencies will lead to major savings in the future, as the free market creates incentives to reduce costs. When Russia's industries recover, their power consumption is likely to increase proportionately less, as power-saving technologies are installed.

The patterns of electric power usage in Russia are different from the West. Industry uses 55% of all electricity consumed in the country, followed by the public sector and residential users with

11% each, then 8% by agriculture and 7% by transport, while a whopping 8% is lost. In the US, industry consumes only 27% of electricity, less than residential users. Russia's residential per capita consumption is less than half that of the US—6,000 kWh in 1996, compared to more than 12,000 kWh in the US. Russians had been starved of consumer goods for generations. They are just now starting to buy color TVs, electric blankets, breadmakers, toasters, air conditioners and the rest of the electricity-consuming gadgetry that creates such a high demand for electricity in the West. A surge in building construction is adding to the residential demand for energy.

Russia exports electricity to all its neighbors—Finland, the Baltics, Ukraine, Belarus, Mongolia, China, and so on. Those exports bring little profit, as most long-term contracts were negotiated by the old Soviet government, which cared more for scoring political points than making profits. Russian electricity exports are likely to become more profitable as old contracts expire and new ones are negotiated. Russia plans to integrate itself into the world electricity system by participating in four "energy bridges"—to Scandinavia, Germany, Turkey, and North America.

The power sector remains one of the very few industries in Russia with prices tightly controlled by the government. It keeps a lid on rates so as not to undermine Russia's economic recovery. Russia's electricity rates are 45% below the US and 90% below Germany. The Russian Federal Energy Commission (FEC) sets wholesale rates each quarter for each power provider based on a cost-plus formula. Regional Energy Commissions regulate local rates in retail energy markets. Those rates cover transmission, distribution, and maintenance costs, so that end-users pay about double the wholesale price.

Residential rates are higher than industrial rates in most developed countries, reflecting higher distribution costs and the price of transforming high-voltage electricity into domestic current. In Russia, the opposite is true. Residential prices are set at about 75% discount from the industrial rates, as the system subsidizes residential and agricultural users. Regulators announced they are only waiting for an improvement in Russia's economy and wages before raising residential rates. A series of residential price hikes is definitely coming; the only question is how soon.

Russia's energy market is burdened with a huge nonpayment problem. Nonpayments have plagued most sectors of the Russian economy since prices were freed in 1992, but the energy sector was hit the hardest. Russian legislation prohibits energos from cutting off electricity to most customers, even those who significantly delay payments. In 1995, only 77% of electricity consumed was paid for, and this ratio fell below 50% in February 1996. By then, the electricity industry was a net creditor of over $2 billion. With real interest rates reaching high double and even triple digits, this amounted to a massive subsidy from electricity producers to the rest of the economy.

Energos try to make up for those losses by using their monopoly position as suppliers of heat to the industry. They can get away with charging higher prices for heat, as there are no restrictions on suspending heat to delinquent industrial customers. The energy industry holds a large volume of *veksels* (see Chapter 7) from industrial customers and receives up to 70% of its payments on a barter basis. Most energos try to stimulate payments by setting special rates at only slightly above cost for industrial users who pay on time and in cash. The problem of nonpayments will only be solved after the overall economy improves.

The stock market has amply reflected the optimism of investors towards Russia's power industry. This sector's shares gained 270% in the bull market of 1996, outperforming the broad averages. Mosenergo was a spectacular performer, rising more than fourfold, from 18 cents a share to over a dollar in four months. With the first waves of investments lifting the blue chips, many lesser energos remain deeply undervalued, with P/E ratios of three or lower in the first half of 1997. Most energy companies issued preferred shares with the dividend rate of 10% of the company's net profit, and those tend to sell at discounts of about 60% from prices of ordinary shares.

UNIFIED ENERGY SYSTEM

UES owns Russia's major thermal and hydropower stations, operates the nationwide high-voltage energy grid, and holds stakes in 69 out of 72 regional energos. UES owns 57 GW of electricity-generating capacity out of Russia's total of 205 GW, while controlling a total of 90 GW through its equity in local energos. The Russian government holds the controlling block of UES shares and uses this company to represent its interests in the power sector. Its capitalization makes it one of the largest Russian publicly traded companies—a true blue chip on the Russian stock market.

UES plays the central role in the Russian power sector thanks to its ownership of all high-voltage transmission lines in Russia—more than 1.5 million miles. The company controls the energos' access to the wholesale market through its central and regional dispatching units and holds stakes of 49% or more in almost all energos. UES influences energos' investment and business policies, helps set development strategies, and distributes investment funds. It has a powerful presence on the Federal Energy Commission and all the regional commissions, setting electricity and heat rates. UES holds stakes in several banks and over 300 construction firms.

The main source of UES income is the hook-up fee it charges local energos for using its high-voltage lines. Those fees accounted for 94% of its income in 1996, with another 4% coming from the UES-owned power stations and 2% from dividends on holdings in energos and subsidiaries. The hook-up income amounted to $1.3 billion in 1995, but nonpayments were a serious problem; in 1995 only 76% of UES invoices had been paid.

The main costs of UES are its payments to the energy industry. In 1995 UES spent 72% of its income by distributing funds among energos and power stations for maintaining and expanding capacity. That percentage tends to remain stable from year to year. UES used 11% of its income to maintain its own power lines and the Central Dispatching Unit.

The future of UES as an investment is tied closely to the cause of deregulation in Russia. The Russian government, with the assistance of the World Bank, has developed a plan for deregulating its energy market. As the economy improves and the government's tight control of energy loosens, UES will profit from its central role in Russia's power markets.

UES has 43.1 billion shares outstanding, 95% of which are ordinary and 5% preferred. The major shareholder is the government, which held 55.9% of UES ordinary shares at the beginning of 1997. Foreign institutional investors held 18.7%, domestic institutions 17%, and individuals held the rest. The government plans to reduce its stake in UES to 51% by the end of the century.

UES shares trade on the RTS; the symbol is EESR for ordinary shares and EESRP for preferred shares. In 1996 UES received approval from the SEC in the US for a Level 1 ADR issue. At the time of this writing, Price Waterhouse was conducting a GAAP audit of the company.

MOSENERGO

Regional energy company Mosenergo produces and distributes electricity and heat in Moscow and Moscow Oblast (region)—the richest and most dynamic area of the country. Real estate investors say there are three main factors in business: location, location, and location. If this applies to energy companies serving that real estate, then Mosenergo has the best location of all Russian energos.

Over 15 million people live in the city of Moscow and the Moscow Oblast—about 10% of Russia's population—but the city and oblast account for a disproportionately high share of industry and wealth. Moscow is to Russia what Hong Kong is to China—a financial and business dynamo. For example, two thirds of Russian banking capital is in Moscow. The population of Moscow has the highest purchasing power in the country. Skyrocketing sales of new electrical appliances and a construction boom in the city and its oblast are fueling an increase in the demand for power.

Mosenergo's annual production fell 20% between 1991 and 1993, as the region suffered in the Depression. It bottomed out and turned up ahead of the rest of the country; the area's consumption of electricity started to rise in 1994. Mosenergo derives 70% of its income from electricity and 30% from heat. Industry buys 25% of its energy and consumers 14%, with the rest split between government, transportation, wholesalers, and agriculture.

Mosenergo produces 10% of Russia's electricity and 13% of its heat; it is the second largest energo in the country, after the Siberian giant Irkutskenergo. Mosenergo owns 11.5 GW of production capacity and leases an additional 3 GW from UES. It produces 1 GW at its hydroelectric power station and the rest at 21 thermal power stations and 16 cogeneration plants. Mosenergo is a net producer of electricity and sells approximately 20% of its output on Russia's wholesale energy market.

Natural gas represents 91% of Mosenergo power plant fuel. It is more energy-efficient and ecologically cleaner than oil. Fuel accounts for 59% of Mosenergo's costs, and the company is working to improve its efficiency and reduce the amount of fuel it needs to produce a unit of electricity. Mosenergo pays its bills promptly, and Gazprom rewards it by charging the lowest rates. While Moscow's demand for power is down from its pre-Depression peak, Mosenergo, currently working at 57% of maximum capacity, is getting ready to meet a future increase in demand. It is installing modern gas turbines and plans to invest about $500 million per year over the next four years in modernization and development. The company employs more than 50,000 persons.

In 1996 Mosenergo became the first Russian blue chip to release financial results audited in accordance with GAAP. Audits by Arthur Andersen and KPMG Peat Marwick showed that profits grew from $129 million in 1994 to approximately $400 million in 1996, even though the company was hit by the nationwide nonpayment problem. It was paid for only 69% of its production in 1996, but half of those payments were in barter. Other energos received up to 80% of payments from their industrial customers in barter, and were forced to waste time and money selling bartered merchandise at a discount. Mosenergo's profitability is likely to increase thanks to improved efficiency, better collections, increased demand, and the coming residential rate hikes. Its industrial rates are unlikely to rise substantially, as they are already at European levels.

Mosenergo issued 2,560 million shares, of which UES holds 49%, foreign institutions 28%, domestic institutions 19%, and individuals hold the rest. Mosenergo trades on the RTS (symbol MSNG). There are no preferred shares. Mosenergo shares have been among the top performers in the Russian stock market. Futures on Mosenergo shares are actively traded on the Russian Exchange (see Chapter 9).

12

THE RUSSIAN
TELECOMMUNICATIONS
SECTOR

I had a friend in Moscow before I jumped ship who was my main supplier of *samizdat*—forbidden underground literature. Igor Guberman, a poet who later became a *politicheskiy* prisoner, told me how he got a phone installed in his apartment. At 17, Igor and his friend both fell in love with the same girl. The girl chose the other teenager, and Igor blamed his loss on not having a phone. The parents of the girl and the other boy had phones, so those kids could talk to each other whenever they wanted, putting Igor at a disadvantage. Smarting from his loss, Igor took a bus to a city office and applied for a phone. Sixteen years later, when Igor was 33 and on his second marriage, a notice came in the mail—his application had been approved. He could get a phone installed after paying the equivalent of $2. This true story helps explain why telecommunications are booming in postcommunist Russia.

Telecoms (this term is used worldwide, while in the US the usual term is telephones) are among the hottest investments in Russia today. The market is fairly open, lightly regulated, and serves 150 million potential customers, most of whom are starved for service. The demand is huge, with waiting lists of 10 years or longer. The outdated system cannot accommodate customers fast enough. A good indicator of demand is the cost of rapid phone installations. In Moscow in

1995 you could jump to the head of the waiting list and have a phone installed in just a few days by paying $1,000. At that time, the average monthly salary was between $100 and $150. The demand was so high that this fee was tripled, raised to $3,000 in 1997, even though the average salary had only risen to perhaps $250/month.

Today, Russia has 18 telephone lines per 100 people. Professionals refer to this as a teledensity ratio of 18/100. This is less than a third of the US 56/100 ratio, and less than half of the 49/100 ratio for all developed countries. What does the future hold? If you expect Russia to remain mired in post-Soviet muck, then its current teledensity is already high enough, above the 10/100 world average. If, on the other hand, you think that Russia is about to advance into the ranks of modern industrialized countries, you can expect the size of its telecoms market to double or triple, creating vast profit opportunities.

City people demand more phone services than the country folk. Russia is an urban country—some 73% of its population live in cities. Moscow has the highest teledensity, with 44 lines per 100 population, close to the industrialized world average. The next three best-served cities are St. Petersburg with 36/100, Novosibirsk with 28/100, and Murmansk with 16/100. Russian telecoms are technologically backward, but they represent valuable franchises. Local telecoms are attractive because any type of service or development within their region must involve them. They are being courted and offered favorable terms by foreign firms, who want to develop and use their infrastructure. International investors are actively improving and expanding Russia's international networks, satellite networks, data transmission, and other services.

Russia has a shortage of phone lines because the Soviets had underinvested in the industry for decades. The KGB did not want people talking to each other too much. Much of Russia's telephone equipment is obsolete—some local stations still use switches installed 50 years ago! Most of that old gear cannot interface with modern technologies. Only 15% of Russia's lines are digital. The transmission quality is poor and the rate of call completion is low. Whenever I work in Moscow, I am appalled by the daily incidence of bad connections, both for incoming and outgoing calls, crossed lines, hissing, and noise.

Up until 1990, the Soviet Ministry of Posts and Telecommunications was responsible for the country's phone system, with the military and the KGB controlling many of its key aspects. In 1992, the newly formed giant Sovtelecom was put in charge, but when the Soviet Union disintegrated the Russian phone services were privatized. The reformist government broke the industry into more manageable segments by creating 89 local providers,[24] plus one large firm, Rostelecom. The latter handles most long-distance traffic, both domestic and international, splitting its revenues with local telecoms. During privatization, the government took 51% of common shares, employees and management received all the preferred shares and 15% of common shares, and the remainder was sold at public auctions.

Local phone rates in Russia are well below international levels. Most customers pay a flat monthly rate—there is virtually no metered local service. Four out of five phones are residential, but they provide only 10% of local telecoms' revenues. Forty percent of revenues come from local calls by businesses, also unmetered but paying much higher rates. Charges for local calls provide half of telecoms' revenues; the other half comes from Rostelecom for handling the local end of long-distance calls, most of which are also made by businesses.

Telecoms suffer relatively little from Russia's nonpayment crisis because the law permits them to disconnect most nonpayers, except for government agencies, including schools, hospitals, police, and so on. For example, in 1996 Nizhnovsvyazinform collected 77% of its bills in cash or equivalents, 3.6% in barter, 5.1% in *veksels*, and 14.3% were bad debts. During that same year the energos, which were not allowed to interrupt service to nonpayers, received only 11% in cash and equivalents, 64% in barter, 2% in *veksels*, and 23% were bad debts. Companies that are paid in carloads of steel or beef carcasses have to waste time and energy trying to turn bartered goods into cash or supplies, while telecoms can concentrate on their primary business.

The Russian telecom industry has set "mass telefonization" as its first goal. It plans to increase the average phone density to 30 access lines per 100 inhabitants by the year 2004 or 2007. After

---

[24] Local companies are usually called by their geographic name plus either *Electrosvyaz* (electronic communication) or *Svyazinform* (communication information).

accomplishing that goal the industry plans to shift its primary focus to modernizing its equipment and broadening its range of services. That process has already begun in the more economically advanced parts of the country, such as Moscow. Modernization usually takes place first in international services, then domestic long distance, followed by local services.

Russia has a rapidly developing cellular phone market, with over 140,000 subscribers at the end of 1996. Cellular services in Russia are based on three standards: NMT-450, AMPS/DAMPS-800, and GSM-900. Two of them, NMT and GSM, have federal status and stand to benefit from state support. Remote regions usually have a single provider, while large cities have several. Most cellular customers are in Moscow and St. Petersburg, but their numbers are kept down by exceedingly high rates. Early in 1997, it costs about $1,000 to get a number, another $1,000 for a cell phone, and then there is a monthly bill, often padded by creative billing, that could easily exceed $1,000. Because of such exorbitant rates, Moscow, with a population of eight million, has the same number of cellular phones as the tiny ex-Soviet republic of Estonia, with 1.6 million population. The number of cellular subscribers is sure to grow as competition drives prices down.

The telecom industry will grow quickly with the addition of more access lines, more services, increased traffic, and higher domestic rates. Stocks of many regional telecoms remain undervalued compared to those in Moscow and St. Petersburg, even though regional telecoms tend to have higher revenues per line. The largest immediate drawback for all telecoms is the looming question of Svyazinvest. Its resolution will clear the atmosphere in this sector of the economy.

SVYAZINVEST

This is a huge state holding company with no operational capability, but a great ability to throw a monkey wrench into any Russian telecom it chooses to fight. Svyazinvest was established in 1995 by a presidential decree with the idea of turning the government stake in telecoms into ready cash, while maintaining the Kremlin's control of the industry.

After the phone industry was privatized in the early 90s, the government held about 51% of the voting shares in each local telecom as well as in the long-distance giant Rostelecom. In 1995, it consolidated its stake in all of these companies by transferring its shares to Svyazinvest. It wanted Svyazinvest to issue its own shares, sell 49% of them to investors, and turn the money over to the government. The government would receive billions, and still control the industry through its 51% stake in Svyazinvest which, in turn, would control telecoms through its 51% stake in each company, while also performing some unspecified central role in running the industry.

That scheme had a dash of brilliance, but was poorly planned and bogged down. Svyazinvest was granted a unique broad license to provide both local and long-distance service, both domestic and international, but it has made no use of it. After receiving a 51% stake in the nation's telecom industry it went to work—with a staff of four! Its staff has grown to over 200 by mid-1997, but Svyazinvest, with all its licenses and mandates did nothing for the telecom industry, other than create a layer of uncertainty.

By offering shares in Svyazinvest, the government thought it could bundle the cats and dogs among telecoms with better companies. It would not allow large investors to cherry-pick companies they wanted. They would have to take shares in Svyazinvest, representing all telecoms, or stay home. But the government could not decide what its share of the telecom industry was worth and how much it could realistically receive.

In 1995 the giant Italian telecom STET agreed to buy a 25% stake in Svyazinvest for $640 million and invest $760 million in the industry, for a total of $1.4 billion. STET wanted to put those funds in escrow until certain agreed-upon conditions had been met, but Russian bureaucrats wanted the money turned over to them unconditionally, and the Italians withdrew. The following year, a consortium of Western investment banks was retained to sell a portion of Svyazinvest. They got tossed out after some well-connected Russian bankers who supported the President in his 1996 election campaign complained that underwriting fees should go to them. The Russian bankers did not get the job either.

Svyazinvest is rich on paper but has little cash. When a prosperous local telecom wants to issue more shares, Svyazinvest has a right to buy a portion of that issue in order to maintain its stake at the 51% level or block the offering. That's exactly what it does. Since it has no money, it blocks telecoms from issuing more equity, like the proverbial dog on a pile of hay that does not eat it itself and does not let others eat it. Until the Svyazinvest situation is resolved, the Russian telecom industry will suffer from a needless level of uncertainty. Local telecoms have had enough of it by now. Many of them have excellent political connections and are lobbying at the highest political levels to resolve the Svyazinvest situation.[25]

ROSTELECOM

If you wanted to make an international call during the communist era, you had to place it through an operator and wait for several hours. The phone system was tightly controlled by the KGB, which limited the number of international calls to the number of agents available to listen in on them.

A person who glimpsed the KGB eavesdropping center at Moscow's main post office in the mid-80s wrote that it could handle 12 simultaneous international calls. The crack in the Iron Curtain was narrow and tightly controlled—12 foreign calls at any given time for the capital region with a population of 15 million! The communists dammed up communications at home as well as abroad. To make a domestic long-distance call, you had to go to the post office, buy a coupon, place your call through an operator, and assume that the KGB could well be listening in.[26] A friend of mine

---

[25] Before this book was published, an announcement came out that a major packet of shares in *Svyazinvest* was sold to a partnership that included a leading Russian bank and George Soros' organization. One of the leading speculators of our era has put a good chunk of his money into Russian telecoms.

[26] KGB eavesdropping deserves its own book. Back in the 1980s the KGB, eager to keep its fingers on the pulse of "social deviants," even bugged the mental health lines that had just begun to spring up in the country. Solzhenitsyn's book *The First Circle* turned on a phone call taped by the KGB and identified by one of the inmates at a secret research center.

called Moscow from his Siberian exile and began to speak Estonian when an operator came on the line and ordered him to speak Russian or get disconnected.

The restrictions on phone calls were swept away by the collapse of the communist system. Today, Rostelecom, the country's primary provider of long-distance services, is benefiting from the slingshot effect of catching up with the West. It finds itself in a key position to profit from the upswing in the Russian economy.

Most phone users in Russia have limited access to long distance—now restricted by backward technology rather than by the KGB. In the countryside, only about a third of phone lines have access to long-distance calls. A Westerner accustomed to picking up his phone and dialing any number in the world may be surprised to hear that in Russia a dial tone in many cases allows you to make only local calls. To make a long-distance call outside of technologically advanced Moscow and St. Petersburg, a Russian still has to go to the long-distance center and place his or her call through an operator. This situation keeps improving, and, as more people get access to long distance, Rostelecom benefits.

Rostelecom does not own any lines to consumers—they belong to local telecoms. It does own 250 million miles of intercity cables, giving it a competitive edge. Landlines are more reliable than satellite connections and have a much greater capacity than the transponders on geo-stationary satellites.

Most Rostelecom lines are still analog—only 30% of them are digital—but the company is working with several international partners in order to go fully digital. Rostelecom owns, leases, and operates satellite channels and digital data-transmission networks, as well as radio and TV stations. The latter are likely to be spun off in the future, as the company concentrates on its core business.

Rostelecom handles 93% of Russia's domestic and international long-distance phone traffic. It derives 90% of its income from those calls, but splits most revenues with local telecoms. Rostelecom keeps 100% of the Russian share of revenues for incoming and 50% for outgoing international calls. It pays between 55 and 88% of its revenues for domestic long-distance calls to local telecoms for handling the local end of international calls. Rostelecom is working to increase its share of revenues for domestic long-distance calls to the world standard of 40–45%.

Rostelecom's incoming international traffic grew from 268 million minutes in 1993 to 404 million minutes in 1995, while outgoing traffic during that time rose from 201 to 234 million minutes. Germany and the US accounted for about one third of those calls, with the rest divided between other countries. International calls are expensive in Russia—one minute from Moscow to New York used to cost $2.67, before declining to the current $2.10. Rostelecom knows it has overpriced its international services and has begun to lower its rates. Kallback-type services are popular, but Rostelecom seems not to mind, since it receives hard currency payments for incoming international calls and, thanks to a quirk in Russian law, finds it easier to use that money for purchases abroad.

Rostelecom's income from domestic long-distance calls has been growing lately at a sluggish 1–3% per year. Only two thirds of Rostelecom's domestic network is considered in working order, but that has not prevented the company from raising domestic rates 79% in dollar terms between 1994 and 1996. Local users are more price-sensitive than foreigners and resist paying Rostelecom's rates, which can be higher between two local cities than an overseas call. Rostelecom knows it must upgrade its services and lower prices in order to experience domestic growth.

Rostelecom expects its share of the long-distance market to decline from 90 to 80% by the end of this century, as more competitors invade its turf. Among them are foreign joint ventures, which are becoming increasingly active, especially in Moscow and St. Petersburg. Since many of those companies lease Rostelecom's lines, their prices are higher, but so is their quality. They are giving a competitive spur to Rostelecom, which is working with foreign partners to lay high-speed fiber-optic cable and install digital telephone exchanges.

Rostelecom finds it easy to obtain credits for equipment purchases from most Western suppliers, including Alcatel, Nokia, Siemens, and many others. It has been planning to float a $100 million Eurobond issue in 1997 and issue ADRs, but the uncertainty over Svyazinvest has slowed down those plans. The government transferred its Rostelecom shares to Svyazinvest, throwing them into the same basket as the local telecoms.

When Rostelecom was privatized in 1993, nearly 200 million shares were issued and later split 5:1. One quarter of those shares were preferred, and given to employees, entitling them to a fixed dividend of at least 10% of the gross profit. By the end of 1996, slightly less than half of the preferred shares were still held by the employees, while the rest were bought up ("sucked up" in the parlance of Russian brokers) by foreign investors. As for ordinary shares, 51% are held by the state through Svyazinvest, 30% by foreign investors, 15% by domestic investors, and 4% by management and employees.

Rostelecom's P/E ratio of 7.5 for 1996 (calculated in accordance with RAS, Russian Accounting Standards) is below Russia's telecom average of 9.9 (which includes stocks with a high of 18.5 to a low of 4.0). Rostelecom's P/E calculated in accordance with IAS (International Accounting Standards) is also close to 7.5, less than half of the world's average for this industry.

Rostelecom's shares trade on the RTS, symbol RTKM for ordinary shares and RTKMP for preferred. The Russian Exchange offers futures on Rostelecom—each contract covers 100 shares. Rostelecom has been audited by Coopers & Lybrand since 1994 under IAS. Once its 1996 results become available, Rostelecom will be eligible under SEC rules to issue Level 3 ADRs and raise capital in the US markets.[27]

MGTS

MGTS (*Moskovskaya Gorodskaya Telefonnaya Set* or Moscow City Telephone Net) is the monopoly provider of all local phone services in Moscow. It is one of the oldest publicly owned companies in the country—established in 1882, stolen by the communists in 1917, and privatized in 1995. MGTS has over 4 million lines, making it the largest local telecom in Russia. The second largest, in St. Petersburg,

---

[27] Rostelecom shares were listed in the US just as this book was being prepared for publication.

has fewer than two million lines, followed by Krasnoyarsk and Nizhny Novgorod with half a million lines each. MGTS is the fifth largest telecom worldwide in terms of the number of processed calls.

MGTS serves a thriving financial and business metropolis of over 8 million people, providing them with teledensity at nearly Western levels. While other Russian telecoms are racing to install new lines, MGTS announced in 1996 that it will direct most of its resources toward upgrading and modernizing its existing network.

This company serves the richest market in the country, but its earnings and profits per line are below almost every other telecom in Russia. This is due to a legal quirk that shuts MGTS out of the lucrative long-distance business. Local telecoms receive about half of Rostelecom's long-distance revenues for handling the local end of long-distance calls. MGTS, like its counterparts in St. Petersburg, Ekaterinburg, and a handful of other cities, is shut out of this profitable long-distance business. Moscow's other local company, MMMT, was set up to provide access to long-distance services, both international and domestic, by switching calls between MGTS and Rostelecom. As a result, MGTS receives only about 10% of revenues from most long-distance calls, a tiny fraction of the 50+% share most other local telecoms get.

The only positive aspect of its being largely deprived of long-distance revenues is that MGTS runs its local business more efficiently. Local rates in Moscow are certain to increase, as the company shifts from flat rate to metered service. MGTS is working to diversify into advanced services—it has invested in 14 related local companies, such as cell phones and digital cable.

MGTS trades on the RTS; its symbol is MGTS for ordinary and MGTSP for preferred shares. At the end of 1996 MGTS had 957,950 common and 319,317 preferred shares. Svyazinvest, representing the Russian government, held 46.7% of voting shares, the agency of the Moscow city government held 22%, while employees held 10% and management 5% of common shares; the rest are held by various investors. Employees owned the majority of preferred shares. MGTS appointed Coopers & Lybrand to perform an IAS audit, widely seen as a precursor to floating bonds or equity in the international capital markets.

MMMT

MMMT (*Moskovskiy Mezhdugorodny i Mezhdunarodniy Telefon* or Moscow Intercity and International Telephone) is in a lucrative business of switching international and domestic long-distance calls between Moscow's local telecom MGTS and the long-distance giant Rostelecom. MMMT processes 1.5 million phone calls daily, and a huge flow of cash passes through its hands. The company pads its profits by requiring customers to prepay their bills or else pay a surcharge of 5% on residential and 25% on business accounts.

MMMT is raking in the money, but finds itself under growing pressure from both Rostelecom and MGTS which want to eliminate this middleman. Both companies want to fold MMMT into themselves, but its managers are fighting for survival by calling on their allies in Svyazinvest, which acts as a defender of the status quo. MMMT is an example of a company that operates in a capitalist environment using old Soviet methods, such as commandeering economic resources by lobbying the state rather than performing a useful service.

Almost 86% of MMMT revenue comes from Rostelecom, which tried to take it over in 1996 before being told to quit by Svyazinvest whose 51% stake in all Russian telecoms gives its enormous power in the industry. After that battle ended, Rostelecom pledged to abandon any takeover attempts for the next five years. Recently, after the government transferred its Rostelecom stake to Svyazinvest, putting it in the same basket with MMMT, the possibility of a takeover has become greater. The MMMT management is scrambling to prevent a takeover and save their jobs. They diversified the company into cellular services and the Internet, set up their own bank, and split their shares, increasing the float 78 times.

MMMT shares trade on the RTS. Rostelecom had hired Coopers & Lybrand to audit MMMT, but its managers tossed the auditors out and stuck to Russian accounting, meaning that an ADR issue is highly unlikely. As Anton Inshutin, a telecoms analyst at CentreInvest Group in Moscow put it, MMMT is a cash cow with very mean horns. This is a type of company that only a politically savvy and extremely well-informed local investor or trader should ever touch.

Vimpelcom

The word *vimpel* means pennant in Russian, and this company has certainly earned one for developing cellular service in Moscow and raising money in the US. Vimpel is a smallish cellular phone company with 56,000 subscribers, primarily in Moscow. Thanks to its superlative political connections in the old military-industrial and security complex, it was the first to obtain all the necessary licenses and radio frequencies for cellular services. Any Muscovite who is not blind or deaf is inundated with Vimpel's ubiquitous advertisements for its trademark Beeline service.

Vimpel took a unique path to the capital markets. All other publicly traded companies in Russia first listed their shares on the RTS, then got themselves audited according to either GAAP or IAS, then issued Level 1 ADRs abroad and are now waiting for the statutory 3 years of audits to issue Level 3 ADRs. Vimpel, on the other hand, got funded, audited, and made its market debut on the New York Stock Exchange in December 1996 with a Level 3 ADR. Its share price (or rather the price of its ADS—American Depositary Shares—each equal to ¾ of an ordinary share) soared within a week from $17.50 to $29 and its market capitalization rose to $750 million, almost a third of the vastly larger Rostelecom. The company brought Russian dancing girls to the New York Stock Exchange on its first trading day, and this Russian beauty was an instant hit on Wall Street.

Russian investors, while admiring Vimpel for its savvy in tapping Western pockets, have been decidedly less sanguine about its value as an investment. Vimpel, listed on the RTS and boasting its own market maker, sometimes goes for two weeks without a single trade and is considered a very minor stock. Convenience comes at a high price—Americans are paying a lot for a listed company, while much better values exist in Russia.

Nizhnovsvyazinform

This company is the local monopolist in the Nizhegorodskaya Oblast (region) in Central Russia. It is one of Russia's most industrialized regions, with auto plants, oil refineries, shipbuilding industry, and pulp and paper companies. There are 3.7 million people living in the *oblast*, 2.9 million of them in the cities, including 1.4 million in Nizhny Novgorod, Russia's third largest city. This region is one of the most prosperous and well-run areas of Russia. Its municipal paper recently received the highest possible ratings from both Moody's and Standard & Poor's (see Chapter 7).

Nizhnovsvyazinform (often called Nizhnov) provides local phone service and connections for international and domestic long distance calls, while also operating radio stations and telegraph. By the end of 1996 the company had over 9,500 employees and served 651,000 access lines. It reduced its waiting list from 350,000 in 1993 to 280,000 in 1996 and bought enough equipment to add another 60,000 lines in 1997. Twenty percent of Nizhnov's network is digital. It is running joint ventures with NEC and Alcatel to install fiber-optic cable and take the entire company digital.

Most of Nizhnov's customers are residential (80% in the cities and 67% in the country), but the company receives most of its income from businesses. Business customers make Nizhnov profitable today, while its residential customers promise a greater profitability in the future, after the company is allowed to raise its rates.

Nizhnov charges all customers a fixed monthly rate for unlimited local service. Its local residential rates are set at just 20% of business rates but are steadily increasing. They rose from $1.80 per month in April 1995 to $3.60 per month in January 1997, outstripping the inflation rate, and regulators promise one or two increases every year. Domestic long-distance calls, most of them made by businesses, bring Nizhnov the lion's share of its revenues. The company receives 57% of all charges for outgoing and 20% for incoming long-distance calls. The number of international calls is likely to grow as this region becomes integrated into the world economy.

Nizhnov has no problems financing its growth. Most major suppliers, such as Alcatel, NEC, and others eagerly finance its purchases at LIBOR. The company also raises funds by selling so-called "phone bonds," offering only 3.5% annual interest rate but entitling their holder to a quick installation of a new telephone. Nizhnov auctions off the rights to rapid installations. A standard installation, for which a customer has to wait for several years, costs $160 for a residential phone and $540 for a business phone, but you can have your phone installed in just a few days by paying $2,000 (more than a year's income for most locals).

Nizhnovsvyazinform is an equal partner with a subsidiary of US West in Nizhegorodskaya Cellular Communications. This company offers the world's most advanced GSM-900 standard but its cellular service is not cheap—$800 to $1,200 to sign up, and then up to $0.72 per minute. The company also provides paging services and access to satellite channels.

In 1996 Nizhnov earned over $30 million in profits on over $90 million in revenues. The company has over 87 million common shares and over 29 million preferred shares, with 26% of shares held by foreign investors. The June 1996 shareholders meeting authorized the board of directors to issue another 29 million of common shares, provided they obtain the agreement of all shareholders holding more than 10% of shares. Svyazinvest is blocking that dilution because it lacks funds to purchase enough new shares to maintain its dominance. Nizhnov executives, highly regarded by most financial analysts, are lobbying to circumvent the obstructionist Svyazinform.

Nizhnov still has not produced a GAAP audit. It has been audited only in accordance with RAS. Nizhnov's 1996 price/earnings ratio of 10.5 is below Russia's 15.3 average. Its shares trade on the RTS, symbol NNSI.

13

THE RUSSIAN
TIGER CUBS

Tigers are born small, blind, and helpless. If you look at them soon after birth, you can easily mistake them for kittens. You see small creatures, wobbly on their feet—it is hard to imagine they will grow into powerful beasts, moving gracefully through the jungle.

Today, many Russian companies—entire branches of the economy—are like newborn tiger cubs. They were born in the muck and slime of privatization, and their parents, huge Soviet government agencies, died after giving birth to them. Left alone to fend for themselves, these tiger cubs seem blind, weak, and disoriented. But make no mistake—theirs is not the weakness of decay—it is the weakness of the young, who will grow into powerful tigers of the economic jungle.

We have already looked at three families of tiger cubs who survived their early childhood and are moving into adolescence. Stocks in the oil and gas industry entered a bull market after those firms found paying customers in the industrial West. Stocks of power companies started to go up as investors recognized their central role in the economy. Telecoms began to rally after foreign companies, experienced in the Third World, rushed into Russia to profit from its pent-up demand for phone services.

Those three families of tiger cubs grew ahead of the rest because of their location in the economic jungle. Initially, each of them appeared disorganized, mismanaged, and with murky financial data. On the other hand, they all had the same powerful common denominator: they were key companies in key sectors of the economy that had shaken off decades of Soviet aimless drift and started moving into the free-market future. Early investors in oil and gas, power companies, and telecoms saw their investments go up hundreds of percent in recent years.

Today, several other tiger cubs are starting to get up on their feet—and the stock market is taking notice. Stocks in several industries—autos, shipping, metals, and mining—are starting to rise from ridiculously low levels. Other industries, such as food, fertilizers, and banking are just starting to stir. Farther out in the jungle are entire industries not yet represented by a single publicly traded stock—entertainment, high-tech, services. Let us poke into the jungle and look for several industries and companies most likely to attract the stock market's attention in the near future.

THE RUSSIAN AUTOMOTIVE INDUSTRY

A car is just a commodity to most Westerners. We take our cars for granted, seldom look under the hood, and complain about traffic. For most Russians, a car remains an object of dreams and yearnings, a gleaming symbol of freedom. As Gogol wrote in *Dead Souls*, his panorama of Russian life in the 19th century, "Oh, what Russian doesn't love a fast ride!" Russians have not had too many fast rides lately. The liberated nation's craving for cars is about to fuel a boom in the Russian auto industry.

The Soviet government's attitude toward private cars was similar to that of Hitler's Germany. Rulers of both countries, with their fleets of chauffeured cars, saw personal autos as needless luxuries, which they barely tolerated and pushed back in favor of grandiose military-industrial projects. By the time the USSR collapsed, the country had only about 50 cars per 1,000 population—one of the lowest car ownership rates in Europe. The local auto industry had been starved of resources, but imports were forbidden. A foreign car parked on a Soviet street always drew crowds, while Brezhnev's personal collection of Lincoln Continentals and Mercedes Benzes probably accounted for a large portion of the country's entire fleet of imports.

Russia's population is two thirds that of the US, but its auto industry is puny by comparison. The largest Russian car manufacturer, *AvtoVAZ*[28] produces only one tenth the number of vehicles made by General Motors, and just a quarter of Chrysler's, the smallest auto maker in the US. This level of output makes it the sixteenth largest car maker in the world. The Russian auto industry suffers from deformities inflicted on it by decades of central planning. Soviet auto plants were not independent car makers but separate departments of a state monopoly, each created to fit a particular niche, such as small cars, larger cars, trucks, and so on. Each was the sole supplier to its segment of the market and never had to compete for customers.

Ordinary Soviet citizens used to spend over ten years on a waiting list for a car. Auto makers could sell any outdated junk because their production was snapped up no matter what. Their quality became so shoddy that many buyers took their brand-new cars apart, engines and all, and fixed and reassembled them prior to driving.

After the Soviet Union collapsed, foreign cars flowed in through the newly open borders, lifting car ownership to about 76 cars per 1,000 people by 1993. Even so, Russia remained behind most countries in Eastern Europe. For example, Poland, which has no auto industry of its own, boasted over 170 cars per 1,000 of population. Only Romania, the basket case of the former Evil Empire, had fewer cars per capita than Russia: 40 cars per 1,000 people.

Alarmed by the influx of imports, the Russian government tried to protect its obsolete auto industry from foreign competitors. It instituted high import duties and taxes, creating both a temptation and an opportunity for organized crime and corrupt officials. The Russian government has an unfortunate habit of putting up a high

---

[28]The names of Russian auto companies usually end in an abbreviation consisting of three letters. The first stands for the city where the company is located, followed by the letters AZ for *Avtomobilny Zavod*, or Auto Works.

import barrier around an industry and then allowing political allies to punch a hole in that fence and collect their own tolls in lieu of customs. That is how the Russian Orthodox Church took over from the disgraced Committee to Support Sports as the largest importer of tobacco and liquor—and that's how foreign cars continue to roll into the country.

Organized crime, working with corrupt customs officials, established pipelines for hustling cars through without paying high customs duties. It is a big and well-organized business. A former relative of mine in New Jersey got the notion in the early '90s that his bilingualism and connections with American used-car dealers were just the ticket for making a fortune importing cars to Russia. A few days after he got off a plane in Moscow, local organized crime figures made it plain to him that he had three choices: to come work for them, clear out of the country, or make his wife a bilingual widow.

After the collapse of the Soviet Union, Russian auto makers had a head-on collision with reality, wearing no seatbelts. Suddenly, customers had a choice, and they rated Russian products at the bottom of the scale. Annual production of passenger cars fell from 969,491 in 1990 to 776,206 in 1994, where it bottomed out and then began to rise. During the Depression of the 1990s car makers suffered the least and truck makers the most. The production of trucks topped out at 642,377 in 1989 and still has not bottomed out; it fell to about 110,000 in 1996. The production of buses also continues to slide, from 57,937 in 1989 to about 30,000 in 1996. Russian factories have no money for trucks and the impoverished municipalities cannot afford to invest in buses.

Most Russian car makers are almost comically inefficient. It takes an American car company an average of 25 man-hours to build a car, while the Japanese do it in 20 hours—but Russians require 400 hours! An average Russian auto factory produces just four vehicles per employee per year. Are Russian auto makers stupid or are workers inept? Not at all. Remember, they work in a country that built better space stations than Americans and infested the oceans with nuclear-powered submarines. Busy with those grandiose pursuits, the Soviets never allocated enough resources to build a decent family sedan!

The financial markets have expressed their opinion of Russian auto makers by awarding them some of the lowest P/E ratios in the market, often between 1 and 2. The Russian auto industry is now trying to rebuild itself, while the government provides life support via customs barriers. Car industries of other Eastern European countries have already attracted foreign capital—GM, Ford, Fiat, Peugot, and others have manufacturing operations in the region. Volkswagen bought a major share in Skoda in the Czech Republic, producing a new zippy compact called Felicia that is taking Eastern Europe by storm. It is taking a long time for the Russian auto makers to shed their old arrogance, ingrained for generations under the Soviets, and sell parts of themselves to foreign companies in exchange for fresh capital and expert management.

Russia's low level of car ownership indicates a huge potential demand for cars. Auto makers benefit from cheap skilled labor and well-established repair and distribution networks. Once Russian auto makers come to grips with market realities, they will be in a strong position to profit from this hungry market. The government recently put car makers on notice to improve or perish, by pushing *AvtoVAZ*, the largest car manufacturer, to the brink of bankruptcy and forcing its hidebound management to change.

GAZ

GAZ (*Gorkovsky Avtomobilny Zavod* or Gorky Auto Works) is the most successful domestic auto maker in Russia today. Its Volga sedan looks remotely like a Volvo and has long been the car of choice among better-off individuals. Its light truck Gazelle is the only success story of the post-Soviet auto industry.

GAZ, along with the rest of the industry, was facing a massive nonpayment problem among heavy truck buyers during the Depression of the 1990s. It turned adversity into opportunity by designing and building a new light city truck, Gazelle.

The heavily centralized Soviet industry used large trucks, while free commerce of the early 1990s needed light trucks to make fast deliveries to "sales tents" that sprung up all over Russia, like mushrooms after a rain. The Gazelle with its 1.5 ton (3,300 lb.) capacity met the demand for an inexpensive, versatile and economical light truck. It found willing customers among small business people. While old heavy-duty trucks went unsold, small enterprises, bootstrapping themselves to success, snapped up the Gazelle.

GAZ has some of the most modern equipment in Russia, including German robotic production lines, although some of its gear had been acquired as far back as the 1950s. It recently began importing Steyr engines from Austria in order to make the Volga and the Gazelle more powerful. While other manufacturers are furloughing workers, GAZ assembly lines operate three shifts per day, six days a week. GAZ produces all of its parts, except for the electronics, rubber, and glass. GAZ owns auto service centers in most large cities and regions of Russia, and Mercedes Benz is currently trying to buy that valuable franchise.

Now Gazelle is starting to age, while GAZ is facing new competitors in the market for light trucks. Will it manage to repeat its success? GAZ is busy developing special trucks for off-road use, named *Asket* (Ascetic) and *Burlak* (Towman—after ancient Russians who used to tow boats upstream with sheer muscle power). Russian country roads can be impassable due to mud several months a year, creating excellent prospects for those trucks. GAZ management is considered to be the most market-oriented among Russian auto makers. They retained Coopers & Lybrand not only to audit them, but to help restructure their financial systems along Western lines. GAZ is the only Russian car company actively managing its finances, for example by investing in GKOs. GAZ common shares are listed on the RTS.

THE PULP AND PAPER INDUSTRY

Much of Russian territory is covered with forests, especially in Siberia and Karelia, north of St. Petersburg. First the tsars and later the Soviets tried to exploit the great wealth of timber, even though their approach bordered on ecological rape. The Soviets earned foreign currency from logging but could never build a sophisticated pulp and paper industry to compete with its capitalist neighbors, such as Finland or Sweden.

Russia's pulp and paper industry imploded as the country slid into the Depression of the 1990s. Between 1988 and 1993 sawed timber production dropped 59%, pulp and paper production 48–54%, plywood production 41%. Pulp and paper manufacturers (PPMs) began to recover ahead of the rest of the economy, thanks to their ability to export to the West. Production began to increase in 1995, when the output of pulp, paper, newsprint, and kraftliner rose 16–45% compared to the previous year. The timber, pulp, and paper industry accounted for over 5% of Russia's GNP and brought in about 4% of the country's foreign-currency revenue.

The demand for paper and forest products is growing worldwide. Paper consumption is directly related to people's standards of living. For example, an average Western European consumes over 700 lb. of paper and paper products per year, while an average Russian consumes only 75 lb. Rich people use more paper—I no longer ask Moscow friends for a paper towel when I spill something, because so few people have them. Russian toilet paper is so rough, it makes you wonder whether it is a secret weapon for toughening the nation by sanding people's bottoms. As the Russian economy pulls out of its Depression of the 1990s, the demand for quality paper products is likely to boom, sending share prices of paper companies up.

Russian production costs are relatively low—timber is cheap, electricity plentiful, and labor well trained and low paid. The demand from the Russian media and book-publishing industries is soaring as a direct result of collapsed communist censorship. The demand for food-packaging board is also exploding—for example, milk and juice cartons, so common in the West, are just starting to appear in Russia.

Initially, all large and small factories in the pulp and paper industry were privatized as separate entities. The logging companies quickly found that they were better off exporting their production, even at low prices, rather than facing nonpayment by local customers. The increased exports of Russian timber starved the processing mills and threatened the industry with collapse. The Russian government responded by reorganizing the industry in 1994, creating 52 vertically integrated pulp and paper holding companies. It swapped shares in previously privatized enterprises for shares in the new holdings.

Roslesprom, the government agent in the industry, is negotiating with Ex-Im Bank and other international agencies to line up long-term credit, while local companies look for joint ventures with local firms. Herlitz International of Germany has taken a majority position in Volga PPM, and Tetra Laval of Sweden has acquired a majority of Svetogorsk PPM.

There is huge pent-up demand for paper and paper products in the country. A striking measure of what the future may hold for Russian PPMs is provided by the ratio of company capitalization per ton of capacity. That ratio fluctuates between $600 and $2,400 for Scandinavian PPMs, while Russian PPMs, some of them just a few hundred miles to the east are valued between $10 and $100 per ton of capacity. As the Russian industry narrows the gap with its Western competitors, its stocks are likely to soar.

SYKTYVKAR TIMBER INDUSTRIAL COMPLEX (SLPK)

SLPK (*Syktyvkar Lesopromyshlenny Kompleks*) is one of Russia's largest paper producers, along with Kotlass PPM, Arkhangel PPM, and Bratsk LPK. Located in the semi-autonomous Komi Republic, the company is in the midst of northern Russian forests and enjoys relatively easy access to foreign markets through the port of Arkhangel, about 900 miles to the west. The company employs over 8,000 people, and has a progressive management team. A strong regional business climate helps make SLPK one of Russia's most attractive pulp and paper companies. Even when this industry was in the throes of depression and operated at only 40–50 percent of capacity in 1994, SLPK functioned at 68% of capacity. The next best utilized PPMs were Kotlass and Kondopoga, with 58% each.

SLPK is vertically integrated. It does everything, from cutting logs to delivering the final products. It operates what in Russia passes for new equipment—European-made machines, acquired in the 1970s and the 1980s and modernized in 1995, with separate production lines for softwoods and hardwoods. It gets all its wood from local forest reserves, established by the Komi Republic to support its industry. The company's own power plants not only satisfy its demands for electricity and heat but even sell to others.

SLPK produces 51% of Russia's printing paper. It is the largest producer of food packaging board in the country, including the pure-pack, tetra-pack, and tetra-grid. These staple products of the West are a huge novelty in Russia and the demand for them is surging. SLPK is known for its high quality and its stable relationships with customers. Most of its production is presold and rarely stocked in warehouses. SLPK was the first Russian PPM to create a marketing department, which may seem unremarkable to Westerners, but represented a radical departure from old Soviet ways, indicating a high level of sophistication.

SLPK shares trade on the RTS, both ordinary and preferred. Management is known to be buying up company shares on the open market and from workers who received shares during the privatization campaign.

THE FOOD AND BEVERAGE INDUSTRY

Millions of Soviets starved to death in this century, as the communist government put its grandiose projects ahead of citizens' welfare. People did not have enough to eat, and what they had was often dirty and contaminated. The Soviet government's public health statistics were a state secret, but when I worked as a physician in the USSR I learned that the incidence of hepatitis, one of the key measures of food contamination, was 400 times higher in the USSR than in the US! The regime was choking on its own dirt. After the collapse of the communist system, for the first time in most people's lifetimes, most Russians received access to quality imported food that was cleanly processed and packaged. The domestic industry is starting to catch up—and a market of 150 million people offers fantastic opportunities for companies that can serve its pent-up demand.

The demand for imported products in Russia and other Eastern European countries skyrocketed in the early days of the free market. Consumers were dazzled by the deluge of new offerings, but gradually many of them realized that imports were not only more expensive, but often of lower quality than traditional domestic brands. Recent market research in Moscow shows that quality, not price, is the most important factor in Russian consumer spending. Russians are no longer buying products in colorful wrapping paper simply because they were made abroad. As the Russian food industry improves and promotes its well-known brand names, the signs "Made in Russia" are becoming more and more attractive to local consumers.

The Russian beer and soft-drink industries are surging ahead. Beer brewers recovered from two vicious blows—the destruction of their capacity during the ill-directed antialcoholism campaign in the waning days of the Soviet Union (which remain a source of abiding hatred of Mikhail Gorbachev by many Russians) and shrinking demand during the Depression of the 1990s. Now production is soaring, the industry is installing new Czech equipment and improving quality. This writer found Russian mass-produced beers on par with good American microbreweries and way above any Budweiser or Miller. The Russian national soft drink, *kvas*, made from bread and water, is starting to give imported soft drinks a run for the money.

RED OCTOBER

Red October (*Krasny Oktyabr*) is Russia's largest confectionery manufacturer. Most Russians, young and old, love its candy and chocolates whose brand names have been impressed in the nation's mind for generations. Its "Pigeon-Toed Bear" and "Crawfish Neck" candy, "Alyonushka" and "Pushkin's Fairy Tales" chocolates, and other brands are synonymous with quality for most Russians. This writer, a confirmed chocaholic, performed extensive testing and found the sweets of Red October below the top Swiss brands, but superior to any Hershey or M&M.

Red October's production has climbed steadily since 1993, reaching 66,000 tons of confectionery in 1996. It is expected to jump to 100,000 per year in 1997, after construction is completed at a new factory in Kolomna, 100 km from Moscow. Red October's main factory has been operating at full capacity for years. It is located in the heart of Moscow, less than a mile from the Kremlin, on the shore of the Moscow River. Its 49-year lease on 5.84 hectares of land was valued at $30 million in 1996.

Red October sales are growing and the company is building satellite factories, taking over small competitors, bringing them up to its standards, and establishing distributorships. Red October is known for its enlightened labor practices, consistently paying its workers about a third more than the average wages in Moscow (it was paying $232 per month in 1995). Its marketing strategy, developed with the help of Western experts, focuses on advertising the Red October brand name in mass media, while focusing on individual products at the point of purchase. This strategy has been so effective that Red October now controls 60% of Moscow's confectionery market. Its products are so eagerly sought in the provinces and abroad that it cannot expand fast enough to meet the demand.

In 1995 Bank Menatep attempted a hostile takeover of Red October, but the company resisted by adopting a "poison pill" defense. As Red October's shares appreciated, the company retained Coopers & Lybrand to prepare a full IAS audit in preparation for issuing its ADRs. In January 1996 Russian banks and funds held 18.4% of shares, other Russian companies 19.4%, foreign banks and funds 19.2%, and the Moscow city government 19.7%; the rest was held by individuals. Shares in Red October (RTS symbol KROT) remained sharply undervalued on the basis of Price/Sales, Price/Earnings, and Price/Book Value when compared with confectioners in other developing countries, such as Thailand, Poland, Indonesia, and Greece.

RIVER SHIPPING

My very last job in the Soviet Union, more than 20 years ago, had been as a ship's doctor. Not long ago I had a nostalgic encounter with the Russian shipping industry—in the Frankfurt airport, where I ran into a group of grizzled Russian seamen, drinking gin at 7 A.M., waiting for the last leg of their flight home. They had been stuck in Namibia, South-West Africa for eleven months, on a ship detained in port for nonpayments, until their company scrounged up enough money to fly them back home. I shared my cigars with them. The mighty Soviet commercial fleet has fallen pretty low in recent years.

Shipping, including river shipping, is used widely in Russia, even though Russian rivers tend to flow from south to north or vice versa, while transport requirements are generally east to west. Most rivers freeze between November and April, allowing only six to seven months of navigation per year. Even so, there are vast areas of Russia where rivers provide the only economical method of transportation. For example, 84% of cargo traffic in the Far North is by boat. The first and the last boats of the season, led by huge icebreakers, are the defining events in the economic and social life of the regions.

In 1992 and 1993 the state-controlled river-shipping monopoly was split into 26 geographically distinct companies and privatized. New shipping companies received not only vessels, but ports, boatyards, and related assets with little or no debt. They could use them as security for borrowing, while transferring Russian tonnage to flags of convenience for easier financing and reduction of legal liabilities.

The early pattern of privatization in this industry had been to offer 51% of the common stock to management and employees at special low rates, while 25% went to the state, and the rest was sold to domestic and foreign investors. The percentages of ownership shifted as stocks began to trade on the open market. In some cases, "Red Directors," Soviet holdovers, went on to accumulate controlling interests by hook or by crook, often cheating workers out of their holdings, in order to keep investors out and protect their turf. Managers of other companies had been more open to outsider ownership and welcomed shareholders' input.

The Depression of the 1990s dealt a blow to the river-shipping industry—its total volume of cargo fell by 75% between 1990 and 1994. Only international shipments remained stable, hauling the exports of iron ore, coke, fertilizers, minerals, ferrous metals, and timber. Most Russian river shipping companies are free to set their rates, except for those with near-monopolies in the Far North. Domestic rates shot up from the artificially low Soviet levels, but are still only about one tenth of international rates.

The shipping industry suffers from typical post-Soviet hang-over. It has too many ships, but most are not good enough by Western standards. Russian river ships are usually self-propelled. The more efficient shippers in the West switched long ago to barges and tugboats. Barges can take their time being loaded and offloaded, while tugboats work full time.

Stocks of shipping companies in the West are priced on the basis of assets, cash flow, and earnings. Russian shipping companies, when compared with other developing and newly developed countries, are vastly undervalued on all those scales. While companies like Yang Ming Marine Transport of Taiwan and First Steamship of Taiwan are selling at almost twice their net asset value, the leading Russian shipping companies are selling at an 80–90% discount from their net asset values. While Precious of Thailand and Yang Ming of Taiwan are selling at more than 10 times their cash flow, no Russian company sells at more than three times annual cash flow, and many sell at less than one! This looks like a gross mispricing in a young and inefficient market, promising great returns to farsighted investors—especially if you think that Russia today is where the East Asian "tigers" were a few decades ago.

VOLGOTANKER

The Volga river is the Mississippi of Russia. This river flows through the industrial and agricultural heartland down to the Caspian Sea. The governments of Russia and three former Soviet republics bordering the Caspian are heatedly arguing over whether it is a sea or a lake. That argument emerged not from any sudden fascination with geography, but from the fact that there are huge oil deposits under the shallow waters of the Caspian and, according to international law, the formula for dividing them depends on whether it is a lake or a sea. While the governments bicker, one thing is certain—much of that oil will be transported to the refineries on Volgotanker ships.

Volgotanker is the largest transporter of oil and oil products in European Russia, with nearly 600 vessels with a total dead weight of nearly 2 million tons. It holds a near-monopoly on Volga oil transports.

The company serves 15 clients, including such giants as Lukoil (see Chapter 10), Yukos, and Rosneft. Volgotanker transports oil and oil products to and from 12 refineries in the region, but 80% of its cargo goes for export, allowing it to collect some payments in advance and shield itself from Russia's pervasive nonpayment problem. Company revenues grew 29% in 1995 and rose again in 1996. The company has retained Western auditors to prepare IAS statements.

Volgotanker shows a steady growth of earnings per share, but as recently as mid-1996 its price/earnings ratio was still only 0.88. At the end of 1995 Volgotanker was included on the government's list of companies that are strategically important for the nation's economy. This means the state will retain a controlling block of shares for several more years. Volgotanker shares trade on the RTS.

MORE TIGER CUBS

The Russian economy is developing so fast, it is sure to overtake any book before it is printed. This and previous chapters are not intended to be a comprehensive overview, only an attempt to show how one analyst goes about trying to recognize new opportunities.

Stocks of Russian companies are catching fire one after the other these days—exploding in fantastic rallies as more analysts and investors recognize their value. Aeroflot, Russia's premier airline, Ingosstrakh, Russia's largest insurance company, and many others are being snapped up as this chapter is being written. There are literally hundreds of companies whose stocks are grossly undervalued, waiting to be recognized by savvy investors.

You need to monitor Russia and its stock market to recognize emerging opportunities. You can follow the news in the media and on the Internet, talk to Russian brokers. It is a good idea to make a few trial investments to give you something concrete to watch in the country. I plan to write updates on the Russian markets after this book is published. To receive a complimentary copy of our latest update, please contact my firm, Financial Trading, Inc. at the address that appears at the end of this book.

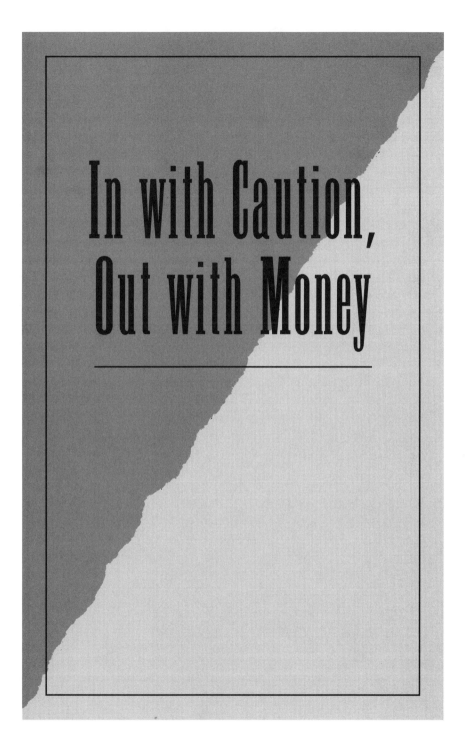

In with Caution, Out with Money

14

HOW TO INVEST IN THE RUSSIAN MARKETS

The recent collapse of the communist system marked the most important transformation of Russia since the nation was Christianized over a thousand years ago. Prior to their conversion people lived in holes in the ground, worshipped fire and made human sacrifices. The monks who walked from Greece across this dangerous terrain began the process that brought Russians into the mainstream of Western civilization.

Now, for the first time in its history, the nation does not have a rapacious ruling class robbing and oppressing people. There are no murderous Mongol archers, no tsars and aristocrats with their secret police, no communists with their labor camps. People can say what they want and keep what they earn. A normal society is emerging in Russia. It is a millennial change for a country whose people suffered for centuries and inflicted suffering upon their neighbors.

This new freedom is igniting an economic boom in a vast land with immense natural and human resources. Russians are working hard—and smart—to catch up with the West. They are rising from a very low economic base, promising huge percentage gains if they succeed. Public perceptions change slowly, and the old reputation of the Evil Empire continues to linger, making Russian assets undervalued in the world markets. The idea of a freedom-fueled Russian boom is so new, it will take years to sink in.

Stephen Jennings, president of Renaissance Capital, said to the group of international investors who came with me to Moscow: "An epochal change is taking place in Russia. When you walk down the street, on one side of the street the past is dying, while on the other side the future is being born. You need to know clearly which is which. This is an exciting time to invest in the future."

If we agree that Russia is in the early stage of an economic boom, let us decide how to profit from it. We need to map out several strategies for profiting from the Russian boom.

We have examined Russia's growing financial markets: fixed income, derivatives, and especially equities. We have studied its leading publicly held companies in major industries, such as oil and gas, electric power, and telecoms. We have glimpsed vast areas of Russia's economy just starting to emerge from the communist morass, such as autos, paper, food, and shipping.

A free market anywhere in the world offers enough choices to confuse and disorient most investors. Trying to choose what to buy or sell can feel like walking through a bank vault or a harem. There are breathtaking temptations at every step, and deadly guards at every turn. An intelligent investor knows he cannot chase every rabbit in his path; he needs a strategy for filtering market information and selecting what and when to buy, sell, or stand aside.

Those who enter financial markets without a plan are doomed to react to events, always a step behind the game—a bad position in life in general and the markets in particular. We cannot control the market—it will do whatever it wants—but we can control ourselves. A good plan does not remove all uncertainty, but it helps us steer the course when markets become stormy. All plans reflect personal preferences, and we will review several of them. These are not rigid prescriptions; you can combine several plans to create your own. Just be sure to write down your plan before entering the market.

It is easy to invest or trade in the US. Just choose your market, select a broker, open an account, and phone in your order. Some day it will be just as easy to invest in Russia, but today an investor needs to jump through several hoops. The early investors who know how to handle the difficulties of young and underdeveloped markets are likely to reap the richest rewards.

THREE STRATEGIES

If you push a ball deep under water and release it, it will rush to the surface and break above it with a splash. Russia had been held under water for two centuries by a brutal Mongol rule, for three centuries by a reactionary dynasty, and for 74 years by bloodthirsty communists. Now, for the first time in the nation's history, Russians are free from oppression—and rushing to catch up with the West at breakneck speed.

The creative energy of a nation—inventive, hard-working, and educated—has suddenly been released. The leg-irons have been broken, and the speed of progress can boggle the mind. Russia still has many serious problems, but it is in a powerful uptrend toward a liberal capitalist society. The ball held deep under water for six centuries began to rush toward the surface just six years ago. When it breaks out, its splash will be heard around the world. Then it will be simpler and easier to invest in the newly prosperous Russia—but today's great bargains will be gone.

The Russian market has been rising in advance of the economic boom. It was the best performing stock market worldwide in 1997 before falling sharply in 1998, when it was dragged down by the Asian crisis. When large international investors get beat up in one market, such as Thailand or Hong Kong, they often respond by reducing their holdings across the globe and retreating home. Their behavior impacts emerging markets worldwide. The small size of the Russian stock market contributes to its volatility—the value of the entire market at the time of this writing is less than the capitalization of General Motors, a single US blue chip.

Buying after a sharp decline is like shopping during a sale. It makes sense to those of us who are bullish on Russia, looking out five years or so, beyond short-term fluctuations.

To profit from the rise of the Russian stock market, consider three strategies—we will call them do-it-yourself low-maintenance, do-it-yourself active, and managed. You can participate in the Russian bull market by turning your money over to professional managers. The main advantage of this approach is that it puts professionals in charge. If you chose them well and monitor their performance, they ought to do a better job than amateurs. The main disadvantage of this approach is that it puts professionals in charge. In today's Russia the pros are likely to charge you an arm and a leg, and not be terribly experienced to boot. Few pros can generate enough profit to offset fees, which often eat up any relative gains of professional management.

If you use money managers, do not be dazzled by extravagant promises and slick advertising, but insist on paying as low fees as possible. Percentages chipped away by managers may seem like small change but they do add up over the years. Researchers in the US have proven that the country's best-performing mutual funds have not been the ones with hot-shot money managers, but those with the lowest fees (I thank Jeffrey Vogel for bringing this point to my attention).

If you plan to manage your own investments in Russia, you'll need to decide how actively to do it. If you control substantial funds and have a great deal of time, you can actively move your money in the Russian markets.

The Russian stock market has a greater tendency than the US market to focus on one or two industry groups at a time. A momentum investor or trader can achieve superior results by closely monitoring the market and switching out of sleepy groups into those on the front burner. For example, last year regional energy companies were all the rage, while at the moment local telecoms are running hot. To play this game, it pays to be located in Moscow, be plugged into the daily flow of information in the brokerage community, and be fluent in the Russian language.

The circle of market professionals in Russia is fairly small and they are constantly talking to one another. Staying in touch with several of them will allow you to keep your fingers on the pulse of the group. The key word here is "several." If you do not speak Russian and depend on a single English-speaking broker to feed you the news, you're likely to get a very slanted picture.

The hurdle of transaction costs, primarily bid-ask spreads, is especially high for active investors and traders. Popular stocks in Russia tend to trade at very tight spreads—less than 0.5% of price among the top ten most active issues. This is because many competing brokers make markets in them. Thinly traded stocks have greater bid-ask spreads, which increase as you go down the list, and may reach a breathtaking 100% for some of the least active shares. In other words, a stock at the top of the popularity scale has to go up 0.5% for a buyer to break even, while a stock at the bottom of the scale has to double in order to break even. The hottest stocks are likely to be among second-tier issues, often hard to buy in size and with wide bid-ask spreads.

Do-it-yourself investors do not have to trade actively. They can take a less stressful low-maintenance approach. If you believe that the Russian economy is poised for a major rise, you can invest in several key sectors and hold your shares for the long haul. You need to monitor your investments, but you will not have to do it daily. It is easier to track a tide than individual waves—and the rising tide of the Russian economy is likely to lift the majority of stocks.

A "RISING TIDE LIFTS ALL THE BOATS" STRATEGY

A low-maintenance approach to investing in Russia means dividing your capital into several equal parts and buying stocks in several major companies in the key sectors. This will allow you to benefit from any sustained rise in the Russian economy. There is a saying on Wall Street—a rising tide lifts all the boats. This "rising tide" approach is less exciting than chasing the next hot stock, but it will reduce your transaction costs and may help a turtle win the race against the hare.

Consider buying several Russian blue chips for your "rising tide" account. Remember, our goal here is to create a low-maintenance portfolio, so that you do not have to check price quotes every day or buy and sell every month. The idea is not to trade but float up on a rising tide. Choose stocks of Russia's largest companies—large boats are less likely to sink in a storm.

Please keep in mind that the suggested list is valid in the beginning of 1998, as this chapter is being written. Use your judgment and consult with experts you trust as you make your choices at a later time.

A long-term portfolio would have to include a utility company, such as Mosenergo (see Chapter 11). Moscow is the richest city in the country and Mosenergo has the monopoly on providing electric power and heat to this thriving metropolis. The demand for energy is likely to grow as the economy gathers steam, and the government has already promised to let this company raise its rates. The stock of Mosenergo is one of the most liquid blue chips on the RTS. The only ADRs at this time are Rule 144A, not available to the public, but that may change by the time you read this book.

A long-term Russian portfolio would have to include telecom shares (see Chapter 12). It is better to avoid Rostelecom whose virtual monopoly on domestic and international long-distance phone calls is being challenged by savvy Western firms. Better to choose a well-run local telecom, with a monopoly in one of the prosperous areas of the country. Nizhnovsvyazinform, run by a well-regarded executive team, located in the economically and politically progressive part of Russia fits the bill. Its stock trades on the RTS, and the company is moving toward issuing its ADRs in the West.

A "rising tide" portfolio would not be complete without shares in the Russian oil industry (see Chapter 10). Lukoil and Surgut are among the largest vertically integrated oil companies in the world. Oil is an international commodity. A barrel of crude under the prairies of Texas, ice floes of Canada, or sands of Saudi Arabia is worth about the same, with differentials due to the costs of pumping and transportation, quality and political risk. The world market still grossly underprices Russian oil. When you divide proven reserves of Russian oil firms by their total capitalization, you find that the market values those companies at about 70 cents per barrel of reserves—about one tenth of the world's average of $6 per barrel of reserves. Shares of Russian oil firms represent a stake in a drastically undervalued key sector of the economy. Lukoil and Surgut are among the most liquid blue chips on the RTS, with ADRs trading over-the-counter in the US.

The above list will need to change as time goes on. New industries and new companies keep coming to the market, and you ought to add shares of new industry leaders to your portfolio. As Fred Berliner, a professional American trader in Moscow, put it: "You have to buy anything in the path of the consumer, as well as agriculture and construction. Consumers had been starved by the old regime and now they are starting to catch up. Look at McDonald's (its Russian franchise is owned by Canadians): they cannot put up their restaurants fast enough, and as soon as they do, they get crowded and stay crowded. The demand for growth in Russia will come from consumers, construction, and farming. They still do not have an auto parts chain, a Home Depot, even a Crazy Eddie. You don't have to be a rocket scientist—buy companies that serve consumers, such as Ingosstrakh (an insurance company) and Sberbank (the largest bank)."

Dan Rapoport, a Texas oilman who now trades professionally in Moscow, points out that "super-returns are in illiquid shares." Sberbank, the country's largest, has been listed on the RTS only a few months ago, at a huge premium above its pre-listing, over-the-counter price. The shares of Aeroflot, Russia's largest airline, are fairly illiquid, as the company awaits its listing on the RTS. With stocks like these, it is better to buy early and hold for the long haul, not trade in and out.

Even a "rising tide" portfolio requires some maintenance. Once you begin to invest in Russia, continue to follow its news and watch its stock market, particularly the new listings. You should readjust your portfolio at least once or twice a year. The money for new purchases may come from fresh funds or from selling existing shares. You should decide in advance that you will sell at least one position in your portfolio by the end of each year. Sell the worst acting stock and invest in a new, promising situation.

AN ACTIVE DO-IT-YOURSELF STRATEGY

Active investors keep switching between investments, holding most positions for several months. This is different from in-and-out trading. Russian markets are not well suited for pure trading today; they are still fairly thin and transaction costs are high. If short-term in-and-out trading is your specialty, you're better off in deeper, more liquid markets, such as US stocks or international currencies.

There are only a few hundred listed shares in the Russian stock market and relatively few professional participants. Many of them are in Moscow, most know one another, and every few months a new investment theme or fad sweeps up the entire group. Suddenly, everyone is rushing into local energos, then telecoms, then the newly listed consumer companies, such as Aeroflot and Ingosstrakh, become hot. If you are plugged into Moscow investment circles, you can do well by buying the newly active sectors.

An active investor in Russia has two options. You can bring money into Russia or an offshore center that serves it, most likely Cyprus, or you can keep your money at home and trade Russian ADRs in the US or Europe. The choice depends, in part, on the size of your account. Remember, the minimum lot on the RTS is between $30,000 and $50,000. If you do not have at least three times that amount, keep your money at home and use ADRs.

An investor with less than $100,000 who wishes to achieve any degree of diversification needs to buy ADRs or else put his money into a Russian mutual fund. Today, there are only two mutual funds in the US dedicated to investing in Russia. Not all US brokers are equally comfortable with ADRs. It is a good idea to work with someone who knows Russian ADRs, so that you do not have to pay to educate him.

ADRs are negotiable certificates representing the ownership of foreign shares (see Chapter 8). Russian ADRs are traded in the stock markets of the US, the UK, Germany, Luxembourg, Austria, and elsewhere. They trade in the US just like US stocks, with the same clearing and settlement rules, and even pay dividends in US dollars.

The US is such a huge and wealthy country that many of us here believe the world ends at the beach; once we come to the Atlantic or the Pacific, there is nothing on the other side. Even those of us who look across the ocean and want to invest abroad often prefer to buy ADRs right here, through our local brokers, without opening an account overseas and dealing with a foreign financial system.

More than a dozen Russian companies have ADRs at the time of this writing, and twice as many are in the process of bringing their ADRs to the market. The Internet is a good place to find an up-to-date list of Russian ADRs and other resources. My firm maintains links to Russian Internet sites at our *www.elder.com* website.

If you trade small lots, ADRs are more convenient than Russian shares. The Russian stock market, at the time of this writing, is dominated by institutional traders who set the minimum size of a round lot on the RTS at $30,000 or higher. If you want to buy a smaller lot, for example, $5,000 worth of Lukoil, many brokers in Russia will not take your order. Even if they do take it, they are likely to skin you on the spread, and do it again, only worse, when you try to sell your small lot later.

ADRs are more liquid than many stocks in Russia, even though they tend to have much higher bid-ask spreads than round lots on the RTS. They cost more to buy and bring less when you sell them. Sitting in a Moscow brokerage, I watched its director punch up numbers on his quote machine. If you wanted to trade Mosenergo in Moscow (the minimum lot size $50,000), the bid was $1.225 and the ask $1.229, a spread of less than 1/3 of one percent. The spread on Mosenergo's ADRs at the same time was 2%. The problem worsened as one moved down the list, toward less liquid shares. The bid-ask spread on Irkutskenergo was 28/28.5 in Moscow—1.78%, while its ADRs traded at a 14/15.5—a spread of more than 10%, a major hurdle in anyone's path to profits.

Many Moscow brokers are active in intermarket arbitrage. They monitor prices of shares and ADRs, looking to buy cheap Russian shares, sell expensive ADRs, and deliver shares bought in Moscow to the custodian bank which delivers ADRs to its customers abroad.

If you wish to bring your money to Russia or an offshore center, you ought to visit Moscow and meet the people with whom you plan to do business. Get a list of the best Russian brokerages and investment banks, call them (most professionals speak English), line up several appointments, then fly to Moscow and see for yourself. A Western investor is still a rare enough bird in Moscow to rate interviews with top executives at most investment houses. Remember that Moscow has the lion's share of investment-related activity in Russia, and, if your time is limited, do not waste it by going anyplace else.

Many professional managers in Moscow are actively turning over their stock portfolios—but in-and-out trading is out. Says Fred Berliner, director of trading at Troika-Dialog: "As a bookie, I make money, but as a trader, this is not a good market. The stocks are too thin, they have trading halts, you have the hassle of dealing with rubles and dollars. If you want to trade, go to the New York Stock Exchange or the NASDAQ. But if you want to buy Surgut at 16 cents and ride it up to 88 cents, you're in the right place."

Dan Rapoport, director of trading at CentreInvest Group tells of a client who opened an account with a million dollars in the beginning of 1996 and actively traded it throughout the year. At the end of that year his account was up 56%, but the market had doubled! "You just have to buy and hold," says Dan, "hold until the story changes."

When Russian brokers quote you a price, they do not add a commission; their compensation has already been worked into the quote. They do it to reduce taxes, because commissions are subject to VAT (value-added tax), but spreads are not.

In theory, a foreigner who wants to bring his capital to Russia to invest in its financial markets must wire funds to a government-approved bank. That bank will convert his currency into rubles and deposit them in a special investment account. Rubles from that account can be used to buy and sell Russian stocks, bonds, and other investments at any brokerage or investment bank. You can repatriate your capital and profits through the same bank which will deduct 20% of profits to pay capital gains tax, convert the rest into dollars and wire them to you in the West. In reality, much of foreign money never enters Russia. Trades are done in Moscow but accounts are settled in Cyprus or a similar locale to avoid taxes.

Centuries of living under harsh regimes made Russians wonderfully inventive in dealing with governments and dodging taxes. Whenever you do business in Russia, you discover a maze of bureaucratic rules, and below it a network of private passages cut out by citizens. "The law is like a telegraph pole," the president of a leading Moscow bank said to me after outlining several tax-avoidance schemes, "You cannot hop over it, but you can walk around it (*nel'zya pereprygnut, no oboiti mozhno*)."

Some investors set up offshore companies in jurisdictions that have agreements with Russia to avoid double taxation but do not tax profits on foreign investments, such as the United Kingdom. Others operate through offshore subsidiaries of Moscow brokerages or investment banks, many of which are domiciled in Cyprus. This Mediterranean island with a 4% tax rate for foreign investors has positioned itself as an offshore haven for Russians. The topic is complex, as laws may change by the time you read this book. Make sure you discuss the tax implications of your trades with trustworthy people in Moscow.

A Money Management Strategy

Investors who want to participate in the Russian stock market without dealing with local intricacies may use professional money managers. More and more of them are waking up to the great bull market of Russia.

Most managers look good in rising markets, but as Wall Streeters say, "Do not confuse brains with a bull market." Some greenhorn investors feel satisfied if their mutual fund goes up 65%, while the stock market as a whole gains 80%. They should be firing their money manager instead of celebrating! If a manager underperforms the market in a great year, what can you expect in a year when the Russian stock market rises only 10%, or even declines 20%?

Many people are careless when choosing money managers. They open accounts after hearing a tip at a cocktail party or seeing a flashy ad in a magazine. Few clients monitor their manager's performance from month to month—they give up control.

When you choose a money manager, consider three measures: his performance for the past five years, his performance in Russia, and the cost of his service. Ideally, you'd focus on the Russian results first, but virtually no money manager has a documented five-year track record in Russia. You have to evaluate performance in other markets in the previous five years to find those who outperformed the markets. It is a joke in the industry that if all money managers lose 15% as a group, then the person who lost only 10% is considered a winner—while you, the investor, are left holding the bag. The only measure of performance is profit, year in and year out. Finally, look at expenses. All other factors being equal, choose the manager with the lowest fees.

Do not relax and sit back after sending your money to a manager. Keep monitoring his performance and that of his competitors. All reputable managers should be happy to supply you with their performance figures. Keep a record of their returns before and after expenses each quarter and compare them with broad market indexes. Do not be shy about moving your account from one manager to another. If this sounds like too much work, find someone who will do it for you. Make sure you are investing on the basis of facts, and not fiction or inertia.

Investors have three basic choices in money management: mutual funds (called unit trusts outside the US), hedge funds, and managed accounts. Mutual funds throw your money and that of thousands of other investors into a pool run by a manager selected by a committee. Hedge funds have much smaller groups of investors and are run single-handedly by a manager with little or no supervision. A managed account, run by a professional as a separate unit, requires an investment of about a million dollars in Russia today.

The first of these three choices is like buying milk in a supermarket, the second like buying a partnership interest in a specific cow, and the third is like buying your own cow and hiring someone to mind it. Each has its advantages and disadvantages. Buying milk in a supermarket puts you under the protection of consumer laws. You are least likely to get food poisoning, but you're not likely to taste great milk either. Hiring someone to manage your cow makes you very dependent on one person's performance. Historically, partnerships—the hedge funds—tend to have the best rates of return.

If you have less than $100,000 to invest in Russia, you are pretty much limited to investing in mutual funds. At the time of this writing, there are only two such funds outside of Russia, and one inside the country. Compare that with more than 5,000 mutual funds in the US! The bull market in Russia has not been recognized by the public, another indication that Russian stocks are undervalued.

In 1997, Russia amended its legislation to allow the creation of domestic mutual funds. Russians were badly burned in the investment pyramids of the early 1990s (see Chapters 3 and 6), and we can expect them to be extremely leery about putting their money into mutual funds. Russians have a saying, "If you burn lips with hot water, you'll be blowing even on cold milk." The first Russian mutual funds, called *PIFs (payevoi investitsionniy fond* or public investment funds) were allowed to invest only in government paper, but the laws are being amended to allow them to buy stocks. Troika-Dialog, a major Russian brokerage firm, just opened a fund in Russia for investing in stocks, called Ilya Muromets, after a legendary folk hero.

As the number of mutual funds investing in Russia increases, consider this strategy: divide your account into three portions and put each in a different fund. At the end of the year fire one manager— sell the weakest acting fund. Then hire a new manager—invest in a new fund. This will help you affirm control of your financial life. This resolution will force you to look for promising new funds and hold a stick over the heads of fund managers you employ.

As your investments in Russia reach into the low six figures, you can start looking at hedge funds. Hedge funds are pools of money whose managers put their own money into the fund and receive no salary but a percentage of profits—as high as 20%. Managers of mutual funds get paid no matter what, but hedge-fund managers receive nothing if they lose money, but can earn a fortune if they make money. Hedge funds are among the favorite investment vehicles of wealthy individuals because historically they have done much better than public mutual funds.

Whether you deal with a hedge fund or a mutual fund, be sure to find out what percentage of its assets is invested in Russia. There is often a wide gulf between a fund's name and activity. You do not want to put capital earmarked for Russia into a fund that invests only 35% of assets in Russia and spreads the rest from Kazakhstan to Hungary.

Find out whether your fund manager is located in Russia and whether he speaks Russian. Generally, the closer to the market, the better. One of the top Moscow money managers said to me that the difference between him and a famous western counterpart was that his "spine was in Moscow"—he could feel the market with his spine. He noticed that the market tended to rise on sunny days in Moscow and sell off on rainy dreary days; he would also hear rumors and news that he could use before they were published and translated into English.

Several investment and brokerage houses in Moscow offer foreign investors personalized money management. You get your own
investment manager, an employee of the firm whose primary job is
to run your account and keep you happy. The amounts involved start
at a million dollars. Management fees are much higher in Russia than
in the West, while purchases and sales are done through the same
investment-management firm, charging full freight. In the crazy bull
market of the recent two years people have gotten away with charging crazy fees, but the caveats I've listed above apply here fully.

Whatever path you take in the Russian financial markets, consider making your first step now. Even a token investment can moti-
vate you to stay focused on what is happening in Russia and its
financial markets.

15

THE ROAD AHEAD

Catching a chairlift at the Mammoth Lakes ski resort in the spring of 1997, I found myself seated next to a 20-year-old-girl. She was a prelaw student whose parents emigrated to California from the Soviet Union while she was still in elementary school. The girl was bilingual, so we switched to Russian, and I mentioned to her that the best opportunities for a young, educated, bilingual person were in Russia. She found that hard to believe. Her parents described the Soviet Union as a dangerous and impoverished hellhole. As crowds of skiers glided below, I told her that Russia is building a liberal capitalist society. Its legal system is developing rapidly, and there is a great demand for educated and energetic bilingual people. New industries are being created. For example, two years ago, Russia had no advertising industry. Today, the people who started agencies in their apartments are at the top of an emerging field.

"International companies coming into Russia need legal support," I say to the girl, "After you graduate, if you look for work in America, you will be trying to take a few crumbs off an essentially stable economic pie. The pie was cut a long time ago and grows slowly—you'll have to fight for your slice. In Russia, they have just begun baking that pie. Anyone with energy and brains can grab a good slice. The pie is rising, it looks irregular; it has burned in spots, but it is rising fast. Now is the perfect time to get a piece!" We hop off the lift and lose each other in the puffs of snow.

The Russian genie is out of the bottle. The people kept down by the Mongols, kept down by the tsars, kept down by the Soviets have busted the lid. A tremendous pressure built up inside the jar over the centuries. Now that Russians have tasted freedom, no one can shove them back into their jar. The nation's energy is going into building, acquisitions, and a mad dash to catch up with the developed West.

The perception of time in Russia has always been different than in the West. In the muck and mire of the Soviet era the Russian attitude was the exact opposite of the American—"Time ain't money." Everybody worked for the state, and people had another charming saying, "Work is not a wolf, it will not run away to the forest." The cold stagnant air of the Soviet regime has been blown away by the winds of change.

Russians have swung to the other extreme. Time has become compressed and everything happens much faster than in the West. Businesses spring up and many disappear so fast that planning for more than 3 months ahead is considered long term. Planning for more than a year ahead is considered a waste of time. In 1996 a group of Russian businesspeople asked me to help them negotiate an exclusive distribution deal with an American software firm. Their positions seemed far apart, as Russians demanded a long-term agreement to protect their investment and the Americans were willing to offer only a short-term deal, to keep control of their product. I was able to bring the parties together by recommending a two-year deal. Russians considered that long-term, while for the Americans it was a nice short-term arrangement.

A banker friend in New York recently asked me to float his idea for a pension fund in Moscow. He would invest Russian money in the US—half in bonds, half in stocks—under conservative management. "What returns should we expect?" Russians asked. When I told them that would be a safe 6 to 8 percent, maybe higher, they laughed, "Per month?" The winds of change blow so fast in Russia, it reminds me of a character in a video game who keeps exclaiming, "Hold on to your ears, Mr. Lemming."

Russia stagnated behind the Iron Curtain; now it is catching up to the West at breathtaking speed. That speed has to be experienced to be believed. Those who look down at the Russians today are making a huge error.

Russia received a tremendous boost from its 1996 democratic presidential elections and the end of its disastrous war in Chechnya. Its 150 million people represent a huge market, its factories and machinery need rebuilding. Where pessimists see inefficiency, others see a tremendous demand for change. Russia has great resources. As David Castillo phrased it, "Timber in the Krasnoyarsk region makes the US Northwest look like a small plantation." Russians are inventive and clever; their kids get higher grades on standardized tests than American kids, and they have more Ph.Ds per capita than any country in the world. Market mechanisms have been formed—exchanges, banks, the stock market. People have survived the depression, learned new skills, changed their attitudes. The current uptrend in Western economies helps send a trickle of investments into Russia.

Thirty years ago, Khruschev pounded his aide's boot on a table at the UN and promised to bury the West. Today's Russians are racing to outbuild the West, guided by Adam Smith's "invisible hand." Moscow is rapidly becoming a normal European city, with a Russian flavor. Russians, liberated after centuries of oppression and smarting from the Depression of the 1990s, have the drive to succeed; they have "fire in the belly."

When my book *Trading for a Living* was translated from English into Russian and published in Moscow in 1995, I wrote in its afterword: "Russian traders sometimes ask me what are their chances in this game. To win, you need knowledge and motivation. This book will give you knowledge. As for the motivation, in a battle between the well-fed and the hungry, I bet on the hungry. They try harder."

MY JOURNEY

When I started telling friends about my plans for writing this book, most looked at me in disbelief. Americans thought the idea of a

Russian boom was beyond bizarre. They saw the country as a hopeless mess. My Russian friends were a bit more optimistic. They expected a mild economic improvement to begin in the 21st century, but the word boom was not in their vocabulary. The widespread skepticism confirmed for me that I was on the right track; I saw something most people have not yet recognized.

One of the advantages of growing older, at least for some of us, is that we learn to trust ourselves. When I was younger, I believed that professors, editors, and government experts knew better. Today, I trust my eyes more than what others say. Having practiced psychiatry for over 20 years has taught me to look beneath the surface in search of reality.

Since I live both in the US (where I have my children and my business) and in Russia (where I am involved in business and cultural life), I had an unusual advantage in writing this book. Those who live in Russia know the minute details of daily life there better than foreigners, but it is hard for them to notice major changes in the country. Caught in the daily flow of life, most people lose track of major shifts; they cannot see the forest for the trees.

On the other hand, a foreigner who visits Russia is overwhelmed by the novelty of it all. Most visitors have no personal yardstick for detecting change. If a visitor does not speak Russian, stays in a hotel, and travels in a chauffeured car, he is even farther removed from what is happening in the country.

When I go to Russia, I live in an apartment building, work in local offices, hang out with local friends, read local papers, eat local food, and hardly ever speak a word of English, unless someone needs a translation or when I call New York.

Coming and leaving every few months has helped me preserve a freshness of view and created a perspective from which to see the fantastic speed of Russia's progress. I land in Sheremetyevo airport, unlock my apartment, go shopping for food and have drinks with locals, all the while looking for changes. I put on a suit and tie and give seminars at exchanges and investment houses that I visited a few months earlier, detecting changes that locals take for granted and most visitors overlook. Speaking fluent Russian and living among locals gets me on the inside in Russia. At the same time, coming to

Russia as an American author of a business bestseller opens the doors of most offices in the country. I can see Russia from an American perspective as well as from the inside.

The disadvantages are personal. The flip side of the excitement of living on two continents is always having to leave. The other side of joy of meeting new friends is the hurt of separations. This complex and bittersweet dilemma is not a subject for this book.

Maxim Sokolov, a leading Russian journalist—bearded, rotund, multilingual, witty—says to me: "We are moving towards a Western-type society. Anywhere you spit, devil knows what's going on, but we keep moving forward—it's a miracle! We keep stumbling and going off on tangents, but we couldn't be moving forward any faster. Everybody criticizes what we've got—but we've got more than anyone expected.

"You've got to give credit to the government—there is no longer an impenetrable wall, no feeling of belonging to separate forms of life. You can have a conversation with the federal leadership—we're beyond the stage of a dialogue with deaf-mutes.

"People are not used to holding officials accountable. They expect them to 'look after themselves' because official salaries are nonsense. A minister officially receives 1.7 million rubles (less than $300), the president 2.5 million (over $400), and the mayor of Moscow 1 million (under $200) per month.

"Ninety-five percent of grief stems from local authorities, but people transfer those feelings onto the central government. The press seldom criticizes municipal authorities—out of fear of being closed down. And why not—municipal governments own much of the property and can give a building to a newspaper or a party, or take it away. The media is afraid of criticizing local authorities—it is safer to pick on the federal government. The opposition are cowards. Our parties have no basis in society—they are based within the Garden Ring (a circle of boulevards in the center of Moscow).

"I have a model for what's happening in our country—in 1993 the federal government decided to start building liberal capitalism, and that same year I decided to build myself a house in the country. So we started building at the same time—and I keep comparing notes. My project is behind schedule and over budget, it is not coming out as elegant as expected, the workers got drunk and stole the boards, and parts of the house had to be redone. The result is far from what I had originally planned—but it is farther still from useless wasteland that was there before the construction. Also, my house is coming up pretty solid. We all dream of one thing and get another. If I think I am so smart and my own house is coming up like that—why should I condemn the government? I am not thrilled with the job it is doing, but it is the best possible job under the circumstances.

"There is a huge number of houses going up all around Moscow—for the first time in decades people have the right to put their money in the ground. Good workers are hard to find. During an economic catastrophe, there should be an oversupply of labor, but there is none of that now. Everyone complains of labor shortages. Russians buy a car, then an apartment, then a country house—those are our priorities; stocks are not among the first three. People have no habit of buying stocks. We should buy them . . . maybe tomorrow . . . we have no such habit. Buying stocks requires a thoughtful approach to life. After 70–80 years of living on a volcano, it will take us a while to learn to plan far ahead."

THE ASIAN DRAGONS

I have lived in Asia, and when I look at today's Russia, I think it is where Hong Kong and Singapore were in the mid-60s. Back then, much of the world viewed them, along with Taiwan and Korea, as economic and social wasteland, populated by backward people. "Back in the early 1960s, when America and Europe enjoyed their golden age of growth, many Western economists viewed Asia as a gloomy place doomed to stagnation," reminds a recent editorial in *The Economist*.

People in what we now call "Asian tigers" have moved from hovels to gleaming high-rises in one generation after the feudal and colonial strictures collapsed in the wake of World War II. All those countries, despite their differences, had one common denominator—

the emergence of free enterprise in an atmosphere of greater protection of personal rights. That is exactly what is happening in Russia today. The old brutal ruling class has been swept out of power; there is true freedom of speech, fair elections, and laws that protect people who open businesses. These essential parallels between Russia and the Asian tigers in the 1960s overshadow any differences of geography or politics.

Can Russia slide back—can a strongman emerge and reverse the tide of reform? The Russians have been so badly hurt by their old rulers that the nation has an abiding revulsion against strongmen. As Harry Panjer, a Dutch businessman and investor, points out, the broad access to modern telecommunications acts as a check against any dictatorial designs. A dictatorship depends on keeping people misinformed. Massive lying and propaganda are impossible in Russia today; people have easy access to the Internet and world media. Russians would not tolerate a modern-day totalitarian ruler any more than they would tolerate the return of Mongol archers, or the tsars, or the communists with their labor camps.

Many Americans to this day have an image of Russia as a poor, dirty, corrupt, and dangerous place. They see it as a country where people do not have enough to eat, criminals rule the streets, the economy is falling apart, and the future is bleak. This is the image I get from scanning American newspapers and magazines. Then I get on a plane and land in Moscow—and see a vibrant developing society. Sure, it has growing pains; but the energy and excitement of a new boom are almost palpable.

I lock up my apartment in Moscow, catch a ride to Sheremetyevo airport, and fly back to New York. I say to my American friends: the country I just left, the country I saw with my own eyes is not the same country I read about in the media. When I started doing research for this book, I said to myself: "I have two eyes, and when I see something, I am going to believe them. I am not going to ask some other guy whether he sees the same thing." This is why I say that Russia is at an early stage of an economic boom, rocketing from a low base, but at a much faster rate than Hong Kong or Singapore in the 1960s.

The economy is booming in Moscow, but the rest of the country is slower to rise. Life is harsh for many outside the Moscow Beltway.[29] Moscow is to Russia what Hong Kong is to China, an economic dynamo, a starter of the engine of economic growth. Changes gradually spread from Moscow across the entire country. In China, first Hong Kong boomed, then Guandong province across the Pearl River (the so-called Shenzen Economic Zone), then other coastal provinces, and now the growth is starting to spread into the country's interior. This process is likely to repeat in Russia, starting in Moscow and a few other progressively managed cities and spreading across the 150-million nation.

Several provincial cities are trying to jumpstart their economies through financial markets, the way Moscow did a few years ago. I was invited by stock and currency traders to come and teach in St. Petersburg and in Siberia. An economic academy in Nizhny Novgorod consulted me on setting up a school for traders, after being swamped by calls from locals looking to staff their trading houses. The great Russian countryside is starting to rev up.

The position of foreigners changes at different stages of the boom. At first, they are treated as valued guests, met with limos at the airports, installed in the choicest hotels, paid high fees, and given opportunities to pick gems in the dirt. That stage ended in Russia in the early '90s.

At the second stage, international companies start coming in. IBM, Kodak, and McDonald's start opening local branches and bring in expats—foreign experts who are supposed to run businesses better than locals. Expats receive tax-free apartments, chauffeured cars, and other perks, on top of generous salaries and "hardship allowances." Expats run businesses through interpreters, and gradually locals realize that with a bit of training and experience they are just as good or better than expats. At that point, parent companies start taking away expats' perks and sending them back home, while locals rise at local offices of international firms. In Hong Kong and Singapore, the locals rose to this level by the mid- to late '70s, about

---

[29] The business-savvy Moscow mayor recently installed a solid centerline barrier and bright lights all along that beltway, sharply reducing traffic mortalities. It takes surprisingly little in Russia to accomplish a lot.

30 years after the war. The Russians are already at that level, only six years after the fall of communism. They are way ahead of the schedule that worked for the Taiwanese, Koreans, and other Asian dragons. There are still expats in Moscow, but they have to compete with the locals. Meanwhile, young Russians are studying in the West, getting their MBAs and western experience, getting ready to run anything there is to run—in Russian.

What's the next stage? A recent article in *The New York Times* tells of English workers scrambling for laborers' jobs on construction projects in Hong Kong. The boom in some Asian countries has come full circle, from exporting shiploads of Chinese coolies for back-breaking labor in faraway countries to importing *gweilos* (foreigners) to dig dirt while locals are busy running banks. This is less likely to happen in Russia because it has 20 times the population of Hong Kong—but that is the direction of change!

UNCLE SAM

While Russia has been going through its most important transformation in centuries, the people who run the Russian policies of the United States have been largely asleep on the job. They have failed, time and again, to help along the process of building democratic liberal capitalism in Russia. Given an historic opportunity to convert an old enemy into a loyal friend and ally, they have largely squandered it and managed to antagonize many pro-Western Russians.

In 1996 I met the director of trading at a leading investment bank in Moscow, a fast-talking, fast-thinking brash New Yorker. Most of his traders were Russian, and I asked him what he thought of them. "They are sharp, very sharp, really sharp. But they have no discipline; I have to teach them—sometimes I feel I am running a kindergarten. And they haven't learned how to be decent to each other. You can't blame them. They are the product of their old country. They have not learned you can't act like that if you plan to be in this business for 20 years. You can't shove a pool stick up a man's ass and break it, because he's gonna take out the piece that broke off and come after you with it." Returning to that investment bank in 1997 I could see that his lessons were learned. I think of that director of trading when I look at US policy toward Russia. Our policy makers could have used his lessons.

In 1991 Russia made its historic break with communism and appealed for help from the West—and the first thing the US did was to send in bill collectors. In November 1991, Yeltsin and his team of reformers had been working to bury communism, taking grave personal risks. That same month, David Mulford, US Undersecretary of the Treasury under George Bush, arrived in Moscow as a leader of a debt-collecting mission. Yeltsin immediately proposed that Russia take over both Soviet liabilities and Soviet assets abroad. It took US bureaucrats more than a year to ratify that sensible proposal.

In 1991, with Russia economically on its back, and reformers under a vicious attack from the communists, the US insisted that Russia continue to service USSR's foreign debt, with no grace period, until a rescheduling could be worked out. Within a few months, the VneshEconomBank—the government bank for foreign transactions—simply ran out of money, deepening the financial crisis and giving a black eye to the reformers. The Bush administration woefully misread Russia. This is hardly surprising, considering the former president's background at the CIA, the genius agency that kept scaring us with the mighty Soviet Empire but was caught absolutely off guard by the collapse of communism in Eastern Europe.

The West has been dragging its feet, failing to give meaningful financial help to Russian reformers, making their jobs more difficult. This goes against the best long-term interests of the West. Free, democratic, and capitalist Russia is an ally of the West, not its enemy. Western politicians seem to realize there is domestic political hay to be made from magnanimous gestures toward Russia, but they are notoriously tardy to deliver on them. Russians are used to waiting and hoping, but now they are more likely to feel disdainful.

During the first three years after the Soviet Union was dissolved in 1991, the West loaned Russia $4.6 billion in "untied" funds, money not linked to any specific project. That was less than one percent of Russia's GDP in any of those years. In 1992, the West announced $24 billion of help to Russia, but delivered $15 billion—$1.5 billion as grants, the rest as export credits and IMF loans. The next year, the

West announced $28 billion of financial aid, but delivered less than a third—$8.1 billion, which included $0.5 billion of grants and the rest export credits and IMF loans. In comparison, during Mexico's latest financial crisis in January 1995, the US came up with $40 billion of aid in just a few weeks.

The US government failed to appreciate an historic opportunity for cultivating friendship with another superpower—by helping its former enemy in its hour of need. Some experts see US actions as basically dumb—and that is a charitable view. Another view, held by many Russians, is that the US wants Russia to remain impoverished—a market for its consumer goods and a supplier of basic commodities. Many Russians say, "The Americans, the Germans, and the Japanese do not want us to rise to the level where we can compete with them."

This meager and belated help to Russia is a bigger problem for the US than it is for Russia. Russia is growing strong and self-reliant, not waiting for handouts, pulling itself up by its sturdy bootstraps. The small-minded and tightfisted approach of one US administration after another represents not only a squandering of a historic opportunity, but a sad reflection on the state of leadership of our nation.

At the end of 1997, the US was busy again doing what the American director of trading taught his Russian employees not to do. The NATO bureaucrats, fresh from their "success" in Bosnia—where they fretted impotently on the sidelines during the three years of a civil war—are busy trying to expand NATO eastward, into the former Soviet satellites and even the former republics of the Soviet Union. The Russian military today is so broke that its fighter pilots are losing their flying certifications because they do not have enough fuel to fly the required number of hours. Much of the military personnel live in tents in the midst of Russian winters, while suicide has become the leading cause of death in the Russian military. At a time when the Russian soldier is no longer a threat to anyone, except some hapless peasants' chickens, the US is trying to take a pool stick to a weak man lying on the ground—by expanding its military fighting machine into his backyard and his front yard, and to the doorstep of his house. The current geopolitical attitude of the US towards Russia is not right.

IN CONCLUSION

The flow of foreign investments into Russia has been thin, and most local businesspeople got used to relying on their own resources. When they ask me what can be done to attract Western investors, I reply that first of all, the country must remove restrictions on the movement of capital across the border. Today, it is not easy to send in money to invest in Russia—and even more difficult to have it sent back. Trying to account for a few hundred dollars in your pocket at the airport is a symbol of an obstacle course for money. When the barriers are removed or at least lowered, more money will flow into Russia. The current barriers reflect old feelings of inferiority, a fear that money would escape from Russia if it could. The government needs to take a closer look at its citizens. When Russians were allowed to travel, many went to visit abroad but very few stayed there. Removing restrictions on the movement of money will bring in more money! Today there are greater opportunities in Russia than abroad. Removing controls will attract foreign investments instead of channeling Russian money to offshore banks.

The second most important step for attracting investments to Russia is to make its tax code more rational and logical. For example, taxes on capital gains are payable immediately after each trade, but there is no provision for deducting losses. A firm or a trader that makes five profitable trades and three losing ones, all the same size, has to pay tax on the winning five, with no reduction for the losing three, making the whole operation unprofitable. No wonder so much Russian stock trading shifts to Cyprus.

Russians envy the American tax system, where a firm can report its income and then reduce its taxes legally, using clever accountants and relying on due process. Russians laugh when I tell them that IRS agents in the US call for an appointment. In Russia they come in bulletproof vests, with a battering ram, knock down the door, lay everyone down on the floor and depart with all the papers, computers, and cash.

The third essential step for improving the investment climate is to strengthen Russia's legal system and fight corruption. As with the previous step, it is going to take years of steady improvements rather than one spectacular change.

Russia is developing at an amazing speed—events are rushing to overtake my book! President Yeltsin has appointed "an economic dream team" in order to push through market reforms. His right-hand man, Anatoly Chubais, was voted the best finance minister in the world in a 1997 poll by *Euromoney* magazine. He was put in charge of UES (see Chapter 11), following a cabinet reshuffle in 1998. Russia has close to full currency convertibility—a more liberal foreign exchange situation than England had before 1979 or France before 1991. Several changes forecasted in this book have already come to pass—most notably the sale of *Svyazinvest* (see Chapter 12) to an investment group led by George Soros. I must rush this book to print before its message turns from a revolutionary idea into a commonly accepted fact.

Many Americans think that people in poor nations are basically dumb, unless they live at a stone-age level in a rainforest, in which case they are thought to possess some special wisdom. As recently as 40 years ago Americans believed the Japanese were stupid. Now we drive Hondas and carry Toshiba laptops.

The Russians are poor today. They are working hard, pulling themselves up by their bootstraps, rushing ahead at such speed that wind blows back their hair. They are coming up from behind, heading into a boom. When they start buying American movie studios, banks, and choice real estate, people will stop, think, and say: Russians are smart. By then you may be driving a Russian car or working for a Russian international firm. When that happens, remember—you read it here first. Meanwhile, do yourself and your kids a favor and buy some Russian stocks.

AFTERWORD

Late in 1997 I was invited to speak at a conference in Russia. I hadn't been there in four months, and the rush of changes hit me in the face like Moscow's bracing autumn air.

The stock market rallied that summer; it nearly tripled for the year, and at the moment was digesting its gains. Trading volume skyrocketed and traders were rolling in dough. Foreigners were beginning to install remote quote terminals for Russian stocks.

Next to the Kremlin wall in the heart of Moscow, where grim-faced armed guards used to chase away the passersby, a gleaming shopping mall was being built, with fountains and hokey statues from Russian folk tales. An American cigarette company set up a ski jump next to the Kremlin gates as a promotional gimmick, and an open-air concert was going on. The forbidden zone in the heart of the "Evil Empire" felt open and festive, like the Mall in Washington or the parks in London.

The economy was gathering steam. The illogical tax system was being reorganized, putting pressure on the "Red Directors." The political system was being cleaned up. Yeltsin went on national TV and ordered his attorney general to send a team of investigators to a provincial city whose mayor had been fingered as an organized crime figure by a leading newspaper.

The government announced a long-overdue move to lop off three zeros from the ruble, bringing it closer to the dollar. A currency reform would have been impossible a year earlier, because of public distrust. Now, the government had earned public confidence. Sociologists reported that longevity of Russian men has jumped up. Bus shelters bore a curious sign of change in a country whose consumer markets had been dominated by imported goods.

251

An ad from a local cigarette company showed a pack of its product hovering above the Manhattan skyline like a space ship with the logo "Return Strike."

Reformers were angry at the Duma, Russia's obstructionist parliament, with everybody waiting for the next elections to throw the rascals out. Complaining and waiting to vote is a normal behavior in the West—but it is a striking change for Russia.

Mindful of my "submachine gun indicator," I kept trying to count guns, but saw only two during my two-week stay, both in the lobby of the MICEX, the country's largest financial exchange. Bandits still ruled the airport, and I had to arrange for someone to come and meet me. Moscow had way too many cars, with traffic jams at all hours, and I did almost all of my traveling by its efficient *Metro*. The subway was spotless with trains arriving every minute during peak hours.

Emerging from the *Metro* on my last Sunday in the city I saw a communist demonstration and crossed the street to join the ragged crowd. Approximately two hundred people gathered at the feet of a huge statue of Lenin with red flags and placards. I scanned their faces—there was not a single young person among them. Many were shabbily dressed. Communists kept milling like sheep, directed by a few leaders with bullhorns, while a few policemen stood by. I noticed a stand with communist publications and went to pick them up, but no, they weren't free, you had to pay. I stood there looking at the covers with pictures of Lenin and Stalin when I saw amidst them a detective/pornographic magazine. The sight of pubic hair next to Lenin's beard and Stalin's mustache was reassuring—the free market had arrived in the communist heartland.

On my last night in Moscow I had dinner with two friends, both of them in wheelchairs. They casually remarked how Russians, especially men, have become more self-assured and helpful in recent years. My friends are constantly being assisted on the streets by the passersby who help carry them and their wheelchairs over steps—there are no ramps in Russia. This is a welcome sign of change from the old years, when Russians, rigid and stiff, shunned disabled people.

As I finish my work on this manuscript, I am already buying my next ticket to Russia. The journey of the new millennium continues.

ACKNOWLEDGMENTS

In writing this book, I was fortunate to have loyal and generous friends, both in Russia and the US. Some have opened new doors for me, offering access to inside information. Others opened doors to a warm shelter, shared their insights, read early drafts of chapters and criticized them, helping me sharpen my focus.

This is a book of stories—most of them happened to me, but a few came from people I trust. If I did not mention you by name, please forgive me, and I'll thank you in person the next time we meet.

In addition to those mentioned in the body of this book, I feel grateful to old and new friends who helped me on this journey: Dr. Barbara Chang, Dr. Boris Goldstein, Dr. Ilya and Natalie Goldstein, Lida Golikova, Alexander Kalinin, Igor and Lora Katansky (and their delightful daughters Olya and Lisa), Robert Ovanesyan, Veronica and Yuri Stein, Estelle Strizhak, Louis Taylor (the friend to whom my previous book was dedicated), Alexander and Rita Volkov, and Valery Zvyagin.

Members of several corporations have been especially helpful. Traders, executives, and support staff of the Russian Exchange have made my stays in Moscow especially productive. In my research on Russian industries and companies I received invaluable assistance from Gavin Rankin's analytic staff at Troika Dialog in Moscow. I'd camp out in Gavin's conference room with my microcomputer and dig through his piles of clippings prior to interviewing his staff. Researchers at two other leading Moscow brokerages—Rinaco Plus and CentreInvest Group—were very helpful. Dr. John Yancey, at the Bank of New York, explained to me the intricacies of Russian ADRs in a lengthy phone interview before both of us had to rush to airports for our flights.

I feel enormously grateful to my staff at Financial Trading, Inc. in New York. It is a unique group of people—each was selected from among hundreds of applicants. I enjoy coming to the office and spending long hours with them. My manager, Julie Ballin, does a great job running the company while I am out of the country for weeks at a time. Inna Feldman, my assistant manager, came from Russia, and her astute comments on several early drafts of this book prompted me to add many important details.

Carol Keegan Kayne, my former manager, left the company six years ago to become a full-time mom, but to this day no writing project is finished until Carol has reviewed it for clarity. I drove out to her house on Long Island for many heated editing sessions, while Eric, her husband, made salmon steaks on an outdoor grill and kept Samantha reasonably quiet.

My children—Miriam, Nicole, and Danny—were born in New York and speak little Russian. All three are excellent writers, but are only now starting to become a little more curious about the country their father came from. I hope this book piques their interest.

Finally, I want to wave hello to people in faraway lands who became trusted friends after reading my previous book, *Trading for a Living*—Colin Nicholson and Tony Reeves in Australia, Phyllis Taylor in New Zealand, and Harry Panjer in the Netherlands.

Dr. Alexander Elder
New York, May 1998

A BRIEF GLOSSARY

Academician A member of the Academy of Arts or Sciences. An academician in Russia is like a general of science or arts, above any professor. The Russians take this title very seriously.

ADR American Depositary Receipts.

Aktsiya A stock, or a share.

Aktsioner A shareholder.

Apparat The ruling establishment (especially during the Soviet years).

Apparatchik A member of the *apparat*. Those who reached the top rungs of the ladder became *nomenklatura*.

Avos Hopefully things will work out for the best.

Baba A peasant woman; also a condescending form of addressing or referring to a female (see *Muzhik*).

Babki Slang for money. The literate term is *dengi*.

Babushka A grandmother; polite form of addressing or referring to an older woman.

Bandit (pl bandity) A gangster (usually involved in organized crime).

Bezopasnost Security (literally, absence of danger, quite different from the American meaning of security). (See *FSB, KGB*.)

Birzha The Exchange.

Blini Blintzes. Thin Russian pancakes.

Brezhnev Head of the Communist party, the ruler of the USSR 1964–1982.

Bytovukha Crime that has to do with everyday life (*byt*)—e.g., violence stemming from interpersonal disagreements.

Chelnok A shuttle trader (fly to Abu Dhabi, bring back two suitcases of sheepskin coats and sell them).

Dacha A country cottage. Anything from a 1-room summer cabin without running water to a 3-story brick mansion. Most Russians either own or crave one.

Dengi Money. Slang terms include *babki, bucksy, griny* (the latter two refer to US dollars).

Druzhinniki Police auxiliaries.

Duma The Russian Parliament (from the verb *dumat*, meaning to think).

Dvoryane The hereditary nobility.

Fondovaya Having to do with shares.

FSB *(Federalnaya Sluzhba Bezopasnosti).* Federal Security Service, the successor agency of the KGB.

GAAP (Generally Accepted Accounting Principles) American accounting standards.

Gaz Gas.

GKO *(Gosudarstvenniye Kratkosrochniye Obligatsii).* "State Short-Term Bonds," or Russian Treasury Bills.

Glasnost Literally, "voice-ness"; openness, speaking up, criticizing mistakes.

Gosudarstvenniye Having to do with the state, belonging to the state, or state-related.

Gosudarstvo The state.

Grin From the English "green," a slang term for dollars (also called *buksy,* the Russian for "bucks").

IAS (International Accounting Standards) Similar to GAAP but more widespread in Europe, particularly in the UK.

IPO (Initial Public Offering) A US term for the first sale of company stock to the public, called "primary placement" in Russia.

KGB (Komitet Gosudarstvennoy Bezopasnosti) Committee for the State Security, or the Soviet secret police (see *Stukach*).

Khalyava, na khalyavu Something for nothing; free goodies at someone else's expense.

Khruschev Head of the Communist party 1958–1964.

Khruschovky 4- or 5-story tenements with small, shoddy apartments, built during the Khruschev era in factory areas (often populated by a rough crowd).

Kinut Literally, "to toss"; to swindle or cheat someone.

Kolkhoz A collective farm.

Komanda A team.

Komitet Committee.

Kontora An office.

Kratkosrochniye Short-term.

Kremlin Literally, a fort; a walled compound, built for defense against invaders in the center of the city. There are kremlins in many cities in Russia, but the most famous is the one in Moscow, occupied by the executive branch of the Russian government.

Krysha Literally, "a roof"; gangster-imposed "protection."

Kulak Literally, "a fist"; a successful peasant who had accumulated wealth before he and his kin got deported to Siberia during the collectivization.

Kustar A small craftsman; also a dilettante or an amateur.

Metro Subway. The Moscow subway is built like the one in Paris, with a dozen radial lines, going from one end of Moscow to its opposite, and the circle line surrounding the city center, connecting all radial lines. An address "inside the circle" is prestigious, especially for a business.

Muzhik (pl muzhiki) A peasant; a casual form of addressing or referring to a male (see *Baba*).

Natsionalnost Ethnicity. A Soviet "internal passport" had a notorious "Item 5" Natsionalnost. Having a "wrong" one closed off several careers.

Neft Crude oil. Names of oil companies often start with the geographical name of their main area of operations and end with *-neft*, i.e., Komineft.

Neftegas Crude oil and natural gas. Names of oil companies often start with the geographical name of their main area of operations and end with *-neftegas*, i.e., Surgutneftegas.

NII (Nauchno-Issledovatelskiy Institut) A scientific research institute.

Nomenklatura The tenured members of the Soviet government, whether its political, military, or KGB branches. They climbed to the top level of the Soviet power establishment (see *Apparatchik*).

NPO (Nauchno-Proizvodstvennoe Obedineniye) A scientific industrial organization.

Oblast A region; a political unit similar to a state in the US.

Obligatsii Bonds.

Obschak Career criminals' "mutual welfare fund," maintained by an especially trusted thief-in-law.

Pavlik Morozov A boy sanctified by the Soviet propaganda for turning in his own father who hid some of the family's grain from communists.

Pechat (pl. pechati) A company seal.

Pereulok An alley, or short narrow street.

Perestroika Rebuilding. Experimenting, during the last years of communism, with new social models, while maintaining the essence of the old system.

Phenya The spoken language of criminals.

Politicheskiy Literally, "political"; a political prisoner.

Prof Professional (a part of many abbreviations; see *Profsoyuz*).

Profsoyuz Trade union (from *prof* + *soyuz*).

Prom (promyshlennost) Industry (a part of many abbreviations; names of companies often start with the name of their industry and end with -*prom*, i.e., Gazprom).

Putch A coup.

Putchist A participant in a coup.

RAS Russian Accounting Standard.

Region An area of the country, or a province.

Rossiyanin A citizen of Russia; the term reflects citizenship rather than ethnicity. A Rossiyanin can be either an ethnic Russian or belong to another ethnic group.

RTS (Russian Trading System) A NASDAQ-like quotation system for Russian stocks.

Ruble Russian currency unit (divided into 100 kopecks).

Russkiy A member of the Russian ethnic group, whether he lives in Russia or not. This term reflects ethnicity rather than citizenship.

Shpana Petty hoodlums.

Sluzhba Service (see *FSB*).

Soviet Having to do with the Soviet Union (see also *Sovok*).

Sovok (sovkoviy) A derogatory term for Soviet (i.e., *sovok* thinking).

Soyuz Union (see *Profsoyuz*).

Stilyaga A person of the quasi-Western style of the '60s.

Struktura A business or government unit.

Stukach Literally, "one who knocks"; an informer.

Subbotnik (pl subbotniki) Unpaid weekend work in the Soviet era.

Svyaz Communication, or connection (the word can also mean an affair).

Torg, torgi Trading.

Tovar Merchandise.

Tovarnaya Having to do with merchandise or commodities (*Tovarnaya Birzha*—Commodities Exchange).

Tseh A small factory or a unit of a large factory (see *Zavod*).

Tsehovik An underground businessman.

Tsentralnaya Central (as in *Tsentralnaya Kontora*).

Ugolovnik A common criminal (as opposed to a *politicheskiy*—a political prisoner).

Ukase A directive from the top.

Vakhter An unarmed residential or industrial guard (see also *Vakhtersha*).

Vakhtersha A watch lady; a ubiquitous Soviet feature, usually an older woman, in the yards of many apartment buildings, watching and reporting all comings and goings.

Veksel Bank, corporate, or local government obligations (promissory notes).

Visitka A business card (do not make the mistake of calling it a "card"—*kartochka*, which refers to a credit card).

Vnesh An abbreviation for *vneshniy*, meaning external, on the outside, foreign. For example, Vneshtorgbank is the bank for foreign trade (see *Torg*).

Vor v zakone Literally, "thief-in-law"; a top-ranked professional criminal (a Russian *made man*).

Vystavka An exhibit.

Vzyatka A bribe.

Zavod Factory, usually a large, self-sufficient one (see *Tseh*). Many company names end in -*zavod* (i.e., Gorkovsky Avtozavod or GAZ).

BIBLIOGRAPHY

Bogdanov, Andrey. *Nizhnovsvyazinform*. Moscow: Troika Dialog, 1997.

Bogdanov, Andrey. *Rostelecom*. Moscow: Troika Dialog, 1997.

Borovoy, Konstantin. *Tsena Svobody*. Moscow: Novosti, 1993.

Brzezinsky, Matthew. "Foreigners Learn to Play by Russia's Rules: Western Firms Find Ways to Avoid Perils of Organized Crime." *The Wall Street Journal*, August 14, 1997.

Chudo: A Periodic Newsletter on Russia and Its Emerging Capital Market, Firebird Management LLC, 1996.

CIA Handbook of International Economic Statistics 1995: The Internet Edition http://www.odci.gov/cia/publications/hes/index.html

Cloud, Daniel. Speech at the Annual Conference of International Professional Economists, July 19, 1996.

Cloud, Daniel. Speech at *Grant's Interest Rate Observer* Conference, April 1, 1996.

Dobozi, Istvan. "Electricity Consumption and Output Decline—An Update" in *Transitions*, a newsletter of The World Bank, Vol. 6, Nos. 9–10, Sep–Oct 1995, as quoted in *Chudo*.

Dunnan, Nancy. *Dun & Bradstreet Guide to Your Investments 1995*. New York: Harper Collins, 1995.

The Economist, March 1, 1997, p. 18.

Elder, Alexander. "A Financial Polka." *Financial Trader,* February 1997.

Elder, Alexander. "Long Freedom, Short Communism." *Financial Trader,* January 1996.

Elder, Alexander. "Making Rubles in the Rubble." *Financial Trader,* December 1996.

Elder, Alexander. *Study Guide for Trading for a Living*. New York: John Wiley & Sons, 1993.

Elder, Alexander. *Trading for a Living*. New York: John Wiley & Sons, 1993.

Falaleyev, Igor. *Gazprom: Leveraged to European Growth*. London: Salomon Brothers, 1996.

Hague, Ian. "Lies, Damn Lies, and Russian GDP Statistics." *Chudo,* September 1996.

Inshutin, Anton. *Moscow MMT: A Tasty Sandwich*. Moscow: CentreInvest Group, 1996.

Inshutin, Anton. "Russian Telecommunications at the Crossroads" (diploma paper). Moscow: Independent Institute of Russian Enterprise, 1996.

Ivanov, A. N. *Obrascheniye i Registratsiya Tsennyh Bumag*. Moscow: Infra-M, 1996.

Koledenkov, Victor, and Gregory Van Beek. *Automotive Production*. Moscow: Rinaco Plus, 1996.

Klyuchevskiy, V. O. *Russkaya Istoriya,* Vols. 1–3. Moscow: Mysl, 1995.

Krasnov, Vladislav. *Soviet Defectors: The KGB Wanted List*. Stanford, Calif.: Hoover Institution Press, 1985.

Krasovskaya, Marina. *Red October*. Moscow: Troika Dialog, 1997.

Krasovskaya, Marina, and Andrey Kulakov. *River Shipping*. Moscow: Troika Dialog, 1997.

Kvateladze, Irina. *Smert Pionera, Dengi,* December 1996, #45.

Layard, Richard, and John Parker. *The Coming Russian Boom*. New York: The Free Press, 1996.

Lynch, Peter. *One Up on Wall Street*. New York: Simon & Schuster, 1989.

Mirkin, Y. M. *Tsenniye Bumagi i Fondoviy Rynok*. Moscow: Perspektiva, 1995.

Modestov, Nikolai. *Moskva Banditskaya*. Moscow: Tsentropoligraph, 1996.

Nurgazieff, Abzal. *Lukoil: Company Profile*. Moscow: Troika Dialog, 1996.

Oganesian, Marina.*The Russian Electricity Sector*. Moscow: Troika Dialog, 1996.

Oganesian, Marina. *Syktyvkar Timber*. Moscow: Troika Dialog, 1996.

"An Open Letter from the Participants in the November 1996 Futures Conference." *Vestnik Rossiyskoy Birzhi* #4, 1996.

Prudnik, Sergey. *Russia: A Real Bear—Front and Back View*. Moscow: Troika Dialog, 1996.

Samoukov, Alexey. *GKO/OFZ Market Summary*, R+ Yield. Moscow: Rinaco Plus, 1996.

Segodnya (Today), December 11, 1996.

Sokolov, Maxim. Private interview, May 1997.

Solzhenitsyn, Aleksandr. *The Gulag Archipelago*. New York: HarperCollins, 1992.

Spicer, Andrew. "Building Markets from Scratch: Institutions and Agency in the Russian Mass Privatization Program" (unpublished article).

Sudoplatov, Pavel. *Razvedka i Kreml*. Moscow: Geya, 1996.

Tolstykh, Milena. *Igra/Skupka Kradenogo*. Moscow: Infox-Internet Securities News, 1996.

"Vimpelcom: v svoyem otechestve proroka net" (editorial). Expert #8 (Moscow), March 3, 1997.

World Bank. *World Development Report 1996: From Plan to Market*. Oxford University Press, 1996.

Yakovets, Yuri V. *Ekonomika Rossii: Peremeny i Perspectivy*. Moscow, 1996.

INDEX

ABOUT THE AUTHOR

Alexander Elder, M.D., was born in Leningrad and grew up in Estonia where he entered medical school at the age of 16. At 24, while working as a ship's doctor, he jumped a Soviet ship in Africa and received political asylum in the US. He continued to work as a psychiatrist in New York City and taught at Columbia University. After becoming involved in financial markets, Dr. Elder founded an educational firm, Financial Trading, Inc. His firm organizes conferences for traders and is one of the largest dealers in books for traders worldwide. Dr. Elder's own book, *Trading for a Living,* published in the US in 1993, has been translated into six languages and became an international bestseller. Dr. Elder is a highly sought-after speaker at financial conferences worldwide. After the collapse of communism, Dr. Elder has traveled extensively in the former Soviet Union, teaching local traders and exploring business opportunities. He is a member of an exchange in Moscow and is currently setting up a fund for investing in Russia.

Readers of *Rubles to Dollars* are welcome to request a "Russian Update" by writing or calling:

Financial Trading, Inc.
PO Box 20555, Columbus Circle Station
New York, NY 10023, USA
(800) 458-0939 or (212) 432-7630
Fax (718) 639-8889
e-mail: info@elder.com